# THE FIRST CROSSING OF GREENLAND •

I'RINTXD BY BA1.LAXTVXK. HANSON AND CO. KDIXBrRGH AND LONDON PREFACE TO FIRST EDITION.

I Feel that I cannot send this book out to meet its fate without attaching to it a hearty expression of my gratitude to all those who gave their help to the expedition with which it is concerned.

Among these I must assign a prominent place to Herr Augustin Gamel, in virtue of the ready liberality with which he offered his support to an undertaking which was very generally considered to be the scheme of a lunatic. And after him I must thank the Committee of the Norwegian " Studentersam-fund," or " Students' Union," who organised the collection of, and the large number of my countrymen who contributed to, the considerable sum which I received on my return home in defrayal of the outstanding expenses of the expedition. And, lastly, I must acknowledge the kindness of all the Danish officials with whom we came in contact, both in Denmark and Greenland, as well as the unbounded hospitality with which we were treated on all sides.

But my chief thanks are nevertheless owing to my five comrades, to whose combined efforts the successful result of our undertaking is of course mainly due. Every one who has conducted an expedition will know how ready the world is to do the great injustice of heaping the vhole praise or blame for its success or failure on the shoulders of the leader alone. And this injustice is greater than usual in the case of an expedition like ours, in which each member serves as one of a team of draught cattle, and the result of which cannot therefore be dependent on the efforts of a single individual.

My comrades, too, I must thank for the terms of good-fellowship on which we lived, and for the many pleasant hours we spent together in spite of ungenial surroundings. On these hours I have often dwelt with peculiar fondness in the course of my narrative. I have once more called to life many a little incident, which to others indeed may seem trivial, but which has a special value to us. If in so doing I have been induced to extend my tale to undue length, I must ask the good reader to bear with me if he can; and if not, to remember that here at least all the blame must be laid on me and me alone.

FRIDTJOF NAN'SEN.

Lvsaker, Christiaxia, *October* 1800.

PREFACE TO NEW EDITION.

In preparing the present edition of Dr. Nansen's account of the first crossing of Greenland in one volume, some curtailment of the larger work has been found necessary. Fortunately I have found it possible to effect this without reducing the space allotted to the narrative of the actual expedition. Dr. Nansen's great work deals with many subsidiary matters of the highest importance to those interested in Arctic travel, both in the historical and the practical aspects of the subject, which is one that has ever possessed a fascination for the English race. It also contains a full account of the Eskimo of Greenland, and an appendix dealing with the scientific results of the expedition. In preparing a popular edition of the work, I have thought it advisable to retain the story of the daring journey through the floe-ice off the east coast, and the heroic crossing to the west coast, intact, referring those who wish to learn Dr. Nansen's views on these cognate subjects to the larger work. Following out this scheme, the chapters in vol. i. on " Equipment," " Ski and Skilobning," "The Voyage to Iceland," "Cruising in the Ice," "The Bladder-nose Seal," and "Life on the *Jason,*" have been slightly abridged, and the historical chapters dealing with previous attempts to penetrate the ice-belt of the east coast of Greenland, and to explore the "Inland ice," have been omitted altogether. On the other hand, the introduction, and the chapters dealing with the attempts to land, the drifting in the ice, and the fortunes of the expedition while working its way up the east coast, have been retained intact. In vol. ii. the account of the crossing of the " Inland ice " until the expedition arrived in Godthaab is reprinted entire, while the chapters entitled "An Eskimo Narrative," "The Eskimo of Greenland," and "A Shooting Trip to Ameralik-fjord," together with the appendix, have been omitted. Nearly all the illustrations given in the larger edition are included in the present one.

C. J. LONGMAN.

Chapter I.

*INTRODUCTION.* OKI- THE KAST COAST OK

GRKENLAND, 1882.

*(From a sketch and a photograph /y the Author.)*

In the summer of 1882 I was on board the *I'iking,* a Norwegian sealer, which was caught in the ice off that part of the east coast of Greenland which is still unexplored, or, more precisely, somewhere in the neighbourhood of lat. 66 50' N. For more than three weeks we were absolutely fixed, and every day, to the terror of the crew, we drifted nearer to the rocky coast. Behind the fields of floating ice lay peaks and glaciers glittering in the daylight, and at evening and through the night, when the sun sank lowest and set the heavens in a blaze behind them, the wild beauty of the scene was raised to its highest. Many times a day from the maintop were my glasses turned westwards, and it is not to be wondered at that a young man's fancy was drawn irresistibly to the charms and mysteries of this unknown world. Unceasingly did I ponder over plans for reaching this coast, which so many had sought in vain, and I came to the conclusion that it must be possible to reach it, if not by forcing a ship through the ice, which was the method tried hitherto, then by crossing the floes on foot and dragging one's boat with one. One day, indeed, I incontinently proposed to make the attempt and walk over the ice to shore alone, but this scheme came to nothing because the captain conceived that he could not in the circumstances allow any one to leave the ship for a length of time.

On my return I was asked to write an article in the Danish " Geografisk Tid-skrift" (vol. vii., p. 76), and in this I expressed it as my opinion that it would be possible to reach the east coast of Greenland without any very great difficulty if the expedition forced-their way as far as practicable into the ice on board a Norwegian sealer, and then left the ship and passed over the floes to shore. I will not say that I had not at this time some notion more or less visionary of penetrating from the coast into the interior, but it was not till a later occasion that the idea took a definite form.

One autumn evening in the following year, that is to say, 1883—I remember it still as if it were only yesterday—I was sitting and listening indifferently as the day's paper was being read. Suddenly my attention was roused by a telegram which told us that Nordenskiold had come back safe from his expedition to the interior of Greenland, that he had found no oasis, but only endless snow-fields, on which his Lapps were said to have covered, on their "ski," an extraordinary long distance in an astonishingly short time The idea flashed upon me at once of an expedition crossing Greenland on "ski" from coast to coast. Here was the plan in the same form in which it was afterwards laid before the public and eventually carried out.

My notion, put briefly, was that if a party of good "skilobers" were equipped in a practical and sensible way, they must get across Greenland if they began from the right side, this latter point being of extreme importance. For if they were to start, as all other expeditions have done, from the west side, they were practically certain never to get across. They would have all the flesh-pots of Egypt behind them, and in front the unexplored desert of ice and the east coast, which is little better. And furthermore, if they did get across, they would have the same journey back again in order to reach home. So it struck me that the only sure road to success was to force a passage through the floe-belt, land on the desolate and ice-bound east coast, and thence cross over to the inhabited west coast. In this way one

would burn all one's ships behind one, there would be no need to urge one's men on, as the east coast would attract no one back, while in front would lie the west coast with all the allurements and amenities of civilisation. There was no choice of routes, " forward" being the only word. The order would be:—" Death or the west coast of Greenland." As these implements and their use will be treated of at length in Chap. III., it will only he necessary here to introduce the terms to the reader. "Ski" (pi. "ski" or "skier"), literally a "billet" or thin slip of wood, and connected etymologically with the Eng. "skid "and "shide,"is the Norwegian name for the form of snowshoe in general use among the northern nations of the Old World. The pronunciation of the word in Norway may le considered practically identical with the Eng. "she." The compounds of the word which will occur in the course of the narrative arc "skilo!er," a snowshoer, and "skiiobning," snowshoeing, both formed from the verb " lobe," to run. The only reason why the established English term "snowshoe" should not have been employed throughout is that this course would have led to inevitable confusion with the very dissimilar Indian snowshoe, of which also frequent mention is made.

Not till the autumn of 1887 did I resolve to give my serious attention to the scheme. My original idea had been to carry out the expedition with private means, but, as I was strongly urged on more than one side to apply to the Norwegian University for the necessary funds, in order to give the expedition a more public and national character, I consented, and sent to the authorities an application for a grant of 5000 kroner, or rather more than £275, in aid of a journey on the lines I have already described. My application received the warmest support from the University Council, and was passed on to the Government for their consideration, and in order that the proposal might be laid by them before the " Storthing," or National Assembly, in the regular manner. The Government, however, answered that they could not see their way to give the scheme their support, and one of the newspapers even went so far as to maintain that there could be no conceivable reason why the Norwegian people should pay so large a sum as 5000 kr. in order to give a private individual a holiday trip to Greenland. Most people who heard of the scheme considered it simple madness, asked what was to be got in the interior of Greenland, and were convinced that I was either not quite right in the head or was simply tired of life. Luckily it was not necessary for me to procure help from Government, " Storthing," or any one else.

At this time I received an offer from a gentleman in Copenhagen to provide the sum for which I had applied to Government. This was Herr Augustin Game'l, who had already contributed to the cause of Arctic research by the equipment of the "Dijmphna" expedition. This offer, coming as it did from a foreigner, and one quite unacquainted with me personally, and in aid of an expedition which was generally considered to be the scheme of a madman, seemed to me so truly generous that I could not for a moment hesitate to accept it.

I first published my plan in January 1888 in the Norwegian magazine *Naturen*, in an article entitled "Gronlands Ind-landsis." Having given some account of the earlier attempts to penetrate to the interior of Greenland, I continued:—" My plan, described briefly, is as follows: With three or four of the best and strongest ' skilobers' I can lay my hands on, I mean to leave Iceland in the beginning of June on board a Norwegian sealer, make for the east coast of Greenland, and try in about lat. 66 N. to get as near to the shore as possible. I should have liked to land farther north in the unknown regions of Scoresby Fjord, but for this it would be necessary to hire a special vessel, and, as it would probably be difficult to raise funds for this purpose, I have for the present given up this idea. If our vessel is not able to reach the shore, though the sealers, who have often been close in under this unexplored coast, do not consider such a thing improbable, the expedition will

leave the ship at the farthest point that can be reached, and will pass over the ice to land. In the summer of 1884, for instance, there was extremely little ice, and the seal were taken almost close under the shore. For the purpose of crossing the open water which will probably be found near the coast, a light boat will be dragged on runners over the ice. That such a crossing of the ice is possible, I feel I can assert with confidence from my previous experience. When I was in these regions in 1882 on board the *Viking,* and we were caught in the ice, and drifted for twenty-four days along the very coast where I now intend to land, I had numerous opportunities while out shooting and for other purposes of becoming familiar with the nature of the ice and conditions of snow, and besides, we were often obliged by sudden ' nips,' or jamming of the ice, to drag our boats over the floes for considerable distances. I therefore think there is every probability of our being able to reach land in this way. I should like it to be for preference somewhat north of Cape Dan, where the coast has never yet been explored by Europeans, and offers in itself much of interest to the traveller. To the south the coast is now comparatively well known, as the Danish ' Konebaad' expedition, under Captain Holm, in 1884 reached a point to the north of Cape Dan, and wintered at Angmagsalik, a colony of heathen Eskimo, in the neighbourhood of the cape. After having examined the coast as far as the time at our disposal will allow, we shall begin the crossing of the 'Inland ice' at the first opportunity. If we reach land to the north of Cape Dan, we shall begin the ascent from the end of one of the fjords close by; if we land farther south, we shall push up to the end of Sermilikfjord before we take to the ice.

" We shall try at once to climb as high as possible on the bare rock, even if the gradient be considerably steeper; for, when we are eventually obliged to take to the ice, we shall thus find it flatter and smoother, and shall escape the worst ice-falls of the glaciers, which with their crevasses and general rough-

ness would be likely to prove troublesome and dangerous. Once upon the ice, we shall set our course for Christianshaab, on Disco Bay, and try to reach our destination as soon as possible. The advantage of making for Disco Bay instead of taking a point farther south is that we shall probably find the snow in better condition farther north. And besides, by Disco Bay, where the land is not much cut up by fjords, it will be comparatively easy for us to find our way to habitations, while Disco Island, which lies off the coast, and will be visible to us with its terraced basalt cliffs, will prove a good landmark and help us to find one of the two colonies, Jakobshavn or Christianshaab, which lie on Disco Bay about thirty-five miles apart.

"The distance from the point on the east coast where I intend to land in Disco Bay is about 670 kilometres or 420 miles. If we calculate that we shall be able to cover on a daily average from fifteen to twenty miles, which is exceedingly little for a ' skilober,' the crossing will not take more than a month, and if we carry with us provisions for double that time there seems to be every probability of our success.

"The provisions will have to be hauled on sledges of one kind or another, and besides the 'ski' we shall also take ' truger,' the Norwegian counterpart of the Canadian snow-shoe, which may serve our purpose better when the snow is wet and soft. We shall also, of course, take the instruments necessary for observations... &c. &c."

It is not to be wondered at that several more or less energetic protests against a plan of this kind appeared in the newspapers, but they were one and all distinguished by an astonishing ignorance of the various conditions of, and the possibility of passage over, extensive tracts of ice and snow.

In this connection I cannot deny myself the pleasure of reproducing some portions of a lecture delivered in Copenhagen by a young Danish traveller in Greenland, and printed in the Danish magazine *Ny Jord* for February 1888. "Other plans," the lecturer says, " have never passed beyond the stage of paper, like the proposals to cross the ' Inland ice' in balloons, which were brought forward at the end of the last century. And among these paper-schemes we must include the proposal which has just emanated from the Norwegian zo-ologist, Fridtjof Nansen, of the Bergen Museum."... " There is much that is at-tractive in the fundamental idea of Nansen's scheme, in his proposal to start from the east coast, and cross to the colonies on the other side instead of taking the reverse way, and in his in-tention, he being a good 'skilober' him-self, to make 'ski' his means of con-veyance. But all who acknowledge the merits of the fundamental idea must, if they know anything of the real condi-tion of things, refuse any further sanc-tion to the scheme. The very method by which Nansen proposes to reach the coast, that is to say, by abandoning the firm ship's-deck and creeping like a po-lar bear from one rocking ice-floe to an-other on his way to the shore, shows such absolute recklessness that it is scarcely possible to criticise it seriously. " ... "Let us suppose, however, that for-tune favours the brave, and that Nansen has reached the east coast of Greenland. How will he now set about getting up on to the real flat expanse of the ' Inland ice,' or, in other words, how will he pass the outer edge, where peak upon peak rise through the ice-mantle, and in all probability present at nearly every point an impenetrable barrier?... " Nansen's proposal to climb the high mountains of the coast and from their summits step upon the expanse of ice which is dammed up against them thus betrays absolute ignorance of the true condi-tions."... "With what can be seen from the shore my experience ends, and I will not attempt to criticise the idea of cross-ing the inner tract of ice on 'ski,' or the possibility of taking enough provisions, or any similar questions. But I think that there is a probability that this part of the scheme may be carried out if Nansen can once pass the outer edge of the ice.

" But there is one very different ques-tion on which I think I am not only qual-ified but bound to speak. And I say that, in my opinion, no one has the moral right, by setting out upon a venturesome and profitless undertaking, to burden the Eskimo of Danish East Greenland with the obligation of helping him out of the difficulty into which he has wan-tonly thrust himself. The few of us who know anything of the condition of things in East Greenland have no doubt that if Nansen's scheme be attempted in its present form, and the ship does not reach the coast and wait for him till he has been obliged to abandon his de-sign, the chances are ten to one that he will either uselessly throw his own and perhaps others' lives away, or that he will have to take refuge with the Eski-mo and be conducted by them along the coast down to the Danish colonies on the western side. And I say that no one has a right to force upon the East Green-landers a long journey, which will be in many ways injurious to them."

There is no doubt that these passages were written with every good intention, but they are, nevertheless, characteristic specimens of the almost superstitious terror with which many people, and among them some who pose as author-ities, and claim to have special knowl-edge of the subject, have regarded the " Inland ice " of Greenland and the pas-sage of tracts of ice and snow generally, even in these latter days. The writer of the above article had himself in the course of several years' exploration passed along the edge of the " Inland ice," but it seems never to have entered into his head to make a little incursion into the interior. The first few steps would certainly have cleared his mind of some of his absurd hallucinations, and he would eventually have learned what an "absolute ignorance of the true conditions " really means.

In another article, which betrays, if possible, even less knowledge of the subject, the writer declared that even if Nansen himself were mad enough to make any such attempt he would not get a single man to accompany him.

In England, too, the press delivered itself of several articles adverse to the plan of the expedition.

But, in spite of these warning voices and in spite of the general opinion that the whole scheme was simple madness, there were, nevertheless, plenty of men who wished to join me. I received more than forty applications from people of all sorts of occupations, including sol-diers, sailors, apothecaries, peasants, men of business, and University stu-dents. There were many others, too, who did not apply, but who said they were more than eager to go, and would have sent in their names, had it been of the slightest use. Nor were these ap-plicants all Norwegians, for I received many letters, too, from Danes, Dutch-men, Frenchmen, and Englishmen.

I could, however, take none who were not thoroughly accustomed to the use of "ski," and men, too, of proved energy and endurance. Finally, I chose three Norwegians: Otto Sverdrup, a re-tired ship's captain; Oluf Dietrichson, first-lieutenant in the Norwegian in-fantry; and Kristian Kristiansen Trana, a peasant from the north of Norway.

As I had originally thought of taking reindeer, and imagined, besides, that some Lapps would be of use to me, as possessing that sense of locality and power of adaptation to all sorts of cir-cumstances which such children of na-ture have as a common birthright, I had written to two well-known men living in Finmarken, asking them if they could find me a couple of Mountain-Lapps willing to join the expedition. I

' As many who have travelled in the north of Norway and Sweden will stip-ulated that they should be plucky men, who were known to be clever moun-taineers and to possess powers of en-durance above the average; that they should be made fully aware beforehand of the dangerous nature of the undertak-ing, and that the fact must be clearly im-pressed upon them that there was just as much probability of their never return-ing home again as of surviving. And I further added that they must be unmar-ried men of an age between thirty and forty, as I considered that at this time of life the powers of both body and mind are best prepared to meet the trials of such an undertaking.

It was a long time before I received an answer to my inquiry. The post among the inland districts of Finmarken is leisurely, and is taken across the mountains in reindeer sledges every fortnight. At last when the time fixed for our start was approaching, I received an answer telling me that I could have two good men from Karasjok, if I was willing to pay them handsomely. I accepted their terms and telegraphed to them to come at once. The next thing I heard was that they were on the way and would arrive on such and such a day. I was exceedingly anxious to see them, of course. They were expected one Saturday evening, and I had some people down at the station to meet them and take them to their lodgings. But no Lapps arrived that day or on Sunday either, and we all wondered what had become of them. Then on Monday I was told that they really had come, and so indeed they had, but by a goods train instead of the ordinary express for passengers. I hurried down to their lodgings at once, found their door, and, as I entered, saw standing in the middle of the room a good-looking young fellow, but more like a Finn than a Lapp, and away in the corner an old man with long black hair hanging about his shoulders, small in stature, and looking more stunted still as he sat huddled up on a chest. He had a much more genuine Lappish look about him than the other. As I came into the room the elder man bent his head and waved his hand in the Oriental manner, while the younger greeted me in the ordinary way. The old fellow knew very little Norwegian, and most of my conversation was with the younger. I asked them how they were, and why they came by the goods train. " We do not understand trains," answered he, "and, besides, it was a little cheaper. " " Well, how old are you both? "I am twenty-six, and Ravna is forty-five," was the answer. This was a pretty business, for 1 had stipulated that they should be between thirty and forty. " You are both Mountain-Lapps, I suppose? " " Oh no! only Ravna; I am settled at Karasjok." This was still worse, as I had made a point of their being Mountain-Lapps. " But are not you afraid to go on this trip? " said I. " Yes,

we are very much afraid, and people have been telling us on the way that the expedition is so dangerous that we shall never come home alive. So we are very much afraid, indeed! " This was really too bad, for the poor fellows had never even been told what they had undertaken to do. I was very much inclined to send them back, but it was too late to get any one else to take their place. So, as I had to keep them, it was best to console them as well as I could, and tell them that what people had been saying was all rubbish. It was no manner of use to discourage them at the outset, for they were likely to lose their spirits quite quickly enough anyhow. Though they did not perhaps look quite so strong and wiry as I could have wished, still they seemed to be good-natured and trustworthy fellows. These qualities, indeed, they have shown to the utmost, and in endurance they have proved little, if at all, inferior to us. In other respects I found them of no particular use, as far as the accomplishments which I expected to find in them are concerned, and, as a matter of fact, they were never used for reconnoitring purposes.

know, ihe Lappish population falls into several more or less distinct divisions. The most interesting section, the real nomadic Lapps of the reindeer-herd and skin-tent, form as a matter of fact a small part of the whole. They are commonly known in Norway as " Fjeldlapper " (" Mountain-Lapps "), and it was from among them that I had intended to take my two men. Far the greater number of the Lapps are settled either on the Norwegian coast as " Solapper " (" Sea-Lapps "), where they maintain themselves chiefly by fishing; or in the interior, at such villages or centres as Karasjok, Kauto-keino, Jokkmokk, Kvickjock, and Karesuando, as well as in most of the upper valleys of northern Sweden. The " Elvelapper " (" River-Lapps "), to whom I refer below in connection with Balto's origin, are merely a small colony settled by the river Tana, and are, as I have said, supposed to be of mixed Lappish and Finnish blood.

Balto, my younger Iapp, on his return home wrote a short account of his ex-

periences while he was away. This has been translated into Norwegian from the original Lappish by Professor Friis, of Christiania, and I propose to include in my narrative those passages of his which seem to me most characteristic and likely to afford most interest to the general reader. After describing his voyage from Finmarken and telling how people on the way discouraged them, and informed them, among other things, that I was a simple maniac, he continues: —" On April 14th we left Trondhjem and reached Christiania on the 16th. Nansen had sent a man to the railway station to meet us. This was Sverdrup, who came up to us and asked: ' Are you the two men who are going with Nansen?' We answered that we were the two. Sverdrup then told us that he was going with Nansen too, and had come on purpose to meet us. ' Come along with me,' he said; and he took us to a hotel, which is in Toldbodgaden, No. 30. An hour afterwards Nansen and Dietrichson came to see us. It was a most glorious and wonderful thing to see this new master of ours, Nansen. He was a stranger, but his face shone in our eyes like those of the parents whom we had left at home; so lovely did his face seem to me, as well as the welcome with which he greeted us. All the strange people were very kind and friendly to us two Lapps while we were in Christiania town, and from this time we became happier and all went well with us."

As through the whole course of my narrative we shall have the company of the five men I have already mentioned, the most fitting thing I can do will be to present them duly to the reader, with some short account of the antecedents of each.

OTTO SVERDRUP.

I will begin with my own countrymen and take them in the order of their age.

Otto Sverdrup was born on October 31, 1855, at the farm of Haarstad, in Bindalen, in Helgeland. His father, Ulrik Sverdrup, a member of an old Norwegian family, was an owner of farm and forest property. Accustomed from childhood to wander in the forest and on the mountains on all kinds of errands and in all sorts of weather, he learned early to look after himself and to stand on his own legs. Early, too, he learned to use his "ski," and a rough and impracticable country like that of Bindalen naturally made him an active and clever " skilober."

At the age of seventeen he went to sea, and sailed for many years on American as well as Norwegian vessels. In 1878 he passed the necessary examination in Christiania and sailed as mate for several years, being during this period once wrecked with a Norwegian schooner off the west coast of Scotland. On this occasion he showed to the full the sort of stuff he was made of, and it was mainly his coolness and perseverance which saved his crew. Since this he has sailed as captain on a schooner and a steamer, and one year spent the fishing season with a smack on the banks off the coast of Nordland. Of late years he has for the most part remained at home with his father, the latter having meanwhile sold his property in Bindalen and moved southwards to the farm of Trana, near Stenkjer. Here he has spent his time at all sorts of work, in the forest, on the river, floating timber, in the smithy, and fishing at sea, where as boat's-captain he was unsurpassed.

Some years ago a man was wanted at Gothenburg to take charge of the Nordenfeldt submarine boat which was to be taken across the North Sea to England. A reward was offered, but no one was found willing to undertake this risky task. Sverdrup at this juncture accidentally appeared, and he offered his services at once. He prevailed upon a relative to go with him as engineer, and the two proposed to navigate the strange craft across the North Sea without further help. The prospect OLL'F CHRISTIAN D1ETKICHSON.

to Sverdrup was one of pure sport, but at the last moment the authorities changed their minds, and the boat was eventually towed across.

It is plain that a man of this type was specially created for such an expedition as ours. In the course of his vagrant and chequered life he had learned to find his way out of all kinds of difficult situations, and I need scarcely add that we never found him wanting in either coolness or resource.

Oluf Christian Dietrichson was born in Skogn, near Levanger, on the 315! of May 1856, and was the son of Peter Vilhelm Krejdal Dietrichson, the official doctor of the district. He was educated at Levanger, Trondhjem, and Christiania, entered the military school as a cadet in 1877, and received a commission as second lieutenant in the Trondhjem brigade in 1880, being promoted to the rank of first lieutenant in 1886. During the present summer he has received his captaincy.

He has all his life been a keen sportsman, and by good physical training he has hardened and developed his naturally strong and well-built frame. Of late years _he has every winter gone long tours on "ski" through the greater part of Southern Norway, has passed through most of our valleys, from Skien in the south to Trondhjem in the north, and there are not many who have seen so much of the country in its winter aspect as he.

The acquirements of his military education stood the expedition in good stead. He undertook our meteorological diary practically single-handed, and the results of our surveys and our maps are due to him. He discharged these duties with an amount of zeal and self-denial which are more than admirable, and the merit of such work as he produced in such circumstances will only be appreciated by those who have had a similar experience. To take observations and keep a meteorological diary with the usual exactitude and punctuality, when the temperature is below-20 F., when one is dead-tired, or when death and destruction are at hand; or to write when the fingers are so injured and swollen by the frost that it is almost impossible to hold a.pencil, needs an amount of character and energy which is far from common.

KKISTIAN KKlSTlANSllN TKANA.

Kristian Kristiansen Trana was no more than twenty-four years old when he joined the expedition. This was considerably below the age which I considered most suitable for such a task; but, as he was plucky and strong and exceedingly eager to go with us, I did not hesitate to take him on Sver-drup's recommendation, and I had no reason whatever to regret my choice.

He was born on February 16, 1865, at a cottage on the farm of Trana, which is now the property of Sverdrup's father. At his home he has been chiefly engaged in forest work, but had been to sea once or twice, and was therefore likely to be a handy man. He proved steady and trustworthy, and when Kristian said that he was going to take anything in hand, I always knew that it would be done.

Samuel Johannesen Balto is a Lapp settled at Karasjok, and was twenty-seven when he joined us. He is of average height, and has none of the outer Lapp characteristics; he belongs, in fact, to the so-called " River-Lapps," who are generally people of some size and have much Finn blood in them. He has spent most of his time at forest work, but for several years he has been out in the fishing season, and for a while, too, he has helped to tend reindeer among the Mountain-Lapps, being for a part of the time in the service of Ravna. He is a lively, intelligent fellow; he did everything he undertook with great energy, and in this respect was very different from his companion Ravna. He showed some powers of endurance too, was always willing to lend a hand at any job, and was thus of great use to us. And, lastly, his ready tongue and broken Norwegian constituted him to a great extent the enlivening spirit of the expedition.

Ole Nielsen Ravna is a Mountain-Lapp from the neighbourhood of Karasjok, and when he joined the expedition was forty-five or forty-six, he not being quite sure of the year himself. He has spent all his nomadic life in a tent, and wandered with his reindeer about the mountain wastes of Finmarken. His herd, when he left it for Greenland, was of no great size, and contained from 200 to 300 deer. He was the only married member of the expedition, and left a wife and five children behind him at home. As I have already said, I did not know this beforehand, as I had insisted upon all my companions being unmarried. Like all Mountain-Lapps, he was pre-eminently lazy, and when we were not actually on the move no occupation pleased him so much as to sit quietly in a corner of the tent with his legs crossed, SAMUEL JOHAN.NIiSEN BALTU. OLL NIELSEN KAVNA.

doing absolutely nothing, after he had once brushed himself clean of snow. Rarely indeed was he seen to undertake any work unless he were directly called upon to do so. He was very small, but surprisingly strong, and capable of any amount of endurance, though he always managed to save his strength and reserve his powers. When we started he knew very little Norwegian, but for this very reason his remarks were extremely comical and provided us with plenty of amusement. He could not write, and had no acquaintance with so modern an apparatus as a watch. But he could read, and his favourite book was his Lappish New Testament, from which he was never parted.

Both the Iapps had come, as they declared themselves, merely to gain money, and interest and adventure had no place in their minds. On the contrary, they were afraid of everything, and were easily scared, which is not to be wondered at when it is remembered how very little they understood of the whole business at the outset. That they did not come back so ignorant as they went will be seen from some of Balto's observations, which I shall subsequently quote.

Ravna and Balto were good-natured and amiable: their fidelity was often actually touching, and I grew very fond of them both.

Chapter II.

*THE EQUIPMENT.*

It was my original intention to take, if possible, dogs or reindeer to drag our baggage. Plainly the advantage of such a course is considerable if one can only get the animals to the spot where the sledging will begin. Many men of experience have maintained that neither dogs nor reindeer are really any help for long sledging expeditions, because they can only drag their own food for a limited period. This argument I do not understand, for, surely, if one cannot use the animals for the whole journey, one can take them as far as their provender lasts and then kill them.

If one has a sufficient number of dogs or deer, and takes as much food for them as they can drag over and above the baggage of the expedition, then one can advance rapidly at the beginning without taxing one's own powers to any extent. At the same time, too, there is this advantage, that one can always procure a supply of fresh meat by slaughtering the animals one by one. For this reason so large a quantity of other food will not be necessary. And so, when one is at last obliged to kill the remaining animals, the expedition ought to have advanced a considerable distance without any exhaustion of the strength of its members, while they the whole time will have been able to eat their fill of good fresh meat. This is an. important point gained, for they will thus be able to take up the work as fresh and strong as when they started. It will no doubt be urged that these advantages will not be gained if dogs are taken. But I can answer from my own experience that hunger is a sufficiently good cook to render dog's flesh anything but unpalatable. The Eskimo indeed reckon it a delicacy, and it is certain that any one who could not in the circumstances bring himself to eat it would not be a fit person to accompany such an expedition at all.

If I could have obtained good dogs, I should therefore have taken them. Dogs are in some important points preferable to reindeer, because they are much easier to transport and much easier to feed, since they eat much the same as the men; while reindeer must have their own provender, consisting mainly of reindeer-moss, which would be a bulky and heavy addition to the baggage. However, it was quite impossible for me to obtain dogs which I could use in the time at my disposal, and I had to give up this idea. I then thought of reindeer, and not only wrote to Finmarken to make inquiries, but even bought moss for them in the neighbourhood of Roros. But then I found that there would be so many difficulties in connection with their transportation, and still more when we should have to land them in Greenland, that I abandoned the scheme altogether, and determined to be content with men alone.

When every scrap of food on which a man is going to live will have to be dragged by himself, it is a matter of course that good care will be taken to make everything as light as possible, and to reduce food, implements, and clothing to a minimum of weight. When one is busy with an equipment of this kind one begins instinctively to estimate the value of a thing entirely with reference to its lightness, and even if the article in question be nothing but a pocket-knife, the same considerations hold good. But care must be taken, nevertheless, not to go too far in the direction of lightness, for all the implements must be strong, since they will have to stand many a severe test. The clothing must be warm, since one has no idea what amount of cold it will have to meet; the food must be nourishing and composed of different ingredients in suitable proportion, for the work will be hard—harder, probably, than anything to which the workers have hitherto been accustomed.

One of the most important articles of equipment for a sledge expedition is, of course, the *sledge.* Considering that in the course of time so many Arctic expeditions have been sent out, and especially from England, one would suppose that the experience thus gained would have led to a high development in the form of the sledge. This is, however, not the case; and it is a matter for wonder, indeed, that polar expeditions so recent as the Second German Expedition of 1869 and 1870 to the east coast of Greenland, the Austrian and Hungarian expedition of 1872-1874 to Franz Joseph Land, and even the great English expedition of 1875 1876 under Nares to Smith's Sound, set out with such large, clumsy, and unpractical sledges as they actually took. Certainly the two latest expeditions, that of Greely in 1881-

1884, and the rescue party led by Schley and Soley, were better equipped in this respect. The general mistake has been that the sledges have been too heavily and clumsily built, and at the same time too large. And as in addition to this the runners were usually narrow, it is not difficult to understand that these sledges sank deep into the snow and were often almost immovable. Some expeditions have certainly made use of the Indian toboggan, which consists of a single board curved upwards in front. It is generally of birch or some similar wood, and is about eight feet long by eighteen inches or more broad.

Even in the beginning of this century these toboggans were used for Arctic purposes, and Franklin had some on his first expedition. The English traveller, Dr. Rae, and after him Greely, used similar sledges with very low and narrow runners, one on each side. Of course, sledges of this type ride well and high in loose snow, and are so far good and practical; but when the surface is not very loose they give rise to too much friction, and are comparatively heavy to pull.

Strangely enough, the organisers of a few expeditions have thpught of placing their sledges on broad runners. Payer, however, in his book upon the Austrian and Hungarian expedition, says that " broad runners make progress in deep snow much easier"; and he speaks of having them 2 inches in breadth. We Norwegians look upon this expedient as simply natural, as we are accustomed to our old-fashioned " skikjaelke," which is a low hand-sledge on broad runners, resembling our ordinary " ski." This was my model for the form of sledge which we actually adopted. Our sledge seemed to possess all desirable qualities: it was strong and light, rode high in loose snow, and moved easily on all kinds of surfaces. I based my design partly, too, upon that of the sledge which is described in the narrative of the Greely Expedition, and was used by the rescue party.

OUR SI.F.DOE.

All the woodwork of the sledges except the runners was of ash, and of as good and tough material as could be procured. And, as picked ash possesses such wonderful strength, we were able to make the upper parts of the sledge light and slender, without reducing their strength too much. The runners of two of the sledges were of elm, and those of the rest of a kind of maple *(Acer philanoides),* as these two woods glide remarkably well upon the snow. This, as it happened, was not a point of much importance, because I had the runners shod with thin steel plates, which I had intended to take off when we were once upon the loose snow, but which were nevertheless used the whole way except in the case of one sledge.

The accompanying drawing will no doubt give a sufficiently good idea of the structure of our sledge, and not much further description will be necessary. No nails or pegs were used, but all the joints were lashed, and the sledges were thus more elastic under shocks and strains, which would have often caused nails to start. As a matter of fact, nothing whatever was broken the whole journey through. The sledges were about 9 feet 6 inches long by i foot 8 inches broad, while the runners, measured from point to point along the steel plate, were 9 feet Sf inches. The fact that they were turned up behind as well as in front gave the whole sledge more strength and elasticity, and there was this advantage besides, that, had the fore end of a sledge been broken, we could have turned it round and dragged it equally well the other way. The chairback-like bow which is shown in the drawing was made of a slender bar of ash bent into position. It proved of great service for pushing and steering purposes, especially when we were passing over difficult ground, and were obliged to take two men to each sledge.

The weight of each sledge without the steel runners was about 25 Ibs., and with them rather more than 28 Ibs. Along the central line of these plates were attached narrow bars of steel with square edges, which were meant to serve as a kind of keel, and to make the sledges steer better on ice and to prevent them from swerving. This is an important point, for when one is passing along the crevasses of a glacier the swerving of a sledge may take it and its load, and even possibly one or more of the party, down into the depths of the ice. These bars were of excellent service while they lasted; but, as they were exposed to continual shocks and hard wear among the rough ice near the east coast, they were soon torn off, and this was especially the case when we climbed into low temperatures, as the steel then became as brittle as glass. Future expeditions, therefore, which make use of these keels under their runners, ought to have them attached in a different way. The strongest method would be, of course, to have them made in one piece with the steel plates, but in this case there would be the disadvantage that they could not be taken off at will.

As the drawing shows, there was a ridge running along the upper surface of each runner. The runners were made comparatively thin for the sake of lightness, and these extra ridges gave them the necessary stiffness and elasticity.

I had calculated that each sledge should be sufficient work for one man; but, as it is a good thing, when one is on difficult ground, to send one of the party on ahead to explore, and as in loose snow the leader has the hardest work to do, I thought it most practical to take only five sledges, and always put two men to the first.

The advantage of having a number of small sledges instead of one or two larger ones is this. On difficult ground, where the work is hard, it is very troublesome to have to manoeuvre large sledges with their heavy loads, and, in fact, we should have often found it a sheer impossibility to advance without unloading and making portages. We, on the contrary, could always put two or three of the party to each sledge, and thus push on without any such delay or inconvenience. Sometimes, indeed, we had to carry them bodily, loads and all.

When we proposed to sail our sledges, as we had several opportunities of doing, we placed two or three of them side by side, laid some "ski" or long staffs across them, and lashed the whole fast. For masts we had bamboo poles brought for the purpose, and for sails the floor of our tent and two tarpaulins. With another bamboo out in front, somewhat after the fashion of a carriage-pole, we could hold a good course and make fair progress. Any one who should equip himself specially for sailing would of course be able to manage things much more easily and successfully than we did. Sailing as a mode of progression was first tried on the " Inland ice" of Greenland by the American traveller Peary, and I think that future expeditions will do well to give more attention to the subject than has hitherto been done. I feel sure, too, that this method of getting over the ground may be adopted with advantage on the great snowfields of the Antarctic continent.

The construction of our "ski," on which we so much depended, was of as much importance as that of our sledges; but, as I intend to devote an entire chapter to the subject of "skilobning" generally, as well as to the part these instruments played in the expedition, I will say no more about them for the present.

We took with us also *Indian snc- nt'shoes,* and their Norwegian counterpart, the so-called "truger." As most of my readers

"truce" And "finxesko." no doubt know, the Indian snowshoe consists of a kind of plaited network of moose-or other sinews stretched upon a frame of ash, or some equally tough wood, the whole construction somewhat resembling that of an ordinary tennis-bat. Ours were some 42 inches in length by 15 i inches in breadth.

The Norwegian "truger" are of much less elaborate structure, and are made of simple osier-work, in the form shown by the accompanying illustration. Ours were small, being only 15 inches in length and ioj inches across. These "truger" are used not infrequently in different parts of Norway both in winter and spring, and on the snow which one finds in the latter season, when " ski" are scarcely so good for practical purposes, they may be very serviceable. In many districts, however, they are employed more for the-aid of horses than

men. These " hestetruger," as they are called, are of exactly the same pattern, though the manner of attachment of course differs in the two cases. Our little mountain ponies soon become accustomed to these aids to progress, and can therefore be used when the amount or condition of the snow would render the employment of less accomplished animals quite impossible.

It will be understood from what follows hereafter that all these forms of snowshoe are, for general use, much inferior to our "ski "on the feet of any one who is accustomed to the use of the latter. The reason why I took these other implements was because I thought they would be of more service when we had to drag our heavy sledges uphill. We used them for this purpose too—that is to say, I myself and two of the others used the Indian snowshoes; our fourth man could never learn to manage these and took to the " truger," though they let him considerably deeper into the snow, while the Lapps expressed a lofty contempt for both kinds, and would have nothing whatever to say to them. But it was not long before we all took to our " ski" for good, and found them preferable even for uphill work. These snowshoes have, however, two advantages as compared with " ski." When the latter are not covered with skin beneath they are more troublesome to use than snowshoes in mild weather, when the snow is sticky, and they are in any case considerably heavier to carry.

To make sure of getting a serviceable *boat,* which should be light enough to drag over the rough sea-ice and yet not weak enough to succumb to the violent shocks and sudden strains which it was sure to be exposed to among the capricious floes, I had one specially built in Christiania. Its length was 19 feet, its greatest breadth 6 feet, and its depth inside 2 feet. The boarding was double, each jacket being g inch thick, the inner of pine, the outer of the best Norwegian oak, the two as carefully riveted together as possible, and the intervening space filled by a layer of thin canvas. The ribs were of bent ash i inch broad and inch thick, and were placed at intervals of 6

inches. Below the boat I had, besides the keel, runners of pine added to support it while it was being hauled over the ice. The boat proved a great success; it was strong and elastic enough to resist the pressure of the floes; but for the future I should be inclined to recommend single boarding instead of double, not only because in the former case the boat is easier to repair, but because the intervening space is liable to hold water and increase the weight. Again, I found that the added runners were really of very little use, while they OUR BOAT.
were always liable to get nipped in the ice, and thus help to destroy the whole boat.

The *sleeping-bag* is, of course, a most important article of equipment for all Arctic expeditions. In our case, the nature of the material of which the bag should be made needed our best consideration, as it was necessary that it should be at the same time light and sufficiently warm. On previous expeditions sometimes wool and sometimes skins have been used. Wool, of course, lets the perspiration through much more readily, and there is not so much condensation of moisture inside as in the case of skin; but, on the other hand, wool has the disadvantage of being very heavy in comparison with the amount of warmth which it affords. For a time I thought of trying woollen bags, but I came to the conclusion that they would not be warm enough, and I now think that if we had taken them we should have scarcely reached the west coast of Greenland alive.

After several experiments I determined to use reindeer-skin, as the best material which I could procure in the circumstances. Reindeer-skin is, in comparison with its weight, the warmest of all similar materials known to me, and the skin of the calf, in its winter-coat especially, combines the qualities of warmth and lightness in quite an unusual degree. This particular skin, however, I could not procure in time, and I was obliged to HALF THE EXPEDITION IN ITS SLEEPING-BAG.
be satisfied with that of the doe, which is considerably heavier. Reindeer-skin

has this disadvantage, that the fur does not stand much wear, and the skin, if exposed much to wet, soon loses its hair. From this point of view, dog-skin is a good deal better and stronger, but it gives nothing like the warmth of reindeer-skin. Wolf-skin is still better than dog-skin, and the only objection to it is its cost. However, our reindeer-skin lasted well through the whole journey and the winter on the west coast. It was specially prepared for us by Brandt, the well-known furrier at Bergen, and I had every reason to be satisfied with it.

We took two sleeping-bags, calculated to hold three men each. This proved a thoroughly practical arrangement, since one bag for three men is, of course, much lighter than three, each for a single occupant, and much warmer, too, because the three mutually profit by each other's heat. In this respect one bag for all of us would have been still better, but I dared not risk the arrangement, for, had the sledge carrying the one bag gone down a crevasse, we should have been left entirely without protection against the low temperature of the nights; while, as it was, if we had been unlucky enough to lose one of our bags, we should still have had the other left, into which we could have put four men under pressure, and so taken turn and turn about.

Our bags had a hood-shaped flap, which could be buckled over our heads when necessary. As long as the cold was not extreme we found it warm enough with this flap just laid over us; but when the temperature got lower we were glad enough to have it buckled as tight as the straps would allow, for the aperture still left gave us quite enough ventilation. Very little, indeed, of the cold night-air of the interior of Greenland inside a sleeping-bag is more than sufficient. To protect the bags against outside moisture I had had some covers made of thin oilcloth, but we abandoned these soon after we started across the " Inland ice."

As our bags were of reindeer-skin, I did not think it necessary to take india-rubber air mattresses, and, as they are very heavy, it was a great advantage to be able to do without them.

In the way of *clothes* we had, except for a few reserve things, very little but what we were actually wearing when we left Norway. With the exception of two tunics of reindeer-skin which the Lapps wore, and a little coat lined with squirrel-skin which I took, but scarcely used, we had no furs, but wore woollen things throughout. Next our skins we had thin woollen shirts and drawers, then thick, rough jerseys, and then our outer garments, which consisted of a short coat, knickerbockers, and gaiters. These were all made of a kind of Norwegian homespun, which gave every satisfaction. Whether the work be hard or not, woollen clothes are far the best, as they give free outlet to the perspiration, whereas cotton, linen, or skins would check it. Above all things, we had to take care that we did not get overheated, because the succeeding chill was so likely to lead to freezing. As we got warm we had, therefore, to gradually abandon one garment after another, and we might often have been seen in fifty and sixty degrees of frost working in our jerseys, and yet perspiring as on an ordinary summer's day.

In wind, snow, and rain we generally wore outside our other clothes a light suit of some thin, brown, canvas-like stuff. This was reputed completely waterproof, but it turned out to be nothing of the kind. In wind and snow, however, it did excellent service, and we used it often on the " Inland ice," as it protected us well against the fine driven snow, which, being of the nature of dust, forces itself into every pore of a woollen fabric, and then, melting, wets it through and through.

To these canvas coats were attached hoods for the head, which were large enough to project well in front of the face. These protected us excellently from the wind, which in a low temperature can be exceedingly trying, not to say dangerous, to one's cheeks and nose.

For *am feet* we took, besides ordinary boots, the peculiar form known in Norway as "lauparsko." The soles of these latter consist of a piece of pliant leather turned up along the sides and at the toe, and sewn to the upper leather on the upper surface of the foot. Inside these " lauparsko " we wore first a pair of thick, well-shrunk woollen stockings, and over them thick, rough goat's-hair socks, which, in addition to being warm, have the excellent quality of attracting moisture to themselves, and thus keeping the feet comparatively dry. The two Lapps had two pair of " finnesko " each, as well as one pair which Balto insisted on presenting to me. These " finnesko " when good are made of the skin of the legs of the reindeer buck, the pieces with the hair on being laid for twenty-four hours or so in a strong decoction of birch or similar bark, or sometimes tanned in tar-water. The skin of the hind legs is used for the soles and sides, and that of the fore legs for the upper leather, the hair being left outside throughout the boot.

These " finnesko," then, which, as I have said, are worn with the hair outside, and which the Lapps fill with sedge or "sennegraes," wrapping their bare feet in the grass and using no stockings, are a pre-eminently warm covering for the feet, and very suitable for use on " ski " or snowshoes. The reason why I had not taken them for our general use was because

"lauparsko."

I supposed we should be much exposed to the wet, which these shoes will not stand. In this respect one has to take very great care of " finnesko," or they will soon be spoilt. As a matter of fact, we were not much in the wet, and the pair of shoes which Balto gave me I wore nearly the whole way across the " Inland ice," as well as during the following winter, and brought them back to Norway with a good deal still left in them. Nor was this all, for they were not new when I got them, as Balto had already used them for a winter. I can therefore speak with confidence as to the suitability of " finnesko" for such expeditions, and can give them the warmest recommendation. They weigh scarcely anything at c all, and one can take a couple of reserve pairs for each of the members of an expedition without feeling the addition.

On our *hands* we used large woollen gloves, as well as in extreme cold an extra pair of dogskin gloves with the hair outside, neither having any separate divisions for the ringers. The lapps used their ordinary gloves of reindeer-skin, which also have the furry side outwards. When these gloves are filled, like the " finnesko,''with " sen negraes," they are exceedingly warm. For use while writing, sketching, and WOODKN EYE-PKOTKCTORS.

taking observations, we also had ordinary woollen gloves with fingers.

On our heads we wore caps of the costermonger pattern, with flaps for the ears and the back of the neck, and, besides these, hoods of cloth as well as those attached to our canvas jackets. With all these three on we were thoroughly well protected against the severest cold, even when the wind was blowing.

The *spectacles,* for prevention of snow-blindness, are another important article of equipment for a sledge-expedition. We used spectacles of dark, smoke-coloured glass, some without and some with baskets of plaited wire to protect the eye against light coming from below and the sides. I myself chiefly used a pair of the latter, which had been given me by Nordenskiold, and which I found excellent. We also used spectacles or eye-protectors of wood with a narrow horizontal slit for each eye, like those commonly used by the inhabitants of Arctic regions. These are very serviceable, especially for the reason that there is no glass to collect moisture and obstruct the sight. They have, however, the disadvantage that the field of vision is very considerably reduced, and it is particularly inconvenient not to be able to see the ground at one's feet when one is travelling on "ski." But I should fancy that this defect might to some extent be met by making a vertical slit as well as a horizontal.

Our *tent,* which was kindly procured by Lieutenant Ryder of Copenhagen, was constructed so that it could be taken into five pieces: two sides, two ends, and the floor, all of them of waterproof canvas. My notion had been that we should be able to use all these sections as sails for our sledges, but the ends and sides were of such thin material that I was afraid the wind would tear them to shreds. The canvas was otherwise most successful against the rain, wind, and driving snow. But as it is necessary to have a thin material for the puqrose of saving weight, I would recommend future expeditions to have their tents sewn in one piece with the floor; the whole would then have the construction of a bag with but one opening, which would serve as the tent-door, as well as two small holes in the floor for the poles, which would be put through them and rammed down into the snow. The strong canvas floor of such a tent can nevertheless be used as a sail, as the thinner pieces can be left to hang down and be gathered together in front. By this means one would avoid the inconvenience of having the fine snow driven in through the laced joins. Our tent was in this respect so imperfect that we would sometimes wake in the morning and find our sleeping-bags completely buried in snow. The floor-surface of our tent was just large enough to hold the two sleeping-bags when they were placed alongside one another, but in opposite ways. The tent-poles were three in number, two being used as uprights, and the other joining them at the top; they were all of bamboo and proved quite sufficient for the purpose, and the two smaller ones were used as staffs while we were on the move. The guy-ropes were fastened with broad iron crampon-like hooks, which gave a good hold. On the whole, the tent stood very well in the snow, though in several storms we were very much afraid that it would go, and I would therefore recommend others to have good storm-guys. We had some, indeed, but one or two of them gave at the point of attachment and were not easy to repair.

The exact weight of the tent, after I had made considerable alterations and reductions, I do not quite remember, though I know that with guys, pegs, and poles it did not altogether exceed eighteen pounds.

The value of a good *cooking apparatus* to the members of a sledge-expedition can scarcely be overrated, for often by its help every drop of drinking-water over and above that which can be melted by the heat of the body must be obtained. The most important qualification is that it shall make the most of the fuel, or, in other words, that it shall render combustion as complete as possible, and let none of the heat escape till it has done its work. In this way the weight of one of the most important articles of equipment is reduced to a minimum.

For/z/?/ there is, no doubt, nothing at all comparable with alcohol, which should be as pure as possible. In addition to other advantages, such as its cleanliness, it has the great merit of yielding more heat than anything else in comparison to its weight. It has certainly two defects, for, in the first place, as a liquid it is easily spilt and wasted, though this may be avoided by using the very best of barrels and taps, and by only giving it into careful hands; and, in the second place, it is drinkable, and at critical times may prove a strong temptation to the best of men. But this, again, may be prevented by adding enough wood-naphtha to make it unpleasant, as we in fact did.

The idea of our cooker was originally taken from that used by the Greely expedition, and after a number of experiments made with the assistance of a friend, I determined finally to adopt the apparatus which is represented by the accompanying drawing. This drawing will, no doubt, make the construction quite intelligible. At the bottom is the heating-chamber, containing a spirit-lamp with several wicks. The air enters by a number of holes at the bottom in sufficient quantity to insure complete combustion, and, as it must itself pass through or near the flames, it is either consumed or heated to such an extent that no cold air can enter the apparatus. Should it be necessary, owing to the overheating of *s*-GL-_ the lamp, to let some cold air in, this can be done by holes in the sides of the hot chamber. This, I am sorry to say, we allowed to happen too often. The boiler, which is placed upon the hot chamber, was of copper and tin-lined. It was a tall cylindrical vessel with a copper flue running through the centre, by means of which the heated air is passed from the lower chamber up to the bottom of a broader and shallower copper vessel, which was placed over the boiler and used to Our Cooker. elt snow in. Thus the air, having delivered a great part of its warmth in the boiler flue and on to the bottom of the snow-melter, eventually escapes through holes in the sides just below the latter.

The boiler and the melter were both cased in thick felt, and the latter was also provided with a lid.

With snow at about-20 Fahr., and with the air at something like the same temperature, it would take an hour or more before I had the boiler full of boiling chocolate, and the upper vessel full of water at a temperature a little above the melting-point of ice. The quantities would be a little more than a gallon of chocolate and rather less water, while to obtain this result I had to use about ten or eleven ounces of spirit; but careful management was necessary. Experiments made after our return home showed me that our cooker made use of only 52 per cent, of the alcohol consumed. This is, of course, a somewhat extravagant use of fuel, though previous expeditions do not seem to have been much more successful. Yet there is no doubt that further improvements in this direction will lead to a considerable reduction in the consumption of spirit.

By way of making the heat of the body do some of the work of melting snow, each of us had a tin flask of a flat and slightly concave form, which could be carried at the breast without inconvenience.

The *provisions* of a sledge-expedition must necessarily consist to a large extent of dried articles of food, as they contain most nourishment in proportion to their weight Preserved things in tins are no doubt more wholesome and easily digestible, but they are much too heavy and can be made little use of.

I had previously reckoned that we should need per day rather more than half a pound of dried meat, about the same amount of fatty food, and a little more of dried bread or biscuit, and that with the addition of various things like chocolate, sugar, peptonised meat, pea-soup, and so on, the whole daily ration would reach two pounds and a quarter, or a little more.

This amount would have proved sufficient if we had only had the proper quantities of each kind of food, but, owing to a misunderstanding, there was a want of fatty stuffs, which caused us a good deal of inconvenience. Herr Beauvais of Copenhagen, who was to provide our pemmican, informed me that he was accustomed to prepare it in the usual way. I had no opportunity of seeing him personally, but supposing that his pemmican, like the ordinary preparation, would consist of dried meat and fat in equal quantities, or would contain at least a third part of the latter, I ordered the necessary amount of him. As I was passing through Copenhagen just before we started I learned that his pemmican was carefully purified of all fat This was an unpleasant surprise; but, as we had a certain quantity of butter, as well as some liver " pate " of a very fatty nature, I thought we should get on well enough. However, it proved a very short supply, and in the end we suffered from a craving for fat which can scarcely be realised by any one who has not experienced it. In other respects Beauvais' dried meat was excellent.

On the advice of Captain Hovgaard, I tried the same manufacturer's " leverpostei," which I may say is not the Strasburg luxury, but a humbler preparation of calf-liver. However, I found it quite unsuited to our needs: in the first place, because it is much too heavy in comparison to its nutritive value; and, secondly, because it contains water, which freezes and makes it unconscionably hard. On ours we broke several knives, and we had eventually to take to the axe; but then it was necessary to go round afterwards to gather up the fragments, which flew far and wide over the snow.

We found Rousseau's meat-powder chocolate especially useful, as it is both nourishing and palatable. I took 45 Ibs. of it, which I ordered of the manufacturer in Paris. The analysis of this chocolate shows that it contains as much as 20 per cent, of meat powder. It certainly had a particularly invigorating effect upon us, and if a sufficient amount of fat were taken with it, and it were given in small quantities, it would prove a most excellent food for men while on the move. As compared with pemmican we found it very easy of digestion. This is a quality which has both advantages and disadvantages. If any substance is too easily digested, it is taken into the body at once, the stomach becomes empty again, and a feeling of hunger ensues. On the other hand, many people will find a substance like pemmican too hard to digest, and in such cases a large amount of nutriment will be passed through without doing its proper work. But easily digestible substances have, on the whole, a greater nutritive value in proportion to their weight than such as are less readily assimilable, and therefore it must be considered that the possession of the former quality in an article of food is a strong recommendation for its use by Arctic travellers.

As bread we used partly the Swedish biscuit known as " knakkebrod," which is very light and has not that dryness of taste which causes a feeling of thirst, and partly meat biscuits. These had to be specially ordered in England, and contained a certain percentage of meat powder as well as flour. They proved palatable as well as nourishing.

For warm drink, which, though no necessity, is undoubtedly a great comfort, we generally used chocolate in the morning and pea-soup in the evening.

We also took tea and coffee, the latter in the form of extract, of which we had rather more than a quart. After having tried this two or three times in the afternoon and evening, and found that, though it made us feel better and cheered us up for the time, we got little or no sleep in the night afterwards, I confined its use to a morning every now and then. But, as it did not seem to suit us even at this time of day, it was finally tabooed altogether, till we had almost reached the west coast, much to the despair of the Lapps. Tea, as far as I can judge, does considerably less harm, and is besides a very refreshing drink. Ve often used weak tea with condensed milk or a little sugar, especially in the morning, after all our chocolate was gone.

My experience, however, leads me to take a decided stand against the use of stimulants and narcotics of all kinds, from tea and coffee on the one hand, to tobacco and alcoholic drinks on the other. It must be a sound principle at all times that one should live in as natural and simple a way as possible, and especially must this be the case when the life is a life of severe exertion in an extremely cold climate. The idea that one gains by stimulating body and mind by artificial means betrays in my opinion not only ignorance of the simplest physiological laws, but also a want of experience, or perhaps a want of capacity to learn from experience by observation. It seems indeed quite simple and obvious that one can get nothing in this life without paying for it in one way or another, and that artificial stimulants, even if they had not the directly injurious effect which they undoubtedly have, can produce nothing but a temporary excitement followed by a corresponding reaction. Stimulants of this kind, with the exception of chocolate, which is mild in its effect and at the same time nourishing, bring practically no nutritive substance into the body, and the energy which one obtains in anticipation by their use at one moment must be paid for by a corresponding exhaustion at the next. It may, no doubt, be advanced that there are occasions when a momentary supply of energy is necessary, but to this I would answer that I cannot imagine such a state of things arising in the course of a protracted sledge-expedition, when regular and steady work is required.

It is often supposed that, even though spirits are not intended for daily use, they ought to be taken upon an expedition for medicinal purposes. I would readily acknowledge this if any one could show me a single case in which such a remedy is necessary; but till this is done I shall maintain that this pretext is not sufficient, and that the best course is to banish alcoholic drinks from the list of necessaries for an Arctic expedition.

Though tobacco is less destructive than alcohol, still, whether it is smoked or chewed, it has an extremely harmful effect upon men who are engaged in severe physical exertion, and not least so when the supply of food is not abundant. Tobacco has not only an injurious influence upon the digestion, but it lessens the strength of the body, and reduces nervous power, capacity for endurance, and tenacity of purpose. With regard to the complete prohibition of tobacco in Arctic work, there is one circumstance to be borne in mind which has not to be considered in connection with spirits, as habitual hard drinkers are scarcely likely to take part in these expeditions: the circumstance that most men are so accustomed to its use that they will keenly feel the want of it. For this reason it would probably be advisable not to make the change too sudden, but to limit the use by degrees, and at the same time, perhaps, not to take excessive smokers and chewers of tobacco upon such expeditions at all.

Among us, four were smokers, Ravna and I being the exceptions, but our supply of tobacco was but small. During the crossing only one pipe was allowed on Sundays and other specially solemn occasions.

Our other provisions, over and above those which I have already mentioned, consisted of butter, some " raekling," or dried strips of halibut, which is of a very fat nature, Gruyere cheese, the Norwegian " mysost" or whey-cheese, two boxes of oatmeal biscuits, some " tyttebaer" or red whortleberry jam, some dried "karvekaal" or caraway shoots, some peptonised meat, eight pounds of sugar, a few tins of condensed milk, and a few other things, all in small quantities.

We were also presented by the Stavanger Preserving Company with some tins of provisions, which we much enjoyed while we were drifting in the ice, and afterwards while we were working our way in the boats up the coast again. This extra supply we had to some extent to thank for the fact that our provisions, which were calculated to last for two months, actually held out for two months and a half, that is to say, from the time we left *thefasott* till Sverdrup and I reached Godthaab. Indeed, we really had a good deal left at the end, especially of dried meat, and some of us used these remnants long after we had reached our winter-quarters. Of the dried meat which had passed the " Inland ice " there was even some left at Christmas.

In connection with the provision supply I may also mention our two double-barrelled guns with their ammunition. Each of them had a barrel for ball of about-300 calibre, and a shot barrel of zo-bore.

The small calibre of these barrels allowed of a considerable reduction in the weight of the ammunition, and I found the guns perfectly satisfactory, whether for seal or sea-birds. They would have been quite sufficient for bear also in the hands of a good shot, for here, as at other times, the most important factor is the man behind the sights. Our guns were intended as well to procure us food on the east coast, especially if it had been necessary to pass the winter there—and with this in view I had thought of leaving a cache of ammunition with one gun on the eastern side—as to give us a supply of fresh meat on the west coast if we did not find people at once. For, given the sea-coast, a gun, and something to put in it, there need never be a lack of food.

The *scientific instruments* of the expedition consisted first of a theodolite, an excellent instrument by a Christiania maker. It was certainly heavy, about 7 Ibs. in itself, and had a stand which weighed little less; but, on the other hand, it proved exceedingly trustworthy for both terrestrial and astronomical observations. In future I should prefer to have the theodolite, as well as other instruments, made of aluminium, which would save much in weight.

The sextant was a nice little pocket

instrument by Perken, Son, & Rayment, of London, which did excellent service. For the artificial horizon we used mercury, which never froze at mid-day. The great weight of mercury leads me to think that oil would be more serviceable for this purpose.

The rest included an azimuth dial with three compasses, for the testing of magnetic deviation as well as for trigonometrical observations; five pocket compasses; three aneroid barometers from the above-mentioned English makers; and a hypsometer, or boiling-point barometer, with the necessary thermometers.

The principle of this last barometer depends upon the accurate determination of the boiling-point of pure water, which, as is well known, varies with the atmospheric pressure, and therefore, of course, with the altitude. I found this a particularly convenient form of barometer, and its inconsiderable weight makes it especially suitable for an expedition like ours, whereas a mercurial instrument would be much too heavy and difficult to transport.

Our thermometers consisted of six special instruments intended to be tied to strings and whirled rapidly round in the air. The bulb is thus brought into contact with so many particles of air that the effect of the sun's rays upon it may be almost disregarded, and the temperature of the air can thus easily be taken in the full sunshine.

If the bulb of one of these sling-thermometers be covered with a piece of some thin stuff like gauze and then wetted, one can readily find the degree of moisture present in the air by comparison with a dry-bulb instrument.

We had, besides the above, a minimum and an ordinary alcohol thermometer, both presented us by a Christiania maker.

Our time-keepers were four ordinary watches of the half-chronometer movement. The usual chronometer watches are scarcely suitable for such work, as in certain positions they are liable to stop. We were in fact exceedingly unlucky with our watches, as one of them, owing to a fall, stopped entirely; another, for the same reason apparently, became somewhat inaccurate; and a third, an old watch of my own, came to a stand-still, probably for want of cleaning. The fourth, however, stood the whole journey well, and proved an excellent time-keeper.

I consider that the expedition was particularly well equipped in the way of instruments, and this was to a large extent due to Professor H. Mohn, the Director of the Meteorological Institute at Christiania, who gave the most unremitting attention to the question of our scientific outfit.

At the request of Professor Pettersson, of Stockholm, I took on his behalf the necessary apparatus for obtaining samples of air during our journey. This consisted chiefly of a number of moderate-sized glass cylinders carefully exhausted of air and hermetically sealed. On being opened they were of course at once filled, and the vessels were so arranged that they could be easily sealed again by the help of a spirit-lamp and a blow-pipe. The air obtained could thus be transported any distance in its original condition.

A necessary addition to the outfit of a modern exploring party is, of course, a photographic apparatus. I took a little camera to use with the theodolite stand, two roll-holders for Eastman's American stripping films, and ten rolls of twenty-four exposures each. The camera alone weighed two and a quarter pounds. I made about 150 exposures, and on the whole was well satisfied with the apparatus and the results. Glass plates would, of course, have been much too heavy and inconvenient. I also had two red lamps, one of glass and the other of paper, for changing the rolls, and a few stearine candles to use in them.

Our remaining instruments, tools, and other things included two pairs of aluminium glasses and a couple of pedometers: an axe, with various smaller implements, such as knives, files, awls, pincers, screwdriver, small screws for the steel plates under the sledge-runners, a sailmaker's palm, sewing materials, and so on; scales for weighing out the rations; Tyrolese crampons or "steigeisen," ice-nails for our boots, Manilla-rope for the crevasses, as well as other cords for the sledges and various purposes; ice-axes with bamboo-shafts, which were also used as " ski "-staffs; a spade for the snow, to screw on to one of these shafts; several bamboos for masts and steering purposes while our sledges and boats were under sail, and block-tackle for hoisting the boats and sledges when necessary; drawing materials, sketch-and note-books; a table of logarithms; nautical almanacs for 1888 and 1889; burning-glass, flint and steel, and matches, which latter were partly packed in air-tight tin boxes, and kept here and there among the baggage in order that, if we lost some, we should still have enough left; three cans of methylated spirit holding rather more than two gallons apiece; tarpaulins, some of waterproof canvas, and others of oil-cloth, to cover the sledges; six bags intended for making portages over difficult ground. but really used as portmanteaus for each member's private effects; long boat-hooks of bamboo, as well as short ones, which could also be used as paddles, and proved exceedingly serviceable in narrow waterways; oars, reserve swivel-rowlocks, and a hand-pump and hose to bale the boats with when they were loaded. Finally, we had a little medicine-chest containing splints and bandages for broken limbs, chloroform, cocaine in solution for the alleviation of pain from snow-blindness, toothache drops, pills, vaseline, and a few other things, all of course reduced to a minimum of weight.

Finally, I may say that four of our sledges when fully loaded averaged some 200 pounds, while the fifth amounted to nearly double as much.

In April we made a little experimental trip up into the woods near Christiania, all the members of the party except one being present. Balto's description of the excursion is worth reproducing:—

"One afternoon we went out of the town up into the woods to spend the night there, and try the reindeer-skin sleeping bags. In the evening, when we had reached the wood where we were to pass the night, we put up our tent. Then it was said that we were going to make coffee in a machine to be heated by spirit. So the pot of this machine was filled with snow, and we lighted the lamp beneath. It went on burning for several hours, but never managed to produce a boil. So we had to try and drink the lukewarm water with coffee extract added to it. It did not taste of anything whatever, for it was almost cold. At night when it was time to sleep, the four Norwegians crawled into the bags, and Nansen offered us places there too, but we were afraid it would be too hot. We did not want bags to sleep in, we thought, and so we lay down outside. In the morning I woke about six and saw our men sleeping like bears in their sacks. So I lay down again and slept till nine, when I woke the others, for I knew that a horse had been ordered to take us back at ten."

This description shows plainly enough that certain parts of our outfit, as our cooking-machine, for instance, were not so satisfactory as they might have been, but there was plenty of time left for improvements. We gave our best attention to the matter, and when we actually started at the beginning of May, after having procured several important things at the eleventh hour, we had nearly everything in the desired state of efficiency, and plenty of time during our voyage to finish all that was not yet ready.

Chapter III.

*"SKI" AND "SKILOBNING."*

The expedition I am about to describe owed its origin entirely to the Norwegian sport of "skilobning." I have myself been accustomed to the use of "ski" since I was four years old, every one of my companions was an experienced "skilober," and all our prospects of success were based upon the superiority of "ski" in comparison with all other means of locomotion when large tracts of snow have to be traversed. I therefore think that I cannot do better than set apart a chapter for the description of "ski" and the manner of their use, since so little is known about the

sport outside the few countries where it is practised as such, and since a certain amount of familiarity with it and its technical terms will be necessary to the full comprehension of some part of the narrative which follows.

It is, of course, not unnatural that those who have never seen the performance should be surprised to learn that a man can by the help of two pieces of wood, shaped for the purpose, progress as rapidly over the surface of the snow as he really does.

" Ski," then, are long narrow strips of wood, those used in Norway being from three to four inches in breadth, eight feet more or less in length, one inch in thickness at the centre under the foot, and bevelling off to about a quarter of an inch at either end. In front they are curved upwards and pointed, and they are sometimes a little turned up at the back end too. The sides are more or less parallel, though the best forms have Sec note to page 3. 8 ON LEVEL GROUND. *(Frew a photograph.)* their greatest width in front, just where the upward curve begins, but otherwise they are quite straight and flat, and the under surface is made as smooth as possible. The attachment consists of a loop for the toe, made of leather or some other substance, and fixed at about the centre of the " ski,'' and a band which passes from this round behind the heel of the shoe. The principle of this fastening is to make the " ski" and foot as rigid as possible for steering purposes, while the heel is allowed to rise freely from the "ski" at all times.

On flat ground the " ski" are driven forward by a peculiar stride, which in its elementary form is not difficult of acquirement, though it is capable of immense development. They are not lifted, and the tendency which the beginner feels to tramp away with them as if he were on mud-boards in the middle of a marsh must be strenuously resisted. Lifting causes the snow to stick to them, so they must be pushed forwards over its surface by alternate strokes from the hips and thighs, the way being maintained between the strokes by a proper management of the body. The " ski" are

kept strictly parallel meanwhile, and as close together as possible, there being no resemblance whatever, as is sometimes supposed, to the motion employed in skating. In the hand most "skilobers" carry a short staff, which is used partly to correct deficiencies of balance, but by the more skilful chiefly to increase the length of the stride by propulsion. In many country districts this pole often reaches a preposterous length, and in some parts, too, a couple of short staffs are used, one in each hand, by the help of which, on comparatively flat ground, great speed can be obtained. When the snow is in thoroughly good condition the rate of progress is quite surprising, considering the small amount of effort expended, and as much as eight or nine miles can be done within the hour, while a speed of seven miles an hour can be maintained for a very considerable length of time.

Uphill the pace is, of course, very much slower, though here-also the practised "skilober" has great advantages over all others. Here the "ski" must be lifted.slightly, as the snow sticking to them counteracts the tendencyto slip backwards. If the gradient be steep, various devices may be employed, the most effectual and characteristic being that shown in the annexed illustration.

t. UP-AND DOWN-HILL. *(By E. Nielsen, after a photograph.)*

The " ski" are turned outwards at as wide an angle as the steepness of the slope renders advisable, and are advanced alternately one in front of the other, the track left in the snow exactly resembling the feather-stitch of needlewomen. This method requires some practice, and cannot be employed if the " ski" are above a certain length, as the heels will then necessarily overlap. By its means a slope of any gradient on which the snow will lie may be ascended quickly and easily, but the position is somewhat too strained to be maintained for long. Another and easier, though much slower way, is to mount the hill sideways, bringing the "ski" almost, if not quite, to a right angle with the slope, and working up step by step. Or again, especially on the open mountain, the " skilober " will work his way upwards by tacking from side to side and following a zigzag course, taking instinctively the most advantageous line of ascent. In any case, if he be up to his work he will cover the ground quickly and without undue exertion, and, as a matter of fact, as Olaus Magnus wrote in 1555, "there is no mountain so high but that by cunning devices he is able to attain unto the summit thereof."

Downhill, the " ski " slide readily and are left to themselves, the one thing necessary being to maintain the balance and steer clear of trees, rocks, and precipices. The steeper the slope the greater the speed, and if the snow be good the friction is so slight that the pace often approaches within a measurable distance of that of a falling body. The author of " Kongespeilet," an old Norse treatise, was speaking not altogether at random when he described the "skilober" as outstripping the birds in flight, and declared that nothing which runs upon the earth can escape his pursuit.

The snow is not by any means always in a good condition for "skilobning," and its moods are very variable and capricious. Wet snow due to a mild temperature is particularly unfavourable, as it sticks fast to the under surface of the "ski," especially if they are not covered with skin, and will often accumulate into a mass ten inches or a foot thick, the weight of which makes progress terribly laborious or well-nigh impossible. This is a.fate which has befallen many an unlucky "skilober" when he has been out on the open mountain, or more especially in the deep loose snow of the forest, and a sudden rise of temperature has surprised him when many miles distant from a habitation.

Nor do the " ski " move readily on newly fallen snow the temperature of which is not sufficiently low, though even when it falls in extreme cold it has a tendency to stick. The same is the case with snow raised from the ground and driven by the wind. The particles are then as fine as dust, and as they pack into drifts they form a peculiar cloth-like surface on which ordinary wooden

"ski" will scarcely move at all. This is worst of all when the snow has originally fallen at a low temperature, as the particles are then extremely fine in the first instance, before the wind has had any effect on them. This was the kind of snow we had to deal with during nearly the whole of our crossing of the "Inland ice," and was the reason why our progress was so very slow and wearisome.

But besides being slippery the surface must also be tolerably firm, or the "ski" will sink too deep. Snow that has fallen during a thaw, has had time to sink and pack well together, and has then been exposed to frost, is in excellent condition for the purposes of the "skilober." Things are even more favourable when a frost succeeding a rapid thaw has turned the surface into a hard icy crust, and if this is subsequently covered with an inch or so of newly-fallen snow, or preferably hoar-frost, the going reaches the pure ideal, and the pace which may then be obtained without effort is simply astonishing. If this crust lie, as it often does, bare of loose snow or rime, the "ski" slide fast enough, but have no proper hold on the surface, and the pace on rough and difficult ground may very soon become uncontrollable and dangerous.

Of all the sports of Norway, "skilobning" is the most national and characteristic, and I cannot think that I go too far when I claim for it, as practised in our country, a position in the very first rank of the sports of the world. I know no form of sport which so evenly develops the muscles, which renders the body so strong and elastic, which teaches so well the qualities of dexterity and resource, which in an equal degree calls for

A STEEP DESCENT IN THE FOREST.
*From a drawing by A. Block.)* decision and resolution, and which gives the same vigour and exhilaration to mind and body alike. Where can one find a healthier and purer delight than when on a brilliant winter day one binds one's " ski" to one's feet and takes one's way out into the forest? Can there be anything more beautiful than the northern

winter landscape, when the snow lies foot-deep, spread as a soft white mantle over field and wood and hill? Where will one find more freedom and excitement than when one glides swiftly down the hillside through the trees, one's cheek brushed by the sharp cold air and frosted pine branches, and one's eye, brain, and muscles alert and prepared to meet every unknown obstacle and danger which the next instant may throw in one's path? Civilisation is, as it were, washed clean from the mind and left far behind with the city atmosphere and city life; one's whole being is, so to say, wrapped in one's " ski" and the surrounding nature. There is something in the whole which develops soul and not body alone, and the sport is perhaps of far greater national importance than is. generally supposed.

Nor can there be many lands so well fitted as ours for the practice of " skilobning," and its full development as a sport. The chief requisites are hills and snow, and of these we have indeed an abundance. From our childhood onwards we are accustomed to use our " ski," and in many a mountain valley, boys, and girls too for that matter, are by their very surroundings forced to take to their " ski" almost as soon as they can walk. The whole long winter through, from early autumn to late spring, the snow lies soft and deep outside the cottage door. In such valleys, and this was especially the case in former times, there are few roads or ways of any kind, and all, men and women alike, whom business or pleasure takes abroad, must travel on their "ski." Children no more than three or four years old may often be seen striving with the first difficulties, and from this age onwards the peasant boys in many parts keep themselves in constant practice. Their homes lie, as a rule, on the steep slope of the valley-side, and hills of all grades are ready to hand. To school, which is generally held in the winter season, they must go on their "ski," and on their "ski"they all spend the few minutes of rest between the hours of work, their teacher often joining them and leading the string. Then, too, on Sunday afternoons comes the weekly festival, when all the youths of the parish, *em !*. THE MODERN "SKADE" OR " SKI "-GUDUESS.

*f/?j /J. Black, after a photograph.)*

boys and young men alike, meet on the hillside to outdo one another in fair rivalry, and enjoy their sport to the full as long as the brief daylight lasts. At such times the girls are present as spectators, notwithstanding that they too know well how to use their "ski," and that many a good feat has been done ere now by Norwegian lasses and gone unrecorded.

Such is the winter life of the young in many of our mountain valleys. The boy has scarcely reached the age of breeches before he knows the points of a pair of " ski": what a good bit of wood should look like, and how to twist a withy to make himself the fastenings. Thus he learns early to stand on his own legs and his own "ski,"' to rely upon himself in difficulty, and grows up to be a man like his father before him. May our sport long be held in honour, may its interests be cared for and advanced as long as there remain men and women in the Norwegian valleys!

But it is especially for the winter pursuit of game that " ski" are an absolute necessity in Norway as well as the North of Europe generally and Siberia, and it is in this way that most of the clever "skildbers" of country districts have been formed.

In earlier times it was a common practice in Scandinavia to hunt the larger animals, such as the elk and reindeer, during the winter upon "ski." When the snow was deep the skilful " skilober" had no great difficulty in pursuing and killing these animals, as their movements, as compared with his, were naturally much hampered. It was an exciting sport, however, and often required considerable strength and endurance on the part of the hunter, as well as a thorough familiarity with the use of " ski. " Now, however, these animals are protected during the winter, and all pursuit of them is illegal, though doubtless there is still a good deal of poaching done in this way, especially in the case of elk, in the remoter forests of Sweden and Norway.

Nowadays the Norwegian peasant has most use for his "ski" in the less exciting pursuit of the ptarmigan and willow-grouse, large numbers of which are shot and snared upon the mountains. The snaring in some districts is especially remunerative, and is often the only channel through which the poor cottagers can attain to the rare luxury of a little ready money. The hare is also sometimes thus hunted and shot, the bear turned out of his lair or intercepted before he has finally taken to his winter quarters, and an occasional lynx or glutton pursued. It is, of course, on "ski" too that the nomad Lapps follow and destroy their inveterate enemy, the wolf.

The Siberian tribes again do all their winter hunting upon " ski," and as with them the winter is the longest season of the year, the great importance, if not absolute necessity, of " ski" to the Arctic and sub-Arctic peoples will readily be seen.

Of late years the sport of " skilobning " has been practised and developed in Norway to quite an astonishing extent. This has been no doubt largely due to the public competitions which

"skilobning" In Thk Old Style.

*(from a tfrawifif by E. Nielsen.)* are now annually held, and above all to the great meeting of the year at Christiania. Here at their first institution the Telemarken peasants appeared and completely eclipsed the athletes of the capital by their masterly skill. In time, however, their arts were learned by the townsfolk, and it has often happened in recent years that the tables have been completely turned, at least in certain parts of the competition. The progress of the sport has on the whole been quite remarkable, and any one who has followed its development step by step, who can remember how empty and desolate the hillsides and forest paths round Christiania were some fifteen or even ten years ago, and who sees how the fields and woods are now thronged on a fine winter Sunday with " skilobers " of all ages, sexes, and conditions, cannot but regard the result of this healthy movement with gratification and pride. In old days the " skistav " or pole of

which I have spoken above was generally considered quite as necessary a piece of apparatus as the "ski" themselves. In those days, when the pace downhill became too hot to be comfortable, the "skilober" rode his pole like a witch's broomstick; to it he had recourse in all difficulties; it was his guide, comforter, and friend in all moments of danger and perplexity. It was a good friend, no doubt, in need, and is so still even to the orthodox; but this unlimited and servile use of an extraneous support and assistance invariably brings the body of the " skilober " into a forced and helpless position, which entirely deprives him of all control over his " ski," and of all confidence in the strength and power of his own legs. But the Telemarken peasant had meantime worked in quite a different direction, and had attained to quite a different form. When he met us in rivalry at Christiania he soon showed us that when one has really learned to control one's " ski" without having continual recourse to one's staff, one obtains a mastery over them which is quite impossible in the other case, and can with ease and speed clear obstacles and difficulties before considered insurmountable. The advantages of the new method were at once apparent, and the grace, freedom, and boldness of the " Telemarking's " carriage and movements generally as compared with the stiff and clumsy manoeuvres of the "skilober" of the old school were very striking.

This new departure led at once to a rapid development of the great art of jumping upon " ski." This, the great feature of "skilobning" from a purely sporting point of view, is really of no direct practical importance, as even the most reckless "skilober" is not in the habit of flying over precipices of unknown depth, but is rather careful to avoid such obstacles when he is using his "ski" in earnest and on unfamiliar ground. Jumping is a sport pure and simple, but at the same time a sport of great use and benefit, as there is no other branch of " skilobning" which tends in the same degree to develop power of balance, control of the "ski," or courage and confident bearing.

JUMPING ON "SKI."

*(From a Jraii'iMf fy A. Blcch.)*

The jumping is done on a steep hillside, which has a gradient of perhaps from 30 to 40. In the middle of the hill a bank of snow is built, or there may be some natural break in the ground or projecting rock which serves the same purpose. The jumper slides down from the top of the hill on to this bank, which, owing to the great pace which he has already attained, throws him far out into the air, whereupon JUMPING ON "SKI." . *Nielsen, from an instantaneous jtlwtogra/li.)* after a longer or shorter journey through space he alights on the slope below and continues his headlong course at an even greater speed than before. The jumper may, and as a rule does, very much increase the length of his leap by gathering himself together and taking a spring just as he leaves the projecting bank. In this way sixty, seventy, or even ninety feet may he cleared when the snow is in good order and the hill and bank of suitable dimensions. A well-known " skildber " from Telemarken, Sondre Auersen Nordheim by name, is reported to have jumped ninety-six Norwegian or ninety-nine English feet from a projecting rock, and to have kept his balance when he alighted below. The perpendicular fall necessitated by such jumps is very considerable, from thirty to forty feet being no uncommon thing, a height which takes one to the roof of an ordinary three-storied house. This comparison will enable the reader to appreciate the magnitude of the performance, which can otherwise hardly be realised by those who have never witnessed it.

While passing through the air the jumper must maintain all his presence of mind, must ke'ep his " ski" straight and under control, and as he touches the ground he will generally shoot out one foot rather in front of the other and sink on one knee, to break in some measure the shock of contact. It is only the enormous speed attained and the elasticity of the snow which make such leaps possible, and therefore it is necessary that the slope of the hill should be quite as steep below the jump as above it, and that

the snow should also be in a condition favourable for the purpose, since if the " ski" are checked in the slightest degree at the moment of contact the difficulty of maintaining the balance is immensely increased. Of course violent falls are frequent, and the spectator who for the first time sees the unfortunate jumper rolling down the hill—arms, legs, and "ski" all whirling round together in a cloud of snow—will naturally conclude that broken limbs must often be the result. As a matter of fact, however, serious accidents are extremely rare.

But the finished " skilober " must be able to do more than jump. At some of the open competitions he is also required to show his skill in turning his " ski" to one side or the other within given marks, and by bringing them quite round to stop short before any given obstacle, both of these manoeuvres having to be executed at full speed, that is to say, in the descent of a steep hill. In these arts the " Telemarkinger"

"FACILIS DESCENSVS AVERNI." AN AWKWARD CORNER.

*(From a dra-.mtig I'f A. Block.)*

are complete masters, and the younger school of Christiania "skilobers" have proved their worthy pupils.

But, apart from these special arts, " ski" must be considered as being first and foremost instruments of locomotion, and therefore the speed which can be attained in an ordinary way across country must be regarded from a practical point of view-as the most important branch of the sport. Though the jumping is always the most popular part of the programme, yet at our yearly meetings equal or greater weight is attached to the long race, for, it must be explained, the chief prizes are given for combined proficiency in the separate branches.

It must not be thought that "skilobning" is a sport which develops the body at all unequally. On the other hand, there can be few forms of exercise which perform this task so uniformly and healthfully. The upper part of the body and arms come into constant use as well as the legs; the arms particularly by the help of the pole. This is especially the case if two poles be carried,

a practice which is common among the Lapps, which has been adopted of late years in the Christiania races, and which was followed by us during our crossing of Greenland.

I have already given some idea of the speed to which a strong and clever "skilober" may attain. But so much depends upon those two most uncertain quantities, the nature of the ground and the state of the snow, that nothing like an absolute standard can be fixed. If the conditions be moderately favourable a good man should be able to cover from sixty to seventy miles in the course of a day's run.

The longest race hitherto brought off in Norway was held at Christiania in February 1888. The distance was 50 km. , or 31 miles 122 yards, twice over a 25 km. course, which was laid out over hilly ground of a very variable character, and included all kinds of difficulties calculated to test the competitors' skill. The race was won by a Telemarken peasant in 4 hrs. 26 min., without much pressure on the part of his rivals. A much longer race, no doubt the longest on record, was that organised by Barons Dickson and Nordenskiold at Jokkmokk, in Swedish Lapland, on April 3 and 4, 1884. The winner was a Lapp, Lars Tuorda, thirty-seven years of age, one of the two who had accompanied Nordenskiold on his Greenland expedition and had then done a great feat on the " ski" on the "Inland ice." The distance on this occasion was 220 km., or nearly 136 English miles, and it was covered by the winner in 21 hrs. 22 min., rests included. The second man, a Lapp of forty, was only 5 sec. behind the winner, and of the first six, five of whom were Lapps, the last came in 46 min. after the first. The course was for the most part level, being laid mainly over the frozen lakes, and the snow must have been in a very favourable condition.

Finally, I will say a few words about the " ski" we made use of ourselves in the course of the expedition, which in the circumstances seem to find their place here more appropriately than in the preceding chapter on " Equipment."

THE "SKI" OK THE EXPEDITION IN PLAN, ELEVATION, AND SECTION.

Our "ski" were not of any fixed Norwegian type, but were specially designed to suit the nature of the ground and state of snow which I expected to find in the interior of Greenland. We took nine pair, two of oak and the rest of birch. The oak " ski" were 7 ft. 6 in. long, while in front at the curve they were 3 in. broad and 3 in. under the foot. On the upper surface was a ridge running the whole length of the " ski," which gave the necessary stiffness without adding too much to the weight. On the under surface were three narrow grooves. The seven pair of birch "ski" were of about the same form and dimensions, except that by the carelessness and negligence of the maker they were made rather narrower in front at the

E- curve, the sides being parallel all through. This want of breadth in front prevents the " ski" from riding so well upon the snow, as they act more like a snow-plough, and move somewhat heavily. These "ski" were delivered so short a time before we left that we unfortunately were unable to get others, and had to take them as they were. These birch "ski," too, were shod throughout with very thin steel plates, and in the middle of the plates, just under the foot, were openings 34 in. by *2-Jy* in., in which were inserted strips of elk-skin with the hair on. The object of the steel plates was to make the " ski " glide better on coarse, wet snow, of which I expected a good deal, and that of the strips of skin to prevent the " ski" from

"LAUPARSKO" AFFIXED TO "SKI," SHOWING THF. FASTENINGS.

slipping back during ascents and the heavy work of hauling as much as the steel-plates would have otherwise caused them to do. We found, however, none of this expected snow, and might well have done without these extra contrivances. The two pair of oak "ski," which Sverdrup and I used, proved in every way satisfactory, and I can thoroughly recommend the pattern for future work of the kind.

The fastenings we used were very simple, and consisted in nothing but a toe-strap of thick, stiff leather, and a broadish band of softer leather running round behind the heel. The stiff fastenings of withies or cane which are commonly used in Norway for jumping and ordinary work generally arc in my opinion quite unsuited to the conditions of a long exploring journey. They are by no means necessary for a complete control of the " ski," and they tire and chafe the feet much more than a soft and flexible fastening like leather. My experience tells me that the less one is conscious of the pressure of the fastenings in these long journeys, the less one draws upon one's stock of endurance.

HOCKS ON THK NORTH COAST OF THK FAROE ISLANDS. *(By Th. Holmtot, ajttr a. fliotirgraflt.)*

Chapter IV.

*THE VOYAGE TO ICELAND.*

As I have already said, I proposed to reach the east coast of Greenland by getting a Norwegian sealer to pick us up in Iceland and take us on further. After negotiations in several quarters I finally came to terms with the owners of the sealer *Jason* of Sandefjord. It was agreed that the ship should call for us in Iceland, and do its best to put us ashore on the east coast of Greenland, while I, on our part, undertook that she should suffer no pecuniary loss by having to neglect her own business on our account. My agreement with the captain of the *Jason,* Mauritz Jacobsen, a coolheaded and experienced Arctic skipper, was that on his way to Denmark Strait, after the season was over in the Jan Mayen waters, he should call for us in Iceland about the beginning of June, at Isafjord for preference, or Dyrafjord in case ice should prevent him getting into the former place.

On May 2 I left Christiania to go by way of Copenhagen and London to Leith, where I was to meet the other members of the party. They left Christiania the day after" me, taking steamer from Christianssand to Scotland, and carrying the whole outfit of the expedition with them.

Many sensible people shook their heads doubtfuHy, and took us sadly by the hand the day we left. They evidently thought, if they did not say: " This is the last time we shall see you, but God grant that you never manage to reach land!" There was a deal of excitement, too, caused by this absurd little expedition, which could not even rise to the dignity of its own steamer, but had to leave home in an ordinary passenger-boat, the owners of which, by the way, had liberally given it a free passage. Of cheering, too, there was plenty in our honour. People thought it was just as well to give these poor fellows some gratification during the short time now left to them for the enjoyment of life. In Ravna's case this enjoyment was for the moment brief indeed, for he had to sacrifice to the gods of the deep or ever he reached the open sea.

Balto thus describes the departure from Christiania: " As we passed out of the town on our way to the quays great numbers of men and women accompanied us, to wish us good luck and cheer us on our way. We were received with similar demonstrations by the people of all the little towns from Christiania to Christianssand, for they thought we should never come back alive. They expected, perhaps, that we should meet with the same fate as Herr Sinklar, when he set out for Norway to plunder and to ravish."

I met the rest of my party in Leith again, and found them enjoying themselves much, thanks to the kindness of their fellow-countrymen there resident. Balto in his narrative speaks of the Norwegian Consul as a " new father" to him, and a hospitable entertainer of the whole party. If the truth be told, Balto managed to find "new fathers" in many different places.

After receiving many proofs of Scottish kindness and hospitality, on the evening of May 9 we went on board the Danish steamer *Thyra,* which lay at Granton, and which was to take us the first stage of our journey to Iceland. It was midnight when we said good-bye to the last of our friends, who saw us off on the deserted quay, and then we steamed out into the darkness on our way northwards.

From the time we left Scotland I began taking daily samples of the air by means of the apparatus I have already mentioned. The object was mainly to measure the amount of carbonic acid prevalent in the different regions. I continued this sample-taking regularly across the sea to Iceland, and thence to the east coast of Greenland, and brought also home with me a certain number of specimens from the " Inland ice " itself.

While we were in the P'aroe Islands, where we were delayed two days by bad weather, we had heard bad news of the state of the ice round Iceland. It was said that it had come farther south this year than had been known within the memory of man, and the east coast of the island was reported inaccessible. This was confirmed only too soon, for we met the ice when we were hardly within 140 miles of shore. We pushed on northwards to see if we could reach land further up, but it was to no purpose, as the ice was everywhere. Several sailing vessels, too, which we met, informed us that it extended a long way to the north.

On Wednesday, May 16. we made another attempt to reach land on the eastern side, though this was off Berufjorden, a long way south; here, too, we were stopped some ninety miles from land. This left us nothing to do but make for the south-west, and we steamed along the rocky and picturesque southern coast with a fair wind behind us. In the evening we passed Oraefajokull, the highest mountain in Iceland, which rises out of the sea to a height of some 6400 feet. As the setting sun cast its last rays upon the mountain's snowy sides, and on the veil of mist which enwrapped its summit, while now and again the breaking of the veil allowed us to see for a moment the soft outlines of the conical peak, the scene was one of unusually impressive grandeur.

On the morning of May 17, we approached the Vestmanna Islands, which lie some miles to sea, off the middle of the southern coast of Iceland. It was a glorious sunny day, and the sea was smooth and bright as glass as we glided in between the lofty precipitous basalt rocks which form this group of islands and lay to off Heimaey, the largest of them all, and the only one inhabited. Here the sea eats away the layers of basalt rock, leaving perpendicular walls which fall sheer into the sea, and are honeycombed with great cavities and grottoes. The whole CLIFFS ON THK NORTH COAST OF THE VKSTMAN.NA ISLANDS.

*(l-'roiu a photograph.)*

scene had a distinctly Mediterranean aspect, and at once suggested a comparison with Capri, not by any means to the latter's undisputed pre-eminence. We were steaming straight for these wonderful cliffs, about which the breakers threw their spray, and the screaming sea-birds wheeled in thousands. There was something strangely fascinating in the whole: a brilliant summer-like day, a bright-green sea as clear as crystal, and right opposite us, on the mainland, the highest peak but one in Iceland, the volcano Eyafjallajokul, whose great white snow-mantle lay before us still glittering in the evening sun. In the background, again, were other peaks and glaciers, among which the huge white dome of Hekla was most prominent.

Later we passed Reykjances, which carries the only lighthouse which Iceland possesses. The spot is one of absolute desolation, and is especially exposed to shocks of earthquake, which have already damaged the lighthouse, and threaten before long to demolish it altogether.

Beyond are a few rocks-and islands which arc chiefly re- TIIK ONLY I.Kiin-ilOL-SK IN Iflil.AM).

*(Ry Th. Holinboc,/roni a sketch ly the Author.)*

markable for the number of Great Auk *Alea impennis)* to which they formerly gave shelter.

After a hard struggle against a head wind and heavy sea, which again and again completely neutralised the *Tliyra's* efforts to push on, we reached Reykjavik, the capital of Iceland, in the course of the night. Our stay was short, but next morning we were allowed some hours on shore.

About midday we left, and now set our course for the promontory of Snefellsnxs, on our way north to Isafjord, our eventual destination. In the evening, just as the sun was setting, we passed Snefellsjokull, an old volcano which lies on the extreme point of the promontory. The peak is most impressive as one passes close beneath it, for it rises out of the sea to a height of more than 4500 feet. It is well known as a most useful sea-mark, and its white cap has guided many a vessel into safety. As we passed it was perhaps at its best, as the last rays of the sinking sun were just reddening its mantle of snow.

Whereas May 18 had been comparatively spring-like, the TIIK "THYKA" PASSING SNKh KLl.SjOKUI.1..

*(/ Til. Holm/we, from .1 sketch by the Author. I*

day following plunged us into the depths of winter again. When we came on deck in the morning we were met by a stiff breeze from the north, with sleet and snow. The high basalt mountains on the mainland were decked from head to foot in white, and the floes which we saw floating by from time to time were precursors which assured us that the main body of ice was not far off. We were now close to Onundafjord, and, as the breeze promised to increase to a gale and the snow was falling thickly, we took refuge in the excellent harbour which the inlet affords, there to await better weather. The storm now increased rapidly, and we had full opportunity of learning what the wind of these northern parts can do. No one ventured on deck who was not obliged. One could keep one's feet there indeed if it were necessary, but to bring one's nose for more than an instant out of shelter was an experiment to which there was little temptation. The ship, however, lay very comfortably where she was, and, as it happened to be Whitsun Eve, we did our best to make things as pleasant as possible down below.

When we woke next morning we were already in Isafjord, where we intended to go ashore. Here, too, winter prevailed no less absolutely, and everything was under snow. Isafjord is the second of the three towns of Iceland, and is a pretty little place, buried, together with its excellent harbour, among the surrounding mountains.

Here I was told that the drift-ice lay not far to the north, as it had, in fact, come south of Cape Nord. Strong northerly winds might bring it still farther south, and block the approach to the fjord. It was extremely rarely that this had happened, but there was just a possibility of it, and the *Jason* might have some difficulty in getting into Isafjord to fetch us. To avoid this risk I made up my mind to go back to Dyrafjord, which lies a little farther south, and is never blocked by the ice, and await her there, as we had agreed to do if it were necessary. So I sent a letter ashore for the *asoris* captain, telling him of our movements, and we started southwards again.

Next morning when we came on deck the weather was splendid, and we were running fast up the approach to Uyrafjord. The winter had now retired to some extent to the mountains, and along the sea-shore there were a few signs of spring to gladden us. We were soon anchored off Thing-eyre, the little trading centre of the fjord, and we now took leave of the captain and crew of the *Thyra,* who had from the first done all they could to make our stay on hoard as pleasant as possible, and who now fired a farewell salute in our honour.

At Thingeyre we were hospitably welcomed by Hcrr Gram, the merchant of the place, who. had kindly offered us shelter while we were to wait for the *Jason.*

At a farm near Dyrafjord I bought a little pony to take with us for the purposes of the expedition. I meant to use it to help us with our boats and baggage in the floes, and if we could get it so far, on the way up on to the " Inland ice." I was not sanguine that it would be of much use to us, but when we were obliged to kill it, it would give us many a meal of good fresh meat. When I left Norway I had thought of buying two ponies, but when I saw what they could do I felt sure one would be quite enough.

As it happened, our little beast was not of much use. In the spring it is not easy to get fodder in Iceland, and in spite of all my efforts I could only scrape together enough for a month.

The pony we took was a very handsome little animal, and, curiously enough, he was used to the work we wanted him for, as he had been put to the plough for a while, which is quite unusual in Iceland, where the ponies are as a rule used only for riding or as pack-horses.

On June 3, in the morning, we could see far out at the mouth of the fjord a little steamer slowly working inwards. At first we could make nothing of her, but soon came to the conclusion that she must be one of the small steamers used by the Norwegian Whaling Company in Isafjord. As she came nearer we made her to be the *Isafold,* which is one of these boats, but what she could want here on a Sunday morning we could not imagine. After saluting the *Fylla* she anchored and sent a boat on shore amid our increasing excitement. I had begun to suspect the truth, when, to my astonishment as well as joy, I recognised in the first who stepped ashore Captain Jacobsen of the *Jason.* Our meeting was almost frantic, but the story was soon told. He had reached Isafjord, and, not finding us there, had thought of coming on to Dyrafjord with the *Jason.* But with the strong w ind blowing it would have taken his heavily-rigged ship a whole day to make the voyage, and, as the Norwegian Company's manager most kindly offered to send the *hafold* to fetch us, he had taken the opportunity of coming too.

We lost no time in getting ready, and there was no lack of willing hands to bring our goods on board. Amid general interest our little pony was led on to the landing-stage. He did all he could to resist, poor little fellow, and had almost to be carried; had he but known the sad fate in store for him, I scarcely think we should have got him on board at all.

When all was done and we had said farewell to Herr Gram, our kind entertainer, and the other friends we had made in Dyrafjord, we steamed out of the fjord and to sea northwards.

The *Jason,* as we learned, had been tolerably successful hitherto, as she was also the whole season as compared with her fellows. Up to this time she had taken 4500 young seal and 1100 old. FORCING Ol'K wav throit.ii ti1k U. K.

*Th. llolmbof, front an instantanfints fh-ptograplt.)*

Chapter V.

*CRUISING IN THE ICE.*

As we leave the land behind us we are followed by hundreds of kittiwakes, in billowy masses of white and blue, chattering in endless chorus, now sinking as they swoop low on extended wing over the vessel's wake, now rising as they soar lightly in their graceful evolutions up towards the blue sky.

It is a glorious northern night. The sun has sunk into the sea; in the west and north the day has laid herself dreamily to rest in her sunlit bath. Above arc the coloured heavens; below, the sea, calm as a mirror, and rocked to sleep in melancholy thought, while it reflects in still softer, gentler tones the mellow radiance of the sky. Between heavens and sea is the black form of the *Jason,* labouring and moaning as her engines drive her westward. Behind us the rocky coast of Iceland, a fringe of violet blue, is slowly sinking into the sea. Behind us lie home and life: what lies before us? We cannot tell, but it must be beautiful. A start on such a night is full of promise.

I am sitting alone in the stern of the vessel and gazing out into the night at the gathering clouds, which, still tinged by the sun, are sailing over the horizon to the north-west. Behind them lies Greenland, as yet invisible.

All nature is, as it were, sunk in her own dreams, and gently and quietly the mind, too, is drawn back into itself to pursue the train of its own thoughts, which unconsciously borrow a reflection of the colours of the sky.

Among all things that are beautiful in life are not such nights most beautiful?

And life—is it much more than hope and remembrance? Hope is of the morning, it may be, but on such nights as this do not memories, all the fair memories of bygone days,, arise dewy and fresh from the mists of the distant past, and sweep by in a long undulating train, sunlit and alluring, till they disappear once more in the melting western glow? And all that is mean, all that is odious, lies behind, sunk in the dark ocean of oblivion.

The very next day, June 5, we reached the ice, which this year has come a long way south.

The impression which the floe-ice of the Arctic seas makes upon the traveller the first time he sees it is very remarkable. Most people will find that what they actually see is not a little different from what they have expected. A world of wonders and enchantments, a complete horizon of wild fantastic forms, ever changing, ever new, a wealth of brilliant rainbow hues playing and glowing amid the cold purity of the crystal ice, such are the features of the picture which the ingenuity of the imagination so often fondly creates. Such, too, are often the illustrations of books, written apparently to give the reader impressions of scenes which the writer can never have beheld himself. But not such is this ice-world. These mighty fantastic forms are wanting; all is monotony and uniformity, features which nevertheless leave an indelible impression on the mind. In small, indeed, it has forms enough and in infinite diversity, and of colours all tints and strange effects of green and blue, flashing and playing in endless variation; but as to its large features, it is just their overpowering simplicity of contrast which works so strongly on the observer's mind: the drifting ice, a huge white glittering expanse stretching as far as the eye can reach, and throwing a white reflection far around upon the air and mist: the dark sea, often showing black as ink against the white; and above all this a sky, now gleaming cloudless and pale-blue, now dark and threatening with driving scud, or again wrapped in densest fog—now glowing in all the rich poetry of sunrise or sunset colour, or slumbering through the lingering twilight of the summer night. And then in the dark season of the year come those wonderful nights of glittering stars and northern lights playing far and wide above the icy deserts, or when the moon, here most melancholy, wanders on her silent way through scenes of desolation and death. In these regions the heavens count for more than elsewhere; they give colour and character, while the landscape, simple and unvarying, has no power to draw the eye.

Never shall I forget the first time I entered these regions. It was on a dark night in March 1882 when we, on board a Norwegian sealer, met the first floes in the neighbourhood of Jan Mayen, and ice was announced ahead. I ran on deck and ga/.ed ahead, but all was black as pitch and indistinguishable to me. Then suddenly something huge and white loomed out of the darkness, and grew in size and whiteness, a marvellous whiteness in contrast to the inky sea, on the dark waves of which it rocked and swayed. This was the first floe gliding by us. Soon more came, gleaming far ahead, rustling by us with a strange rippling sound, and clisappearing again far behind. Then I saw a singular light in the northern sky, brightest down at the horizon, but stretching far up towards the zenith. I had not noticed this before, and as I looked I heard a curious murmur to the north like that of breakers on a rocky coast, but more rustling and crisper in sound. The whole made a peculiar impression upon me, and I felt instinctively that I stood on the threshold of a new world. What did all this mean? Were these the fields of ice in front of us and to the north? But what were the sound and light? The light was the reflection which the white masses of ice always throw up when the air is thick, as it was that night, and the sound came from the sea breaking over the floes while they collided and grated one against the other. On still nights this noise may be heard far out to sea.

But we drew nearer and nearer, the noise grew louder, the drifting floes more and more frequent, and now and again the vessel struck one or another of them. With a loud report the floe reared on end, and was thrust aside by our strong bows. Sometimes the shock was so violent that the whole ship trembled and we were thrown off our feet upon the deck. Not long, indeed, were we allowed to doubt that we were now voyaging in waters new and strange to us. Ve shortened sail, and for a day or two cruised along the edge of the ice. Then one evening it blew up for a storm, and, as we were tired of the sea, we resolved to push into the ice and ride out its fury there. So we stood straight ahead, but before we reached the margin of the ice the storm fell.upon us. Sail was still further shortened, till we had but the topsails left, but we still rushed inwards before the wind. The ship charged the ice, was thrown from floe to floe, but on she pushed, taking her own course in the darkness. The swell grew heavier and heavier, and made things worse than ever. The floes reared on end and fell upon each other; all around us was seething and noise; the wind whistled in the rigging, and not a word was to be heard save the captain's calm but vigorous orders, which prevailed over the roaring of the sea.

F

Precisely and silently were they obeyed by the pale men, who were all on deck, as none dared risk his life by staying below, now that the ship was straining in every joint. We bored steadily inwards into the darkness. It was no use trying to guide the vessel here; she had to be left to herself, like the horses on the mountains at home. The water seethed and roared round our bows; the floes were rolled over, split in pieces, were forced under or thrust aside, nothing holding its own against us. Then one looms ahead, huge and white, and threatens to carry away the davits and rigging on one side. Hastily the boat which hangs in the davits is swung in on to the deck, the helm is put down, and we glide by uninjured. Then comes a big sea on our quarter, breaking as it nears us, and as it strikes us heavily we hear a crash and the whistling of splinters about our ears, while the port is thrown across the deck, a floe having broken the bulwarks on the weather-side. The ship heels over, we hear another crash, and the bulwarks are broken in several places on the lee-side too.

But as we get further into the ice it grows calmer. The sea loses its force, the noise is deadened, though the storm tears over us with more fury than ever. The wind whistles and shrieks in the rigging, and we can scarcely keep our footing on the deck. The storm seems to rage because it cannot roll at its will in the open sea; but here at last we can ride at our ease. We had played a dangerous game by taking to the ice in a storm, but we had come out of it unscathed and were now in smooth water. When I came on deck next morning the sun was shining, the ice lay white and still around us, and only the broken bulwarks grinning in the morning sun called to mind the stormy night.

This was my first meeting with the ice. Very different was it indeed this second time. We saw it now on a fine bright day, a dazzling white expanse quivering and glittering in the sunshine far away towards the horizon, while the sea rocked gently and peacefully against its edge.

It must not be supposed that this drifting ice of the Arctic seas forms a single continuous field. It consists of aggregations of larger and smaller floes, which may reach a thickness of thirty or forty feet or even more. How these floes are formed and where they come from is not yet known with MV FIKST MKMTINC. WITH THE I'OI.AK ICK (1882).

*(By Th. ffolmboc.)*

certainty, but it must be somewhere in the open sea far away in the north, or over against the Siberian coast, where no one has hitherto forced his way. Borne on the Polar current, the ice is carried southwards along the east coast of Greenland. Here it meets the swell of the sea, and the larger solid masses are broken into smaller and smaller floes as they come farther south. By the pressure of the waves, and consequent packing, the floes are sometimes also piled one upon another, and then form hummocks or crags of ice which may often rise twenty or thirty feet above the water.

It is this broken and scattered polar ice which the sealer meets in Denmark Strait, and it is among these floes, which can indeed be dangerous obstacles enough, that he forces his way with his powerful vessel in pursuit of the bladder-nose.

For several days we worked southwards, skirting the ice. On Wednesday we see the point of Staalbjerghuk in Iceland, and estimate that we are about thirty miles distant from it.

On Thursday, June 7, we get into a tongue of open ice. and see here and there seals, bladder-nose, upon the floes. There is life on board the *Jason* at once. " It is a good sign to see seal so soon, on the first ice we get into. We shall have a good season this year very likely, and we want it too, after all these bad years," and so on. And visions of a real handsome catch, as in the good old Greenland days, arise in the lively imagination of many a sealer. The men are all deeply interested in the success of the vessel, as their earnings are dependent thereon. Hope too, luckily, has a tendency with many folk to follow the direction of their wishes. Easily is it raised, but just as easily disappointed.

We saw more seal on the ice, and our captain determined to try for a little haul. So the boats of one watch were sent out. Sverdrup and Dietrichson, vho had never been out before, were of course consumed with eagerness to see and try their rifles on these masses of game. They were no little delighted when they had received the due permission and the boats were under way, but as beginners they were put in charge of skilled shooters. We soon heard reports on various sides of us, but only a shot now and again—no lively firing, nothing like the continuous blaze and rattle all over the ice which is the accompaniment of a good haul. They were evidently youngsters and mainly small seal which lay scattered hereabout.

In the afternoon, when this detachment had come back, the boats of the other watch were sent out. I stayed on board the whole day, and shot a number of seal from the stern of the vessel. Curiously enough, one can, as a rule, get nearer to the seal with the larger vessel

than with the boats. They have learned to fear the latter, and often take to the water quite out of range, while one can sometimes bring the big ship right up to the floe on which they lie before they decamp.

We got 187 seal altogether that day, which is no great bag. They were chiefly youngsters, though there were some old ones among them. Dietrichson's boat got twenty seal, and Sverdrup's thirty-six.

That day, too, we saw several sealers in the ice to the west of us, and next day we had a talk with some of them. Of course they all wanted to talk with the *Jason,* which had the Greenland expedition on board. The captain of the *Magdalena,* of Tonsberg, came to see us and carried off the post we had brought from Iceland for the other vessels, promising to have it delivered, as the *Jason* was bound for the east coast of Greenland, and it was uncertain whether we should see the other sealers for some time. The postal system of the Arctic Sea is managed in a somewhat remarkable way. If any of the vessels touch at Iceland they carry off the post for the rest of the fleet. The reader will perhaps think that the Arctic Sea covers a large area, and that it would be doubtful whether one vessel would find the others in these parts. But it is not really so. The sealing-grounds are not so extensive that one is not quite as well informed about one's fellow's actions and movements as one generally is about the business of one's neighbour in a small town at home. The sealers like to keep close together, and no one will separate any distance from the rest for fear the others may come in for a haul while he is away. He dare not run the risk of getting nothing while the others are taking seal, on the mere chance of getting a larger haul all to himself another time. The struggle for existence is here maintained in the same way as elsewhere in the world.

Later in the afternoon we passed the *Geysir* of Tonsberg. The captain came on board and had supper and a glass of grog with us. He was in such high spirits that none of us had the heart to tell him that he had lost three of his children from diphtheria since he sailed from home. Captain Jacobsen had been told it in a letter which he got in Iceland, but the father had heard nothing of it, nor did he learn it from us. One can thus live up here in the Arctic Sea without a suspicion of what is going on in the world. One's joys and sorrows are hound up in the seal and sealing, and the whole of Europe might well collapse without the knowledge or regard of this section of its population.

On Sunday, June 10, we have thick and foggy weather. For several days we have been unable to take an observation and cannot tell how far we have advanced, though the current, which is strong here, must have carried us far to the west at the same time that we have made a good deal of way south. We must have reached that point where, if there is to be any prospect of getting to land at present, the edge of the ice should be taking a more westerly or north-westerly direction. Of this there is no sign; there are masses of ice extending in a south-westerly direction. This does not look at all hopeful. The real sealing season begins to get very near, and it may take the *Jason* a long time to make her way to the northeast again against the current, especially as it has begun to blow from the east. Meantime the other ships may be taking seal, and I had bound myself not to let my expedition interfere with the vessel's real business.

So that morning we came to the conclusion that we must give up all attempts to land for the present, and wait for a better chance. Ve turn eastwards for the ordinary sealing-grounds, but wind and current are now in our teeth, and we have to beat up against them.

Next day it clears up and we get a sight of land, the first alluring sight of the east coast of Greenland. We see high, jagged mountain tops, evidently the country north of Cape Dan. We are not so far away as we expected, perhaps rather more than sixty miles.

We find a narrow inlet cutting deep into the ice in the direction of land. It seems to stretch far inwards, and we cannot see the end of it even from the

masthead. We THE FIRST SIGHT Ol' GREENLAND ON JUNE II.

f *from a sketch by the Aiittiar.)*

determine to try how far we can get, and it is possible that we may find seal there too. We have the wind in our favour and make our way in quickly. We soon find the way blocked, but a sealer does not lose heart at such trifles. We force a passage, and the floes of ice have to give way before the stout bows of *OhK-jasoH.* Then we get into a large open pool with no ice in sight between us and land. This looks promising. We take our latitude and longitude, and at noon find ourselves at 65 18' N. and 34 10' W. We are still some fifty miles from land, but our hopes begin slowly to rise as we think that we may perhaps after all be able to effect our landing without further waiting.

But after steaming inwards for another couple of hours at good speed we again sight ice from the masthead right in front of us. We go a little way into it and see that it is packed, so that our vessel will find it difficult to force a passage through. We are now some forty miles from land, and, as the ice ahead is rather heavily packed and rough, it seems scarcely advisable to try and land now. It will be better to wait till later in the year when the ice will have diminished.

It certainly seems to us that the ice farther north is more open, and that we shall be able to get considerably nearer land that way, but, as I have said already, the *Jason* is out sealing, and if she forces her way through up there she will run the risk of getting stuck and losing the best of the season. This risk is not to be thought of, so we make our way out again, and say farewell to the east coast of Greenland for the present. The fog soon hides the land again from our sight.

Balto's description of his first sight of Greenland shows that the impression it made upon his mind was not altogether satisfactory. He writes: "After sailing for some days in the direction of Greenland we at last came within sight of land, but it still lay far in the distance, some sixty or seventy miles away be-

yond the ice. That part of the coast which we could now see had no beauty or charm to the eye, but was dismal and hideous to look upon. Mountain peaks terrifically high rose like church-steeples into the clouds which hid their summits."

Next day we have a good proof of the strength of the current in these seas. We have been beating up to the north-east the whole night long with a strong easterly breeze. Next dayat noon we again see land in the same direction as on the day before, and, if possible, we are a little way still farther south. The current has been bearing us to the southwest all along.

The next few days we beat up to the north-east along the edge of the ice, but make little way, as the wind is strong against us and the current carries us back. As hitherto, we see a great deal of whale. They are chiefly the " bottle-nose," several of the larger species of whalebone whales, most of them probably the blue-whale, and most of them moving westwards, possibly towards Greenland. Whales have evidently their migrations, though we know little or nothing about them. Now and again we see one of the smaller kinds of whale-bone whale, which our sealers sometimes called " klapmyts "-whale, as they maintain that it is in the habit of frequenting the grounds where the "klap-myts," *i.e.,* the bladder-nose seal, is caught. It seemed that it might possibly be the same species as that found on the coasts of Finmarken, where it is called the "seie "-whale *(Balanoptem borealis).* Once or twice, too, I saw the killer-whale *(Orca gladiator),* the little species so readily known by its prominent back-fin. It is an unusually powerful little whale, is active in its movements, and provided with a set of dangerous teeth. It is the terror of the big whales; when it appears they flee pell-mell, and one of these little gladiators alone is enough to put the giants of the sea to flight, and even to drive them ashore before him. Nor is this terror the big whales have for their enemy all ungrounded, as he pursues them and attacks them from the side. The killer generally hunts in companies, the members of which rush straight in upon the whales and tear great pieces of blubber out of their side. In pain and despair the big whales lash the water and break away with the speed of lightning, but closely followed by these little monsters, who do not desist until their victims, exhausted by loss of blood and exertion, throw up the game. Not only the whale, but the seal too, is the victim of the killer's rapacity. The Eskimo have told me that they have seen this animal—"ardluk," as they call him—devour a seal in a single mouthful.

The killer of our coasts seems to some extent to lead a more peaceful life. He is an habitual visitor at our herring-fisheries, and then seems to live on nothing but herring and coal-fish, among which, however, he causes a deal of panic and confusion. He seems to show no tendency to attack the great whales with whom he comes into contact daily on these occasions, nor do they seem to have any fear of him. The reason of this mutual relation is not quite certain. Possibly at these times the killer gets enough fish-food and feels no desire for whale-blubber, but it is also probable that the great whalebone whales which appear at the herring-fisheries, viz., the fin-whale *(Bakenoptera musculus),* and the pike-whale *(Balanoptera rostraia),* are not the particular species which he is accustomed to attack. I am inclined to think that these two species are too quick for him, and that he therefore prefers the larger but less strong and speedy blue-whale, and possibly, too, the hump-backed whale *(Megaptera hoops).*

Now and then we see seals asleep in the water. As they bob up and down with the waves they look like live ship-fenders floating on the surface. A few we see, too, on the scattered, drifting ice-floes. This probably means that there are more on the ice inside, but the air is thick and we have no time to look. We are impatient to see our fellows again; it may be that they are hard at work, while we should be here poking about in the ice, and very likely catching nothing, while they are in the

thick of it. That would never do.

At last we got a little wind from the west, and a couple of days' sail brought us to the rest of the fleet again. There was a general sigh of relief on board-the *Jason* when it was known that the others had caught nothing since we left them. NAVIGATION IN THE ICE—" HARD A-STAKBOARD." *By the Author, from a photograph.)*

Chapter VI.

*THE BLADDER-NOSE SEAL AND ITS CAPTURE.*

The bladder-nose, the "klapmyts" of the Norwegians and *Cystophora cristata* of naturalists, has its nearest connections among seal-kind in the sea-elephants of western North America and the Antarctic Ocean, one point of resemblance being the hood which the male bears upon its nose, a feature which makes it strikingly distinct from all other Arctic seals. It oftcns attains considerable size, and next to the blue-seal *(P/ioca barbata),* is the largest of the seals found in Arctic waters from Greenland to Spitzbergen. It takes to the water immediately after birth, when it carries a coat of smooth hair, light or nearly white below, and grey on the back. At the first change this becomes somewhat spotted, and gradually as the young seal grows it becomes more and more dappled, till at maturity the coat has a greyish-white ground with numerous black spots, large and small, irregularly distributed over the whole body. These spots are smallest upon the head, but they are here so closely set that the effect is often that of a continuous black.

As I have already said, the male seal has a kind of hood MAI.K OF THE BLADDER-NOSE SEAL. (// *E. Xiebai,/rom a sketch tji the Author.)* or bladder on its nose, which can be blown out to a size which is quite astonishing, and then gives the head a most extraordinary appearance. But it is seldom that this is done, and I have only seen it when the animal is excited or irritated, as for instance by being shot at. At ordinary times the hood is folded, and generally hangs over the end of the nose like a short proboscis.

This seal is an excellent swimmer and

diver, and to obtain its food, which consists chiefly of fish, it sometimes descends to extraordinary depths. How deep it will go is not known, but some idea may be formed from the fact that I once found between Spitsbergen and Jan Mayen some of the peculiar Norwegian red fish, the " bergylt" *(Scbastes norvegicus),* in the stomach of a bladder-nose. This is quite a deep-sea fish, its habitat ranging from sixty to ninety fathoms below the surface. If the pressure at this depth, which amounts at least to eleven atmospheres, be realised, it will be seen that this seal must possess a chest of considerable strength. As another proof of its immense power, I may mention that it can jump out of the water on to a floe the edge of which lies as much as six feet above the surface. I have often seen them shoot suddenly KKMAl.K AND YOL'XG OK TIIK Til. ADDER-NOSK SEAL.

*(By E. Nielsen, ftvni sketches by the Author.')*

out of the sea, describe a curve in the air, and plump down some way inside the edge of an ice-floe, which was quite as high above the water as I have said. The impetus necessary for this purpose implies an amount of power which the observer is scarcely likely to realise at first.

The bladder-nose is almost entirely a seal of the open sea. It does not keep much to the coasts, but follows the drifting floes in its migrations, and occurs all over the Arctic Ocean and the northern Atlantic, from Spitzbergen to Labrador and Baffin's Bay. It is not quite certain whether it goes further west, but it is not likely to do so to any great extent. Its easterly limits seem to be the neighbourhood of Spitzbergen, for it is not found off Nova Zembla.

The tract which this seal chiefly frequents is the stretch of sea which lies between Iceland and Greenland. Here during the moulting-season they gather in enormous numbers, and here it is that the Norwegian sealers get their best hauls.

The bladder-nose season generally begins in June, at which time the sealers arrive in Denmark Strait after their season with the saddleback-or harp-seal *(P/ioca Green!andica),* which is taken in the neighbourhood of Jan Mayen. Even before this some of them have also been engaged in the capture of the bottle-nose whale *(Hyperoodon diodoii)* off the northeast of Iceland.

The first thing, of course, is to find the seal, and this is often a difficult task, for it must not be supposed that they are at all generally distributed over the ice. The sealers often have to search for weeks, skirting the edge of the icefields and examining every bay or inlet which admits of a passage in. The glasses are in constant use' in the crow's-nest on the main-top. Then, if after long search signs of seal are at last discovered far away among the floes, and the ice does not lie too close to make a passage possible, the engines are at once put to their highest speed. The one object is now to push in and anticipate one's competitors. Just as at the card-table there is no fellowship, so among the sealers of the Arctic seas altruism is a virtue unknown. Every ship does its best to outwit its fellows, and nothing brings so much satisfaction as the success of an ingenious trick. So, if there happen to be several vessels in one's neighbourhood when one discovers seal, and there is reason to believe that the others are still in ignorance of the find, the first thing is to entice the others away and set off in pursuit alone. To gain this object recourse is had to the most extraordinary stratagems. To steam off at full speed in quite a different direction, as if one already saw or expected to see seal in that quarter, so draw the others off, and then a while afterwards sneak back and start off to make one's capture alone, is an artifice in daily use at these times.

When the vessel is then being driven with all the speed she can bear onwards among the floes, and the crew begin to suspect that seal have been sighted from the look-out, there is soon life on board. The men gather in the bows and along the ship's side to get the first sight of their prey from the deck, and then all hands are set to work to get the boats ready and to see whether the bread and bacon lockers and beer-cask are proper-ly supplied, whether there are cartridges enough in the box, and the rifles are all clean and in good order. Every detail is now seen to, and if there is nothing else to be done the skinning-knives have their last edge put on, that they may do their work well upon all the seal in prospect. Then up the men go on deck again to have another look ahead, following the direction of the long glass up in the crow's-nest above. Then, when one seal at last appears, they talk and gesticulate, and as more and more come gradually into sight, scattered like black dots among the floes, the excitement increases, and the men gather together into groups and eagerly discuss the probabilities of a real haul.

Meanwhile the ship pushes slowly and steadily on, and the captain shouts his orders from above, with now and again an oath or execration directed at the two poor wretches who are standing at the wheel and striving their utmost to do what they are told with promptitude and care. The curses, indeed, pass in at one'ear and out at the other as they stand there working, till the sweat runs off them, while the ship, amid noise and crashing, labours from floe to floe, and at each shock trembles in every joint, sometimes so violently that it is no easy matter to keep one's footing upon the deck. All the time the engines are pushed to the utmost, and the screw leaves its swirling eddies, which are soon obliterated by the ice. The captain sits in the crow's-nest and feasts his eyes on the crowds of seal ahead, laying his plan of campaign the while and directing the vessel's course. It is an exciting time, this approaching of the seal, and expectation and anxiety prevail throughout the ship.

Then, when at last the order to get ready comes, there is a shriek of joy from one end of the vessel to the other. In the forecastle the confusion is at its highest; no more sleep is allowed, the men get into their sealing-clothes, and a good meal is prepared on the crackling stove to give the boats' crews heart for their work. By this time, perhaps after several hours' steam through the ice, the ship is well among the seal, which are to be seen lying on all sides about the floes. But she still pushes on, till she is in the very midst of them, and the final order for the start is given. At once all hands drop into the boats, which are hanging clear in their davits over both sides of the ship. Then the shooters— there is only one in each boat's crew, and he takes command— receive their orders from the captain, and the boats are lowered away. The ship has meanwhile slackened speed, and all life is transferred to the boats. Quickly they drop into the water and bear away, each in its own direction. It is a fine sight to see a sealer's ten boats thus get under way. The shooter stands up in the bows with his eye fixed on his seal. The coxswain stands in the stern at his post, and the other three or four men of the crew bend eagerly to their oars; all is excitement and expectation, more intense than before.

When the seal are actually reached the fusillade begins, often with all the liveliness of a hot brush between skirmishing parties. If the day be fine and sunny, and there are plenty of seal around, lying basking lazily upon the floes, there is a fascination about the scene which will never cease to charm the mind of one who has been present at it.

The main object of the shooter is, of course, to be the first back to the ship with a load of seal, and he tries to excite his men to the same ambition and urges them to their best efforts. The mode of approach is interesting. It is no use stalking the seal or drawing warily near under shelter of the floes, for this method is nearly certain to make them take to the water. On the contrary, one must avoid bringing one's boat behind a piece of ice which will conceal it from view, after the seal have once caught sight of it. It must be taken along in as open water as can be found, and as directly as may be in the face of the seal which are to be first approached. They ought to be able to see the boat, if possible, from the very first, for if they are taken at all by surprise they disappear at once.

As a seal catches sight of a boat in the

distance he generally raises his head, but if it is not near enough to alarm him he will very likely lie down at his ease again. Then, as the boat comes nearer, he lifts his head again, shows a certain amount of uneasiness, and looks first up at the strange object and then down at the water below him. The boat is brought still closer, the oarsmen rowing with all their power; the seal grows restless, drags himself still further out towards the edge of the floe, and gazes in his uncertainty at the boat and the water alternately. Now that he gives unmistakable signs of disappearing, the boat's crew, at their captain's order, set up a series of most terrific yells. The seal is at first petrified with astonishment at this strange phenomenon, but he soon recovers and drags himself still nearer to the edge. More yells, still more unearthly and longer sustained than the first, stop him once more, and he stretches out his neck listening intently and staring in wonderment at the boat, which is all the while pressing in nearer and nearer to him. But now he bends over the edge of the floe, stoops down, and stretches his neck towards the water in spite of repeated yelling from the boat. He has now made up his mind to go, and if the boat is not yet within range the only thing the shooter can do is to raise his rifle quickly and put a ball into the side of the floe just below his head, scattering the snow and ice in a shower over his chest and face. This is a new danger, and in terror he draws back again and drags himself on to the floe, gazing intently at the edge, where evidently a malicious and unseen enemy lurks c close at hand. While the seal is still pondering upon this new mystery, the boat has been brought by its vigorous oarsmen well into range. At the words " Well rowed! " the oars are shipped and the boat glides on, the crew sitting still as the shooter raises his rifle, at the report of which the seal, shot in the forehead, lays his head down upon the ice for the last time.

If there arc more seal on the same floe or the surrounding SIIOOTING BLADDER-NOSE.—"THE OTHERS I-1F. QUIETLY GAZING AT THEIR DEAD COM-

RADES...." *(By E, Neiken, from a sketch by the Anther.)* ice, a large number may be shot then and there. But the chief point is to hit the first ones so as to kill them on the instant. If this is done one can proceed at one's leisure, and if there are really many seal about one can make a good haul straight away. When I was out in 1882 I remember shooting my whole boat's load on the same spot, and I could have multiplied the number again and again if I had been able to go on shooting. For when one is once well in among the seal, and has the dead bodies of those one has shot lying round one on all sides, the others lie quietly gazing at their dead comrades, whom they take still to be alive. They evidently think that, if these can lie there so quietly while the enemy is in their midst, there can be no reason for them to move. On the other hand, if the shooter is unlucky enough not to hit the first seal or seals in an immediately fatal spot such as the head, so that any of them begin to jump about the floe in their pain, or fall splashing into the water, it is pretty certain that the rest will take alarm and disappear too. For this reason it is much better to shoot wide altogether than to wound a seal, and it will easily be understood how important it is for a sealing-boat to be in charge of a really good shot.

As soon as the seal are shot they are skinned, and if there are several on the same floe the whole crew disembark and set to work. The great thing is to get them all done with the least possible delay, lest the other boats should get a chance of pushing on before. The object of every shooter is therefore to get quick and clever skinners among his crew.

A good skinner will get through his work in an incredibly short space of time, and I have often seen the whole process completed in a couple of minutes. First comes a long slit down the front from head to tail, and a few cuts on each side to separate the layer of blubber from the flesh: then, with a few more gashes by the head and hindlimbs, the whole skin is drawn off; the fore-limbs are then cut away, and the process is complete. Only the skin and

the thick layer of blubber which lies between it and the flesh are taken, the rest being left on the ice as food for the seabirds.

The capture of the bladder-nose in Denmark Strait is not an industry of very long standing. It was inaugurated by the Norwegians in 1876, and their example was followed by a few English and American vessels. For the first eight years the venture was an unprecedented success: the seal were more than plentiful, and were shot down in thousands. During this period something like 500,000 head were captured, and it is probable that quite as many were killed and lost. After these years of plenty came a change, and ever since the pursuit has been practically a failure, all the vessels alike being equally unsuccessful.

The reason of this change has puzzled the brain of many a sealer. He looks to unfavourable conditions of wind, sea, and ice, but in none of these can he find consolation or encouragement to hope for better things in the future. It might be the case that the conditions were unfavourable for a year or two, but the ill success of summer after summer for a period of four or five years can scarcely be explained in this way. For instance, as regards the ice, I can testify from my own experience that *the Jason* made her way several times into ground which would undoubtedly have been called good when I was out in 1882, but on these latter occasions we found no seal. When we did find them they lay always farther in, where the, ice was packed closest, and whenever it happened to open they invariably moved off, and always again farther inwards.

The question now arises whether the bladder-nose still exists in its original multitudes. All who look upon the subject impartially must at once acknowledge it as obvious that there has been a considerable decrease in the numbers of the seal owing to the simple butchery to which they have been exposed. To me, who have had opportunities of visiting the sealing-grounds in two different periods, the difference between past and present was very striking. Here, on the very same ground where in 1882 I saw seal on all sides as soon as we had pushed a little way into the ice, and where I helped to shoot them down by thousands, there was now scarcely a sign of life to be seen. That there is a decrease in their numbers is certain, but I was no doubt inclined at first to consider this decrease greater than it really was, and to attribute to it alone the failure of the industry in recent years.

On July 3, 1888, I was induced to modify my opinion on this point. We had penetrated, as my narrative will subsequently show, a long way into the ice, and came within sight of seal in numbers quite as great as anything I had seen before. But they lay where the floes were packed closest, and we could not get within reach of them. Here they were, then, in all their numbers, on ice which we should never have searched in earlier years, because there were always enough and to spare on the outer floes, where they are now as good as extinct. As soon as I saw this unexpected abundance I was obliged to admit that the decrease could not be so great as I had hitherto supposed.

The failure of the sealers must, therefore, allow of some other explanation. The conclusion I have gradually come to is that, while the decrease of the numbers of the seal owing to excessive slaughter is a factor of no little importance, there is, nevertheless, another which has at least an equal bearing upon the result. This contributive cause seems to be the alteration of the seal's habits and way of life, which may be due both to actual education and experience, and to the imperious laws of the ordinary struggle for existence.

In earlier days the seal had a glorious time of it up here on his fields of ice. He ate, slept, and, in short, enjoyed himself, and multiplied exceedingly. The old males had their internecine struggles indeed, and fought desperately for the females, but this is a state of things common upon the face of the earth, and it serves besides to make life more lively. Only one enemy had the bladder-nose in this his golden age, and this was the polar bear. But it was not often the bear

troubled them, for, as he is not much of a swimmer, he prefers to keep to the closely packed ice well inside, while the seal in those days, for that very reason, frequented the outer floes. But in the year 1876 a polar bear of another kind, bigger and more voracious than the seals' familiar foe, paid its first visit to Denmark Strait. This was the Norwegian sealing-vessel *Isbjorn,* or the *Polar Bear,* which was sent to these parts by Sven Foyn, the veteran among the sealers of Norway. The *Isbjorn* found heaps of seal, and carried off with her several thousand skins. The life of peace which the bladder-nose had hitherto enjoyed was now a thing of the past. Every summer, at the end of May or beginning of June, fleets of Norwegian sealers found their way hither, and, as their victims were tame and unsus-

Tiik Oni: Knkmy 01 The Bi.auukk-nose In The Good Old Days. *(By E. Xitlu.)* peeling, great numbers were secured. So tame and confiding were they, indeed, the first few years, that it was not necessary to shoot them. They were simply knocked upon the head where they lay, and some captains did not even allow their men to take rifles out in the boats with them. This period of bliss for the sealers was not, however, of long duration. The bladder-nose had not yet learnt the danger threatened by these vessels with their crow's-nests on the maintop and swarms of boats. But his experience soon taught him, and it was not long before he grew shyer. He would no longer let the boats come close in before he took to the water. The rifle had now to be used, often at long ranges, and even so it was not easy to fill one's boats. The most remarkable thing was that it was not only the old seal that grew shy, but the youngest animals were now astonishingly wary. The parents must have imparted their experience to the offspring, or the same result must have been brought about by heredity, though this seems scarcely likely to have happened in so short a time. Whichever be the true reason, the fact remains that these seal have grown shyer year by year, or, in other words, have learnt to protect themselves from

an enemy hitherto unknown, and what is more, they have learnt this lesson in the short space of a decade. But I believe myself that the bladder-nose has learnt even more than this: that he has discovered that it is among the outer floes, where before he was safest, that danger now awaits him. He has found that if he wants to be undisturbed in the moulting-season, when he likes to be at his ease upon the floes, he must resort to the closely-packed ice inside. Here, indeed, he exposes himself to the ravages of the bear, but he avoids a far worse enemy, the Norwegian sealer.

Chapter VII.

*ATTEMPT TO LAND—DRIFTING IN THE ICE.*
On June 28 we were far in the ice, about 66 24' N. and 29 45' W. We could see land to the north, N.E. E. magnetic, and two mountain tops were especially prominent. However, we could not tell their real form, since, owing to the "looming" or optical distortion so common over these ice-fields, and due to the refraction of light through the different layers of warm and cold air, they were much altered, and looked like abruptly truncated peaks rising out of an embrasured parapet. They must have been the peaks by the Blosseville coast, though they lay more to the west than those marked on the map. I had a talk afterwards with Captain Iversen of the *Stcerkodder,* who had been further into the ice to the north. He could there see land quite distinctly: a very mountainous coast—this was probably at about 68 N. L. —not low, as it was farther down, *i.e.,* at about 67 N. L., where he had been in near shore in the year 1884. This account agrees to some extent with the description which Captain Holm had from the Eskimo of Angmagsalik, and on which he based his sketch of the east coast farther north. This shore, in fact, is one of the least known regions on the earth.

On the evening of June 28 we saw a great number of seal far in among the ice. About this time we used to see them daily, but could never get at them. On July 3 we at last got a long way in amid a quantity of seal, but the ice lay so close that it was impossible to work the boats, and we consequently got nothing. In the middle of the night, when the sun gets down to the horizon, one can see a long way and very distinctly across the fields of ice. One night I went up to the masthead to look at the seal. I turned my glasses towards land, and saw them in greater numbers than I remember to have ever seen them before. They lay, as the mate said, "scattered about the ice like coffee." From north-east to north-west, wherever I turned my glasses, there were seal lying as close as grains of sand, stretching away to the horizon and probably much further still, and the further away they were the thicker they seemed to be. It was glorious to see such an amount of life. The seal are not yet extinct, but they have learned wisdom, have altered their habits, and retired to the remoter pack-ice, and we get none of them.

Next day was foggy, and the floes lay closer still, while the swell of the sea began to reach us. In the course of the afternoon we got out of the ice again.

On July 11 the ice was moving violently, as we had come into one of the stronger currents. As two or three of us were sitting in the mess-room the *Jason* was struck so heavily by a floe on the bows that she was literally driven back. We rushed out and saw another big floe advancing with great speed upon her quarter. The shock comes, the whole vessel quivers and heels over, we hear a crash and the rudder is gone, but luckily the damage is no worse. Had the floe struck us full in the side, there is no telling what might have happened, as it would have found the sealer's weakest point.

Next day we spent fixing the spare rudder which these vessels always carry, and we were soon as seaworthy as before. But the summer was now so far advanced that there was little prospect of our getting more seal. So on July 13 it was resolved, to the satisfaction of us all, to leave the ice and make westwards for Greenland. That day, however, and the next, we did get some seal, in all about a hundred, which we passed on the outer ice.

On the night of the I4th the mate had

sighted land, and the same again in the morning, and then at no very great distance. Later, however, it grew foggy, and we could not tell how near we were, though we thought we could not be far off, as we had been sailing all day towards it in open water.

Our baggage is brought up upon deck, all preparations are made for our departure, and our despatches and letters are SEAL HUNTING. THE CAPTAIN ON THK LOOK-OUT.
(Ac *ike Authet'iJ'roin a photograph,*) written. Towards dinner-time, as I sit down below busy with my correspondence, I hear the magic word "land" from the deck. I rush up, and a glorious sight meets my eyes. It seemed, so to say, to set the finest chords of my heart vibrating. Right before me through the veil of mist lay the sunlit shore of Greenland, the glorious array of peaks which lie to the north of Cape Dan. Ingolfsfjeld is especially prominent, but further to the north there seem to be still higher tops. Never have I seen a landscape of more savage beauty, or nature in wilder confusion, than here—a landscape of sharp peaks, ice, and snow.

We were probably about thirty-five miles from land, but as we see ice ahead we turn southwards, continually drawing nearer. It looks as if we could get right into shore down by Cape Dan, as the belt here trends inwards. But as we get nearer we find that there is more ice than we expected.

On our way south we pass several enormous icebergs, and on one or two of them we saw rocks. When one first sees these monsters at a distance they look like tracts of land, and several times we thought we saw islands lying right ahead, though when we came nearer we found them to be nothing but ice. South of Cape Dan especially were numbers of these giants lying aground.

However, we could make no attempt to land that day, nor on the next. There was too much ice, the belt being from fifteen to twenty miles wide, and it seemed better to see how things looked further south.

On the 16th we passed Cape Dan, which is unmistakable with its round

dome-like form. The ice still lay far out to sea, the belt being over fifteen miles in width. Further west, however, the blue tint of the air suggests that there is a deep inlet stretching landwards. We pin our hopes on this channel, make for it, and in the course of the night actually reach it.

When I came upon deck on the morning of the i yth I saw plainly enough that the landing must be attempted that day, and a climb to the masthead only served to strengthen my resolve. The mountains round Sermilikfjord lay enticingly before us. Further west we could see the " Inland ice," the goal of our aspiration, stretching far inwards in a white undulating plain. This was the first time we had come within sight of it.

It could not have been much more than ten or twelve miles to the nearest land, and for the first bit the ice was fairly practicable. Further in certainly it seemed to be somewhat closely packed, but I could see small pools here and there, and on the whole the ground looked as if it might well have been worse. At places I could see a good deal of small ice, which makes the portage of the boats difficult, though, again, it is better to deal with than the larger floes, which are often hard to move when it is a case of forcing the boats through the water.

But what especially struck me as making the outlook hopeful was the reflection from open water which I could see from the masthead beyond the ice, and between it and land. The probability, therefore, was that when we had broken our way through the middle of the ice-belt, where the floes lay closest, we should then find looser ice merging into the open water beyond. It would, no doubt, have been an easy matter for a boat like the *Jason* to push her way through this little belt, for often before we had gone through much worse ice. But then it had been a case of seal, the real business of the ship, while now things were in a somewhat different position. Had the vessel been mine I should not have hesitated a moment about taking her in; but we were only guests on board, and, besides, she was not insured against the risks of effecting a landing in Greenland. The currents and soundings of these waters are as yet unknown, and if the *Jason* were to lose her propeller in the ice she would probably be gone beyond all chance of salvation. She could not well supply its place, and, worst of all, in case the ship had to be abandoned here, it might be very difficult for her crew of sixty-four men to make their way to inhabited parts with the small stock of provisions they had on board. And furthermore, as I believed that we could get through without help, I never thought for an instant of asking the captain to take us further than to the edge of the ice, but gave orders to have our things packed and the boats got ready.

As I have already said, we had brought one boat with us, which had been specially made for us in Christiania. But, as this would have been heavily laden with the somewhat voluminous equipment of the expedition, I gladly accepted the captain's kind offer of one of the *Jasorfs* smaller sealing-boats. So we had the two lowered and brought alongside, and there arose an unusual bustle on board with the opening of our cases and the packing of the boats. I cannot say which were more eager to help, the members of the expedition or the ship's crew; but I think I may assert with confidence that the eagerness of the latter was not due to their anxiety to see the last of us, but to simple goodwill of the most unselfish kind.

The last touches were given to our despatches and home letters; and if any of us had a specially dear friend to whom he wished to send a final farewell, it was sent, I take it, for it was not quite certain when the next meeting would be. But my companions seemed in a particularly cheerful humour, and there was no consciousness to be seen in the little band of preparation for a serious struggle. Nor was this to be wondered at, seeing that after six weeks of waiting and longing the hour of release was now at hand. The sensation which the sight of land that morning gave me was nothing short of delicious. As I then wrote to a friend, our prospects looked

brighter than I had ever dared to hope. I had a sense of elasticity, as when one is going to a dance and expecting to meet the choice of one's heart. A dance indeed we had, but not on the floor of roses which we could have wished, and our heart's choice certainly kept us a long time waiting.

Towards seven o'clock in the evening everything is ready for our start. Sermilikfjord lies now straight in front of us. According to the results of cross-bearings taken from points on shore we ought to be about nine miles from its mouth. I go up to the mast-head for the last time to see where the ice looks easiest, and what will be our best course. The reflection of open water beyond the ice is now more clearly visible than before. In a line somewhat west of Kong Oscars Havn the ice seems most open, and I determine to take that course.

More confident than ever I descend to the deck, and now the hour of departure is at hand. The whole of the *Jason's* crew were assembled. It spite of our joy at the prospect of a successful start, I think it was with much regret that we bid farewell to these brave seafolk, with whom we had now spent six weeks, and among whom we had each of us found many a faithful friend, who at this moment assumed a doubtful air, or turned away his head with an expressive shake. No doubt they thought they would never see us again. We shook hands with Captain Jacobsen last of all, and in his calm, quiet way this typical Norwegian sailor bid us a kind farewell and wished us God-speed.

Then down the ladder we went, and into the boats. I took charge of our *Jason* boat with Dietrichson and Balto at the oars, while Sverdrup steered the other with Ravna and Kristiansen.

" Ready? (live way then!" And as the boats rush through the dark water before the first vigorous strokes, the air rings with three lusty cheers from sixty-four voices, and then come two white clouds of smoke as the *Jason's* guns send us her last greeting. The report rolls heavily out into the thick, saturated air, proclaiming to the silent, solemn world of

ice around us that we have broken the last bridge which could take us back to civilisation. Henceforth we shall follow our own path. Then good-bye! and our boats glide with regular strokes into the ice to meet the first cold embrace of that nature which for a while is to give us shelter. All of us had the most implicit faith in our luck; we knew that exertion and danger awaited us, but we were convinced that we must and should get the better of them.

When we had got some way into the ice a boat and twelve men in charge of the second mate overtook us. They had been sent by Captain Jacobsen to help us as far as they could the first part of the way by dragging our boats or forcing a passage. They kept with us for a while, but when I saw they could be of very little use to us, as we worked our way through as fast as they did, I thanked them for their kindness and sent them back. We then reach a long stretch of slack ice, wave farewell to the boat, and push on with unabated courage.

At first we advanced quickly. The ice was open enough to let us row our way to a great extent among the floes, though now and then we had to force a passage by the help of crowbars and axes. There were few places where we had to drag our boats over the ice, and then the floes were small. It had begun to rain a little before we left the *Jason;* it now grew heavier, and the sky darkened and assumed a curiously tempestuous look. It was an odd and striking sight to see these men in their dark-brown waterproofs, with their pointed hoods, like monks' cowls, drawn over their heads, working their way surely and silently on in the two boats, one following close in the other's wake, amid the motionless white ice-floes, which contrasted strangely with the dark and stormy sky. Over the jagged peaks by Sermilikfjord black banks of cloud had gathered. Now and again the mass would break, and we could see as if through rents in a curtain far away to a sky still glowing with all the lingering radiance of an Arctic sunset, and reflecting a subdued and softer warmth upon the edges of the intercepting veil. Then in a moment the curtain was drawn close again, and it grew darker than ever, while we, stroke upon stroke, pushed indefatigably on, the rain beating in our faces. Was this an image of our own fate that we had seen, to have all this radiance revealed to us and then hidden and cut off by a veil of thick, impenetrable cloud? It could scarcely be so, but the soul of man is fanciful and superstitious, ready to see tokens on all sides of him, and willing to believe that the elements and the universe revolve on the axis of his own important self.

The ice now gave us rather more difficulty, and we had often to mount a hummock to look out for the best way. From the top of one of these look-outs I waved a last farewell to the *Jason* with our flag, which she answered by dipping hers. Then we start off again, and quickly, as we have no time to spare.

From the first we had had a big iceberg far to the west of us, but now for a long time we had been astonished to see how much nearer we were getting to it, though we were not working in its direction, as our course lay considerably to the east. We saw it must be the current which was taking us west. And so it was; we were being carried along with irresistible force, and it soon became plain that we could not pass to the east of this iceberg, but would have to go under its lee. Just here, however, we drift suddenly into a tearing mill-race which is driving the floes pell-mell, jamming them together and piling them one upon another. Both our boats are in danger of destruction. Sverdrup drags his up on to a floe, and is safe enough. We take ours on towards an open pool, though every moment in danger of getting it crushed. The only course is to keep a sharp look-out, and clear all the dangerous points by keeping our boat always over the so-called " foot," or projecting base of the floe, or in a recess or inlet in its side, when a nip is threatened. This is not easy in these irresistible currents, but by our united efforts we succeed, and reach a large open pool to the lee of the iceberg, and are for the time secure. Now comes Sverdrup's turn; I signal to him to follow us, and

he succeeds, keeping his boat in calmer water than we had.

We now find many good lanes of open water on our way inwards. The ice jams only once or twice, especially when the current carries us against one of the icebergs which lie stranded round about us, but it soon opens again, and we pass on. Our prospects are good, and our hearts are light. The weather is better too: it has ceased to rain, and the king of day is just rising behind the jagged background of Sermilikfjord, setting the still clouded heaven in a blaze, and lighting his beacons on the mountain tops.

Long stretches of water lie in front of us, and I already fancy I can see from the boat the open water beyond the ice. We are very near the land to the west of Sermilikfjord, and I can clearly and distinctly see the stones and details of the

H rocks and mountain side. It does not seem possible that anything can stop us and prevent our landing, and we are so self-confident that we already begin to discuss where and when we shall take our boats ashore. Just at this moment the ice packs, and we are obliged to find a place of safety for our boats, and drag them up. This we do, Sverdrup a little way off us. We have not secured a very desirable harbour for our boat, as the approach is too narrow, and when the floes part again and we are taking her out, a sharp edge of ice cuts through a plank in her side. She would no longer float, and there was nothing to be done but unload her and pull her up on to the floe for repairs. Sverdrup and Kristiansen took her in hand and mended her again with really masterly skill, and with little loss of time, considering the wretched implements they had to use. We had nothing to give them but a bit of deal which had formed the bottom board of one of the boats, some nails, a hatchet, and a wooden mallet. This broken boat, however, settled our fate. While we were at work the ice had packed again, the clouds had gathered, and the rain began to pour down in torrents, enveloping all around in gloom and mist. The only thing to be done was to get up our tent and wait.

It is now ten o'clock on the morning of the 18th of July. The best thing we can do is to crawl into our sleeping-bags and take the rest which is not unwelcome to us after fifteen hours' hard and continuous work in the ice.

Before we turned in it grew a little clearer seawards, and through a break we caught sight of the *Jason* far away. She was just getting up full steam, and a while later she disappeared in the distance, no doubt comfortably believing that we were now safe on shore. This was our last glimpse of her.

"When Ravna saw the ship for the last time,'"' writes Balto, " he said to me: ' What fools we were to leave her to die in this place. There is no hope of life; the great sea will be our graves.' I answered that it would not have been right for us two Lapps to turn back. We should not have been paid, and perhaps the Norwegian consul would have had to send us to Karasjok out of the poor-rates. This would have been a great disgrace."

While we were asleep it was necessary for one of us to keep watch in order to turn the others out, in case the ice should open enough to let us make further progress. Dietrichson at once volunteered for the first watch. But the ice gave little or no sign of opening. Only once had I to consider the possibility of setting to work again, but the floes closed up immediately. Dragging our boats over this ice was not to be thought of; it was too rough, and the floes were too small. So, while the rain continues, we have more time for sleep and rest than we care for.

In fact, we were already in the fatal current. With irresistible force it first carried us westwards into the broader belt of ice beyond Sermilikfjord. Here it took a more southerly direction and bore us straight away from shore, at a pace that rendered all resistance on our part completely futile. Had we not been detained by our broken boat, we should probably have been able to cross the /. one where the current ran strongest and get into quieter water nearer shore. As it was, the critical time was wasted, and we were powerless to recover it.

The force of the current into which we had thus fallen was considerably greater than had been previously supposed. That a current existed was well known, and I had taken measures accordingly, but, had I had a suspicion of its real strength, I should certainly have gone to work in a different way. I should in that case have taken to the ice considerably further to the east, and just off Cape Dan, and had we then worked inwards across the line of the stream we should probably have got through the ice before we were driven so far west, *i. e.,* past the mouth of Sermilikfjord, and into the broader belt of ice where the current turns southwards. Then we should, as we had expected, have reached shore all well on July 19, and chosen our landing-place where we had pleased. But now it was our fate to see how well we might have managed. We had seen the open water under the shore, we had seen the rocks on the beach; a couple of hours of easy work, and we should have been there. But Paradise was barred in our faces; it was the will of Destiny that we should land many miles to the south.

Meanwhile the rain is descending in streams, and we are constantly at work keeping our tent-floor clear of the pools of water which finds its way in through the lace-holes. After we have spent nearly twenty-four hours in the tent, mainly engaged in this occupation, the ice opens enough to tempt us to continue our efforts to reach land with renewed courage and restored vigour. This was at six o'clock on the morning of July 19.

The rain has abated somewhat, and through an opening in the fog we can see land somewhere near Sermilikfjord. We are much more than double as far distant from it as we had been—some twenty miles, in fact; but we look trustfully forward to the future. For even if we did not reach shore at Inigsalik, as we had hoped, we can still do so further south at Pikiudtlek. All we have to do is to work resolutely across the current, and we must get to shore sooner or later. As far as we could see, this was plain and simple reasoning and gave us no

ground for apprehension, but experience was to show us that our premises were not altogether in accordance with fact. The main factor in the calculation, the strength of the current, was unfortunately an extremely uncertain quantity.

However, determination and courage were not wanting. We worked with glee, got to the lee of a huge iceberg, found lanes of open water stretching far inwards, and pushed a good way on towards land.

Then the ice packs again, and we have to take refuge on a floe once more. The sun now finds its way through the clouds from time to time, so we pull our boats right up on to the floe, set up our tent, and settle down as comfortably as we can, get a change of clothes on, and dry a few of our wet things. This was a process I had especial need of, as in the course of our day's work I had fallen into the water, owing to the breaking of the edge of a floe as I was jumping into the boat. An involuntary bath of this kind was, however, an almost daily experience to one or other of the expedition. Later on in the day the sun comes out altogether, and we pass a really pleasant afternoon. We do thorough justice to the tins of provisions sent us from the Stavanger Preserving Factory, and we have no lack of drink. Had we had no more beer in our keg, we could have found plenty of the most delightful drinking-water in pools on the floes.

Our keg, I may say, belonged to the boat the *Jason* had handed over to us. All the small boats attached to the sealers are provided with a keg of beer and a chest of bread and bacon. The keg and chest the captain had let us carry off well supplied, much to our present comfort.

We now for the first time can hear rather clearly the sound of breakers on the edge of the ice towards the sea, but pay no particular attention to the fact. We seem to be drifting straight away from land, and the tops of the mountains by Sermilikfjord gradually diminish.

That evening I sit up late, long after the others have crept into their bags, to take some sketches. It is one of those glorious evenings with the marvellously

soft tones of colour which seem to steal so caressingly upon one, and with that dreamy, melancholy light which soothes the soul so fondly, and is so characteristic of the northern night. The wild range of jagged peaks in the north by Sermilikfjord stands out boldly against the glowing sky, while the huge expanse of the " Inland ice " bounds the horizon far away to the west, where its soft lines melt gently into the golden background.

The evening was lovely, and the " Inland ice " lay temptingly and enticingly just before me. Strange that a narrow strip of drifting floes should be able to divide us so hopelessly from the goal of our desires! Is not this often the case in life? The land of enchantment looks so alluring and so near. One spring would take us there, it seems. There is but one obstacle in our way, but that one is enough.

As I sit and sketch and meditate I notice a rumbling in the ice, the sound of a growing swell which has found its way in to us. I turn seawards, where it looks threatening, and, thinking that there is a storm brewing out there, but that that is of small consequence to us, I go at last to join my slumbering comrades in the bags to sleep the sleep of the just.

Next morning, July 20, I was roused by some violent shocks to the floe on which we were encamped, and thought the motion of the sea must have increased very considerably. When we get outside we discover that the floe has split in two not far from the tent. The Lapps, who had at once made for the highest points of our piece of ice, now shout that they can see the open sea. And so it is; far in the distance lies the sea sparkling in the morning sunshine. It is a sight we have not had since we left the_/rw?H.

I may here reproduce the entries in my diary for this and the following day:—

" The swell is growing heavier and heavier, and the water breaking over our floe with ever-increasing force. The blocks of ice and slush, which come from the grinding of the floes together, and are thrown up round the edges of our piece, do a good deal to break the violence of the waves. The worst of it all is that we are being carried seawards with ominous rapidity. We load our sledges and try to drag them inwards towards land, but soon see that the pace we are drifting at is too much for us. So we begin again to look around us for a safer floe to pitch our camp on, as our present one seems somewhat shaky. When we first took to it it was a good round flat piece about seventy yards across, but it split once during the night, and is now preparing to part again at other places, so that we shall soon not have much of it left Close by us is a large strong floe, still unbroken, and thither we move our camp.

" Meanwhile the breakers seem to be drawing nearer, their roar grows louder, the swell comes rolling in and washes over the ice all round us, and the situation promises before long to be critical.

" Poor Lapps! they are not in the best of spirits. This morning they had disappeared, and I could not imagine what had become of them, as there were not many places on our little island where any of us could hide ourselves away. Then I noticed that some tarpaulins had been carefully laid over one of the boats. I lifted a corner gently and saw both the Lapps lying at the bottom of the boat. The younger, Balto, was reading aloud to the other out of his Lappish New Testament. Without attracting their attention I replaced the cover of this curious little house of prayer which they had set up for themselves. They had given up hope of life, and were making ready for death. As Balto confided to me one day long afterwards, they had opened their hearts to one another here in the boat and mingled their tears together, bitterly reproaching themselves and others because they had ever been brought to leave their homes. This is not to be wondered at, as they have so little interest in the scheme.

" It is glorious weather, with the sun so hot and bright that we must have recourse to our spectacles. We take advantage of this to get an observation, our bearings showing us to be in 65 8' N. and 38 20' W., *i.e.,* 30 minutes or

about 35 miles from the mouth of Sermilikfjord, and from 23 to 25 minutes or about 30 miles from the nearest land.

" We get our usual dinner ready, deciding, however, in honour of the occasion, to treat ourselves to pea-soup. This is the first time we have allowed ourselves to cook anything. While the soup is being made the swell increases so violently that our cooking apparatus is on the point of capsizing over and over again.

"The Iapps go through their dinner in perfect silence, but the rest of us talk and joke as usual, the violent rolls of our floe repeatedly giving rise to witticisms on the part of one or other of the company, which in spite of ourselves kept our laughing muscles in constant use. As far as the Lapps were concerned, however, these jests fell on anything but good ground, for they plainly enough thought that this was not at all the proper time and place for such frivolity.

" From the highest point on our floe we can clearly see how the ice is being washed by the breakers, while the columns of spray thrown high into the air look like white clouds against the background of blue sky. No living thing can ride the floes out there, as far as we can see. It seems inevitable that we must be carried thither, but, as our floe is thick and strong, we hope to last for a while. We have no idea of leaving it before we need; but when it comes to that, and we can hold on no longer, our last chance will be to try and run our boats out through the surf. This will be a wet amusement, but we are determined to do our best in the fight for life. Our provisions, ammunition, and other things are divided between the two boats, so that if one is stove in and sinks we shall have enough to keep us alive in the other. We should probably be able to save our lives in that case, but of course the success of the expedition would be very doubtful.

" To run one of our loaded boats into the water through the heavy surf and rolling floes without getting her swamped or crushed will perhaps be possible, as we can set all our hands to work, but it will be difficult for the crew of the re-

maining boat to get their ship launched. After consideration we come to the conclusion that we must only put what is absolutely necessary into one boat, and keep it as light as possible, so that in case of extremity we can take to it alone. For the rest, we shall see how things look when we actually reach the breakers.

" We have scarcely half a mile left now, and none of us have any doubt but that before another couple of hours are passed we shall find ourselves either rocking on the open sea, making our way along the ice southwards, or sinking to the bottom.

" Poor Ravna deserves most sympathy. He is not yet at all accustomed to the sea and its caprices. He moves silently about, fiddling with one thing or another, now and again goes up to the highest points of our floe, and gazes anxiously out towards the breakers. His thoughts are evidently with his herd of reindeer, his tent, and wife and children far away on the Finmarken mountains, where all is now sunshine and summer weather.

" But why did he ever leave all this? Only because he was offered money? Alas! what is money compared with happiness and home, where all is now sun and summer? Poor Ravna!

" Yal ar farviil det svaraste bland orden
Och mycket skont dcr finnas an p4 jorden."

" It is but human at such moments to let the remembrance dwell on what has been fairest in life, and few indeed can have fairer memories to look back upon than yours of the mountain and reindeer-herd.

" But here, too, the sun is shining as kindly and peacefully as elsewhere, down on the rolling sea and thundering surf, which is boiling round us. The evening is glorious, as red as it was yesterday, and as no doubt it will be tomorrow and ever after, setting the western sky on fire, and pressing its last long passionate kiss on land and ice and sea before it disappears behind the barrier of the ' Inland ice.' There is not a breath of wind stirring, and the sea is rolling in upon us ruddy and polished as a shield under the light of the evening sky. The words of our good old song come unconsciously into my mind:—

" Havet er skjont naar det roligen hv;vlver
Staalblanke skjold over vikingers grav."

" Beautiful it is, indeed, with these huge long billows coming roljing in, sweeping on as if nothing could withstand them. They fall upon the white floes, and then, raising their green, dripping breasts, they break and throw fragments of ice and spray far before them on to the glittering snow, or high above them into the blue air. But it seems almost strange that such surroundings can be the scene of death. Yet death must come one day, and the hour of our departure could scarcely be more glorious.

" But we have no time to waste; we are getting very near now. The swell is so heavy that when we are down in the hollows we can see nothing of the ice around us, nothing but the sky above. Floes crash together, break, and are ground to fragments all about us, and our own has also split. If we are going to sea we shall need all our strength in case we have to row for days together in order to keep clear of the ice. So all hands are ordered to bed in the tent, which is the only thing we have not yet packed into the boats. Sverdrup, as the most experienced and cool-headed among us, is to take the first watch and turn us out at the critical moment. In two hours Kristian-, sen is to take his place.

" I look in vain for any sign which can betray fear on the part of my comrades, but they seem as cool as ever, and their conversation is as usual. The Lapps alone show some anxiety, though it is that of a calm resignation, for they are fully convinced that they have seen the sun set for the last time. In spite of the roar of the breakers we are soon fast asleep, and even the Lapps seem to be slumbering quietly and soundly. They are too good children of nature to let anxiety spoil their sleep. Balto, who, not finding the tent safe enough, is lying in one of the boats, did not even wake when some time later it was almost swept by the waves, and Sverdrup

had to hold it to keep it on the floe.

" After sleeping for a while, I do not know how long, I am woke by the sound of the water rushing close by my head and just outside the wall of the tent. I feel the floe rocking up and down like a ship in a heavy sea, and the roar of the surf is more deafening than ever. I lay expecting every moment to hear Sverdrup call me or to see the tent filled with water, but nothing of the kind happened. I could distinctly hear his familiar steady tread up and down the floe between the tent and the boats. I seemed to myself to see his sturdy form as he paced calmly backwards and forwards, with his hands in his pockets and a slight stoop in his shoulders, or stood with his calm and thoughtful face gazing out to sea, his quid now and again turning in his cheek—I remember no more, as I dozed off to sleep again.
o _4-
"I did not wake again till it was full morning. Then I started up in astonishment, for 1 could hear nothing of the breakers but a distant thunder. When I got outside the tent I saw that we were a long way off the open sea. Our floe, however, was a sight to remember. Fragments of ice, big and little, had been thrown upon it by the waves till they formed a rampart all round us, and the ridge on which our tent and one of the boats stood was the only part the sea had not washed.

" Sverdrup now told us that several times in the course of the night he had stood by the tent-door prepared to turn us out Once he actually undid one hook, then waited a bit, took another turn to the boats, and then another look at the surf, leaving the hook unfastened in case of accidents. We were then right out at the extreme edge of the ice. A huge crag of ice was swaying in the sea close beside us, and threatening every moment to fall upon our floe. The surf was washing us on all sides, but the rampart that had been thrown up round us did us good service, and the tent and one of the boats still stood high and dry. The other boat, in which Balto was asleep, was washed so heavily that again and again Sverdrup had to hold it

in its place.

" Then matters got still worse. Sverdrup came to the tent-door again, undid another hook, but again hesitated and waited for the next sea. He undid no more hooks, however. Just as things looked worst, and our floe's turn had come to ride out into the middle of the breakers, she suddenly changed her course, and with astonishing speed we were once more sailing in towards land. So marvellous was the change that it looked as if it were the work of an unseen hand. When I got out we were far inside and in a good harbour, though the roar of the breakers was still audible enough to remind us of the night. Thus for this time we were spared the expected trial of the seaworthiness of our boats and our own seamanship.

Chapter VIII.
*STILL DKII-TING.*
"THE 2ist of July is a quiet day following a stormy night. All is rest and peace; we are drawing steadily away from the sea, the sun is shining kind and warm, round us stretch the fields of ice in silence and monotony, and even the Lapps seem relieved.

" One thought only consumes me: the prospect of the expedition failing for this time, and of a year being thus thrown away. Well, we can only do our best, and for the rest, as we say at home, 'anoint ourselves with the good virtue of patience.'

" We take advantage of the sun to get an observation. We found ourselves to be 64 39' N. and 39" 15' W. We can still see the peaks by Sermilikfjord, and the 'Inland ice' from Pikiudtlek northward toward Inigsalik stretches majestically in front of us, looking with its flat unbroken horizon like one vast white expanse of sea. No peaks rise from its surface except a fringe of dark tops and rocky points here and there along its outer edge.

"Down here the coast is very different from the surroundings of Scrmilik, Angmagsalik, and Ingolfsfjeld. There, further north, the land rose high, abrupt, and wild out of the sea, the calm surface of the ' Inland ice' hidden behind a glorious range of Titanic peaks, whose sublime beauty captivated and held the eye, and whose summits the all-levelling ice-mantle has never been able to envelop, destroy, and carry with it to the sea. Here, on the contrary, the land is low, the ice-sheet has brought its limitless white expanse down to the very shore, and the few projecting points that do appear arc humble and unobtrusive. They have been planed by the ice, which by its overpowering might has bome all before it seawards. Wild-ness there is here too, but the wildness of desolation and monotony. There is nothing to attract the eye or fix its gaze, which therefore roams helplessly inwards over the alluring desert of snow, till it is lost in the far distance, where the horizon bars its further range. Sad to say, it is all too far distant from us. It is strange that we should have been so near our goal and then driven so far to sea again.

"The floes now part a little, and we see a stretch of slack ice leading inwards. We launch one boat and try to make some way, but to little purpose, as the slush of ice and snow that lies between the floes and comes from their grinding together in the swell is so thick that our heavily-laden craft will make no progress. So we abandon the attempt; to drag our sledges and boats over the floes is out of the question too, as the channels between them are too wide. We still hear the breakers in the distance; the swell still rolls in and keeps the ice packed close."

This day, the first on which we found time to do anything but simply work our way ahead or sleep, our meteorological record was begun. It was kept mainly by Dietrichson, who always, even in the most trying circumstances, devoted himself to it with most praiseworthy ardour. We noted chiefly the temperature, the pressure, the moisture of the air, the direction and force of the wind, and the extent and form of the clouds. Observations were taken as often and as circumstantially as possible, but of course on such an expedition, every member of which is as a rule fully occupied with work of an arduous kind, many gaps are likely to occur in the meteorological record. This is especially the case at night, when one takes the rest earned by a day of real exertion. Yet I think I may say that the record we brought home is in spite of all remarkably complete, and contains many valuable observations, thanks to Dietrichson's indefatigable zeal.

The days that now follow, spent in drifting in the ice southwards along the coast, are somewhat monotonous, each much as its fellow. Every day we watch intently the direction we are drifting, the movements of the ice, and every gust of wind, in the hope that a lucky turn may bring us in to land. From the darkness of the air overhanging the ice, we feel sure there must be open pools along the shore, or else in the ice to the south of us. It is a life of hopes and disappointments, and yet a life not without pleasant memories for many of us.

As some of my readers may find it interesting, and especially such as may contemplate future expeditions in the ice, I will give a short extract from the entries in my diary at this time.

"Late in the afternoon of July 21, from a high hummock of ice, we can see a very narrow channel stretching far away to the south of us. As far as we can judge we are drifting along this towards its end, which seems to be far in towards shore. Our hope of a change in our luck, and a speedy landing, naturally at once increases.

"July 22.—In the night a fog comes on and hides everything from us. We cannot tell which way we are drifting, but the breakers sound no less distinct than they have been. Later at night, however, we do not hear them so plainly, and the swell quiets down a little.

"The fog continues the whole day, and the rolling as well. At noon, however, it clears up so much overhead that, by the help of a pool of water on our floe as an artificial horizon, I can take an observation. I find our latitude to be 64 18' N., so we arc moving well southwards.

"As in the course of the morning the ice opens a little, we try an empty boat in the slush between the floes. We can get on, but it is very slowly, and we think it is better to save our strength, as in the fog we cannot see which way we had better work. Possibly a good chance of pushing for land may offer, and we shall then want all our energy.

" In the afternoon it clears, and we seem to be possibly a little nearer land. A gentle breeze from the magnetic N. by E., or about the true W. by N., begins to blow, and we hope it may increase and part the ice, though the rolling still goes on. What we want is a good storm from land, which would kill this swell which is rolling in and holding the ice together, and would carry the floes seawards instead, while we should be able to push in between them.

" We see a number of big seal, bladder-nose, lying on the floes around us. Many of them bob their big round heads out of the pools close alongside our floe, stare wonderingly at these new dwellers on the ice who have thus appeared, and then, often with a violent splash, vanish again. This is a daily experience. We could easily shoot them, but, as we do not want them now, we leave them in peace. We have enough fresh meat as yet, a big haunch of our little horse which we brought off the Jason. Through the afternoon the ice remains packed.

""July 23. — During the night we keep watch, two hours apiece, and we get a good laugh at Ravna. He does not understand the clock, and did not know when his two hours were up. So to make safe he willingly kept at it for five or six hours before he turned the next man out, with the innocent inquiry whether he did not think the two hours were over.

" At half-past seven Dietrichson calls us up. We find the ice open, and, though there is slush between the floes, practicable. After loading our boats and waiting half an hour on account of the ice packing again, we really get some way in to some pools which I can see from a high point stretch landwards. For a time we get on fast. Before we left our last floe a flock of some black duck flew past us, making north. The sight was like a greeting from land, and served to raise our hopes still further. It is quite astonishing, otherwise, what a scarcity of bird-life there is up here. There is not even a gull to be seen.

"We work inwards towards land the whole day, wait patiently while the ice packs, but push on all the harder when it opens again. As we get near land our hopes rise. A raven comes flying from the south-west and passes over our heads, making northwards. This is another greeting from land, and we are still more encouraged.

"We see several big seal, full-grown bladder-nose, lying about the floes round us. The temptation is too strong for a sportsman to withstand, and Sverdrup and I start off to shoot an old ' /uet-tefnnt, ' as we call him, *i.e.,* an old male with the bladder on his nose, who was lying close by. I managed to stalk him successfully and shot him, but when we got up to him he was not quite dead. In my zoological zeal I wish to improve the occasion by making observations on the colour of the eyes, the form of the bladder in the living animal, and other points which are not yet clearly known to science. While I am thus engaged the seal flaps along towards the edge of the floe, and before we know what he is about he is slipping off the ice into the water. As he is falling I drive the seal-hook 1 am carrying into him, and Sverdrup does the same with his boat-hook. It is now a case of pull-devil, pull-baker between us, and we try and hold up the seal's tail and hinder parts, in which his strength lies, so that he shall not get a stroke in the water with them. For a time we succeed, but with difficulty, for in his death-agony his strength is great. So, finding that we have not a really good hold of him, I tell Sverdrup to take the rifle and shoot him, and I will try and keep him up meanwhile. He thinks, however, that his hold is better than mine, and that I had better leave go, and, while we are hesitating, both our hooks come away, the seal gives a couple of violent flaps, and is gone. Crestfallen and discomfited, we look now blankly in each others faces, now helplessly into the dark water, where an air-bubble rises mockingly here and there to break on the surface, and to give us our seal's last greeting. Though he would have been of no great use to us, we felt not a little foolish at having lost

so fine a booty in so silly a way. Sverdrup, too, thought he was the biggest seal he had ever seen. Compassionate readers may console themselves with the thought that his sufferings were of no long duration. His struggles were but the last convulsions of his death-agony. The bullet had certainly been of somewhat small calibre, but had hit him in the right place, in the head.

" As the evening wears on we are stopped. We have got into some unusually rough and difficult hummocky ice, which is closely packed, and makes the hauling of the boats almost impossible. So we spread our tent with the sleeping-bags on the top in order to be more ready for a start in case the ice opens. We then get into our bags, setting the usual watch, but as it turns out the ice does not open. The dew is very AT WORK WITH THE BOATS.

*(By E. Nielsen, after f/mtagrafhs.)*

heavy during the night, so that the bags are found very wet in the morning.

*"July* 24.—To-day the ice is packed just as close, and we determine to drag the boats and sledges landwards. Most of our baggage is laid on the sledges, so that they can be put into the boats when we come to open water. Just as we are ready to start, the ice opens, and we manage to punt ourselves along a good way, though eventually we have to take to hauling. We get on but slowly, as the ice is not at all good; but this is at least better than nothing, and we are steadily approaching land. Our hopes are at their culmination. It is the coast north of Igdloluarsuk which we sec before us, and we begin at once to reckqn how long it will take us to reach Pikiudtlek, where we shall be able to begin our journey over the ice. To-day, too, we sec more birds: a raven and a flock of eight short-tailed skuas. Birds arc always a comfort to us, and make our life much brighter.

"As the ice is difficult and the sun hot in the middle of the day, we halt and pitch our tent while dinner is being prepared. It consists to-day of raw horse-flesh and marrowfat peas. The preparation gave rise to a comical scene. From the horse's leg which we brought with

us from the *Jason* I proceeded to cut off as much meat as I thought was enough for six men, chopped it up on the blade of an oar, turned it into one of the divisions of our cooker, sprinkled some salt on it, added the contents of a couple of tins of peas, stirred the whole mixture up, and our dinner was ready. Bnlto had been standing by my side the whole time, watching every movement intently, and indeed now and again giving me his assistance. He was hungry, and was looking forward to a good dinner, as he told me. Though, like the Lapps and other unenlightened folk generally, he had very strong prejudices against horse-flesh, yet, when he saw me pour the peas in, he informed me that it looked uncommonly good. 1 said nothing, and gave him no hint that it was going to be eaten raw, but when it was all ready took the dish and put it down before the others, who were sitting outside the tent, and told them to help themselves. Those who had the good fortune to see it will not easily forget the face that Balto assumed at this juncture. It first expressed the supremest astonishment and incredulity, and then, when he discovered that it was bitter earnest, there followed a look of disgust and contempt so intensely comical that it was quite impossible for us to restrain our laughter. Balto now told Ravna in Lappish how matters stood, and he, up to this time an indifferent spectator, now turned away with an expression of, if it were possible, still greater scorn.

"The rest of us, not letting this spoil our appetites, fell to with vigour, and did full justice to this nourishing and wholesome dish, with which we were more than satisfied. The two Iapps, had they said anything at all, would have called us heathens, for, as they explained one day afterwards, it was only heathens and beasts of the field that ate meat raw. But at the time they said nothing, but maintained an attitude of dumb despair at the fate which had thrown them into the society of savages, who had, as they often used to say, ' such strange ways, quite different from those of the Lapps.' They could scarcely endure to see us eating. I could, of course, easily have cooked some of the meat for them, but we had to be sparing of the spirit. We were likely to want it all later on, and it was only two or three times during our wanderings in the floe-ice that we allowed ourselves the luxury of cooking anything. As a rule all our food was cold, and for drink we had either plain water, of which we had an abundance in larger and smaller pools on the floes, or else a mixture of water and preserved milk, which made a pleasant and refreshing beverage. This time the Lapps were treated to tinned beef instead of the horse-flesh, and they seemed quite consoled for the first disappointment, the beef being pronounced by Balto to be 'good clear, food.' How common it is to see things in this life turned completely upside down by prejudice!"

In connection with the above I will quote an answer Balto gave one day after we reached home to some one who asked what his worst experience had been in the course of his travels. " The worst thing," said Balto, " was once when we were drifting in the ice and were just being carried out into the Atlantic. I asked Nansen whether he thought we should get to land, and he said ' Yes.' Then I asked him what we should do if we did, and he said we should row northwards. 1 wanted to know what we should live on if we did not get over to the west coast, and he said we should have to shoot something. Then I asked how we should cook it when we got it, and Nansen answered that we should have to eat it raw, which made Balto very depressed."

" Towards evening we again advance a little, but, as the ice is not close-packed, and the swell is heavy, while the eddies and suction caused by the rolling of the floes are nasty for the boats, we soon resolve to camp for the night and wait for better times. There was a thick wet fog about us which soaked our clothes through, and a biting north-west wind, a message from the 'Inland ice,' which I hoped presaged the opening of the floes.

"in: Stopped, Regarded us For AX IN-STANT, AND..." "*Jufy* 25.—At half-past four I am woke by Kristian-sen, the watch, calling in at the tent-door, 'Nansen, there is a bear coming.' I tell him to get a rifle out of the boat, slip my boots on meanwhile, and run out in a very airy costume. The bear was coming at full speed straight for the tent, but just as Kristiansen came back with the rifle he stopped, regarded us for an instant, and suddenly turned tail. At that moment he was no doubt within range, but the rifle was in its case, and before I could get it out it was too late. It was very annoying, hut the others at least had the pleasure of seeing a polar bear, which they had long sighed for.

" Balto was the only one who did not wake at the alarm in the night. In the morning he told us that during his watch, which came just before Kristiansen's, he had been so afraid of bears that he had not dared to stir from the tent the whole time. He was much astonished and very incredulous when we told him there really had been a bear about the place.

"After breakfast we started off hauling again, but had to give up at the very next floe, because the swell was increasing. Ever since the day we were out among the breakers we have had more or less of this rolling, which besides keeps the ice packed and prevents our getting to land.

"During the day the ice opens very much from time to time, but soon packs again. I dare not try to push on, as there is so much brash between the floes, and as there are no safe harbours of refuge for us to take to when the ice nips with the extreme suddenness which is its way now. The ' feet' or projecting bases of the floes are at other times safe resorts, but now they arc quite spoilt by these nasty eddies, which are most destructive to boats.

" As we can find nothing better to do we set to work to clean the sledge-runners of rust, so that they will move better. When this is done we get our dinner ready, which to-day consists of bean-soup, to which the remains of yesterday's raw meal and some more meat are added. During the cooking we take the latitude, which is 63 18' N.; and the longitude, taken later in the afternoon, proves to be about 40 15' W. We are thus about eighteen minutes, or nearly twenty miles, from land, and have drifted considerably further away than we were yesterday. Our hopes, which were then so bright, grow dim again, but a raven passing us to-day too brings us some consolation.

"Dinner is at last ready and the soup poured out into the few cups we possess, which are supplemented by meat-tins. We fall to, and all—the Lapps even included—find the soup excellent. Then to his horror and despair Ravna suddenly discovers that the meat in the soup is not properly cooked. From this moment he refuses to touch another morsel, and sits idle with a melancholy look on his face which sets us all laughing. On such occasions his puckered little countenance is indescribably comical. Balto is not much better, though he manages to drink the soup, which he finds ' first-rate'; but the meat he gently deposits in a pool of water by his side, hoping that I :.

DOMESTIC I.1FK ON TIIK FLOE-ICF.. t*Twin a fifiotf'ffrapti.*) shall not notice it. He now declares that he can say, in the words of the prophet Elias: ' Lord, that which I have not eaten, that can I not eat.' I tried to make him understand that Elias could certainly never have said anything of the kind, because he did eat what the Lord sent him, but that another man, known as the Apostle Peter, no doubt did say something like this, though it was in a vision, and the words were meant figuratively. Balto only shook his head doubtingly, and still maintained that none but heathens and beasts of the field would eat raw meat. We console the Lapps by giving them a meat-biscuit each. It is, of course, no use trying to teach old dogs to bark, and I really believe they would both have died of starvation rather than eat raw horseflesh.

" To-day both Dietrichson and Kristiansen complain of irritation in the eyes, and I recommend every one to be careful to wear their glasses henceforward.

"The ice remains about the same during the afternoon, while we drift fast southwards. In the course of the previous night we had been carried away from land, but we now seem to be drawing nearer it again. In the afternoon we are right off Skjoldungen, an island well known from Graah's voyage. Since we have come south of Igdloluarsuk we have again had a glorious Alpine region in view, with sharp and lofty peaks, and wild fantastic forms, which in the evening and sunset glow-are an especially fascinating sight.

"The rolling is increasing in an astonishing way, though we are far from the edge of the ice. There must be a very heavy sea outside.

" We begin to find it cold at night, and put all the tarpaulins and waterproofs we can spare under our sleeping-bags. We may just as well make things as pleasant as possible.

" When the rest go to bed I take the first watch in order to finish my sketches of the coast. This is very difficult, as we are so far south that the nights have already begun to darken considerably. My thoughts, however, soon desert pencil and sketch-book for contemplation of the night.

" Perfect stillness reigns, not a breath of wind is stirring, and not even the growing swell can destroy the prevailing peace. The moon has risen large and round, and with a strange ruddy glow, up from the ice-fields to the east, and in the north there is still a narrow golden strip of evening light. Far away under the moon and above the ice is a gleaming band which shows the open sea; inside this and all around is ice and snow, and nothing but ice and snow; behind lie the Greenland Alps with their marvellously beautiful peaks standing out against a dusky, dreamy sky.

" It is strange indeed for a summer night, and far different from those scenes that we are wont to connect with moonlight and summer dreams. Vet it has fascination of its own, which more southerly regions can scarcely rival.

"On the ice before me stand the boats, the sledges, and the NIGHT AMONG THK FI.OF.S.

' *Hy E. Niclsctt. front a sketch by ttic*

*Author.*

tent, in which my tired comrades are lying in sound slumber. In a pool of water by my side the moon shines calm and bright. All nature lies in an atmosphere of peace. So lately we had the day with all its burning eagerness and impatience, with its ponderings and restless designs upon the goal of our undertaking—and now all is stillness and repose. Over all the moon sheds her soothing light, her beams floating through the silence of the polar night, and gently and softly drawing the soul in their train. The thoughts and powers of Nature herself seemed to pervade all space. One's surroundings of place and time vanish, and before one appears the perspective of a past life instead.

"And, when all comes to all, what is our failure to be reckoned? Six men drifting southwards on a floe, to land eventually at a point other than that contemplated. And cither, in spite of this, we reach our goal—and in that case what reason have we to complain?—or we do not reach it, and what then? A vain hope has been disappointed, not for the first time in history, and if we have no success this year we may have better luck the next.

"*July 26.*—No change, except that we are nearer the edge of the ice and the open sea. The swell seems to have gone down considerably, and, though the sea is much nearer, we feel the rolling less than yesterday.

" We are drifting southwards along the coast, apparently at great speed.

" For the time there is nothing for us to do, as the ice does not lie close enough to let us haul our boats and sledges while this rolling is going on, but is packed too close to let us row or punt our boats through.

"We are kept in the tent by the rain.

"We have to encourage the Lapps, who seem to lose their spirits more and more, because they think we shall end by being driven out into the Atlantic. We are sitting and talking of our prospects of reaching land, and we agree that in any case we shall be able to manage it at Cape Farewell. We calculate how much time this will leave

us, and come to the conclusion that we shall still be able to work up the coast again and cross the ice. Some of the others maintain that even if we are too late this year it will be best to start northwards at once, get through the winter as we best can, and then cross over to the west coast in the spring. My opinion is that this will not be a very prudent proceeding, as it will be difficult for us to keep the provisions intact which we have brought with us for the crossing. Dietrichson thinks that this will be the only course open to us, as he considers a return entirely out of the question, and as he says, ' We shall risk nothing but our lives, anyway.'

" While this discussion is going on, Balto says to me: ' Don't talk about all this, Nansen; we shall never get to land. We shall be driven out into the Atlantic, and I only pray to my God to let me die a repentant sinner, so that I may go to heaven. I have done so much wrong in my life, but regret it bitterly now, as I am afraid I shall not be saved." I then asked him if he did not think it necessary to repent of his sins, even if he were not on the point of death. He said that he had no doubt one ought, but there was not so much hurry about it in that case. However, if he came out of this alive, he would really try and lead a better life. This seemed to me a naive confession of a peculiar faith, a faith which is, however, probably not uncommon in our society. I then asked him if, in case he reached his home again, he would give up drinking. He said he thought he would, or at any rate he would drink very little. It was this cursed drink, he told me, that was the cause of his being here in the ice. I asked how that was, and he said that he was drunk when he met a certain X., who asked him whether he would join the Greenland expedition. He was then in high spirits, and quite thought he was equal to anything of the kind.

" But next morning when he woke up sober, and remembered what he had said, he repented bitterly. He thought then that it was too late to undo it all, but he would now give any amount of money not to have come with us at all.

Poor fellow! I consoled him and Ravna as well as I could, though I must freely confess that their despondency and cowardice often caused me considerable annoyance. But as a matter of fact the poor fellows did not enter into the spirit of the undertaking at all. I do not feel sure whether my consolation was of much avail, but 1 have reason to think so. They used often to come to me after this, and appeared relieved when I gave them any information about the continent of Greenland, and the drift of the ice, things of which they seemed to have little or no comprehension.

" Otherwise our spirits are excellent, and we are really comfortable as we sit here in the tent. One or two of us are reading, others writing theif diaries, Balto is mending shoes, and Ravna, as usual, and as he prefers, is doing nothing. Nevertheless, our prospect of soon being carried out to sea again cannot be called entirely pleasant.

" In the afternoon it clears a little, the rain holds up, and we can see land, which looks quite as near as it did before.

IIAl'UNG AMONG THB HUMMOCKS.

*(By A. Block, from a. sketch ty the A ui/iar.)*

" A little later we determine to push in through the ice. It is dangerous work, but we must make the attempt, as we are being carried towards the open sea at great speed. We make a good deal of way inwards, though we are in constant risk of getting our boats crushed. We have to keep all our wits about us if we are to get the boats into shelter when the ice packs. One time we take refuge at the very last moment on a thin little floe, which splits into several pieces under the pressure, though the fragment on which we stand remains intact.

"As the ice continues packed, we begin hauling, though this is no easy matter while this rolling goes on. The floes at one moment separate, at another arc jammed together, and it is very difficult to get the sledges safely from one to the other without losing them in the sea. Often we have to wait a long time before we can get back and fetch the rest of the train from the floe on which we

have left it. By moving cautiously, however, we manage to push on at a fair pace. But it is all of little use. It serves to give us exercise, which is an important thing, but otherwise our work does little good. The sea works faster than ve do, and there is every probability of our being carried out into the breakers again. Well, so let it be; but we must first find a good ship to carry us. We set about carefully surveying all the floes round us, and we now understand pretty well what the points of a good floe are. At last we find one, of solid blue ice, thick, but not large, and in shape something like a ship, so that it will ride the seas well, and without breaking across. . It has high edges, too, which will keep the sea from breaking over it, and at the same time there is one lower place which will let us launch our boats without much difficulty. It is without comparison the best floe we have been on as yet, and on it we propose, if we are driven out, to remain as long as we can stick to it, however furiously the breakers rage around us.

" Of course we had as usual made sure, before we decided upon this floe, that there were pools of water upon it. Such there are indeed on most of these floes, for the snow which covers the ice melts and provides the most excellent drinking-water, which collects in pools of larger or smaller size.

" Nevertheless we looked very foolish this time when we were filling our boiling-pot, and, happening to taste the water, found it was brackish. It had not struck us that most of the snow was now melted away, and that our water came from the underlying salt-water ice. However, on examining the highest points of the floe, where the snow still remained, we found plenty of good water.

" This evening we had an excellent cup of coffee and were all in high spirits. If any one could have put his head into our comfortable tent, and seen us encamped round our singing coffee-pot and carelessly talking about all sorts of trifles, it would never have struck him that these were men who were on the point of engaging in a struggle with ice,

sea, and breakers, which was not likely to be altogether a joke. But let us enjoy the moment, look just so far in front of us as is necessary, and for the rest leave the day to attend to its own evil.

"We are now just off the mountains of Tingmiarmiut. Along the whole of this magnificent coast of East (Ircenland one group of wild Alpine peaks succeeds the other, each more beautiful than the last. Really it is not so bad after all to lie drifting here in the ice. ' We see more of the coast and more of the beauties of nature altogether than we should have otherwise.

" To-night it is fine, still, and cold, with a bright moon, as it was yesterday.

" It must be that coffee which is making me sit out here and talk nonsense, instead of creeping into my sleeping-bag as I ought, in order to gather strength for the exertions of to-morrow. Good-night!

*"July* 27.—Did not go to bed after all till well into the morning. There is no doubt it was a clear case of coffee-poisoning.

" Walked about talking to Sverdrup through his watch and afterwards, recalling our school-days. Life and the world seem so strangely distant to us as we drift in the ice up here.

*"July* 28.—Yesterday we did nothing, and the same is the case to-day. Our fear of being driven out into the breakers again was by no means groundless. Yesterday we were within much less than half a mile, and yet we almost wished to go, as by putting out to sea we should bring this life in the ice to an end. The sea was moderate and the wind fair, and we might thus have reached Cape Farewell within twenty-four hours. When there we should certainly have been able to push through the ice and get to land. However, we were not to go to sea after all. After we had drifted along the ice at its outer edge for a time, we began to move inwards in a field of floes, which seemed to extend away south. The ice-belt is here very narrow, and on taking our bearings upon several points on the coast we found that, though at the outer edge of the ice, we were not more than eighteen miles from land at Mogens Heinesens Fjord.

"The weather, which was yesterday bitterly cold with a wintry and clouded sky, is bright again to-day. The sun is shining warm and encouragingly down upon us. The ' Inland ice' north and south of Karra akungnak lies stretched before us pure and white, looking to the eye a level and practicable plain, with rows of crags peeping through the ice—the so-called 'nunataks'—away behind, more of them, by the way, than are marked on Holm's map. The expanse of snow beckons and entices us far into the unknown interior. Ah, well! we too shall have our day."

With this sanguine expression of confidence, which was perhaps remarkable considering the number of times we had been disappointed, my diary for this section of our journey curiously enough concludes. The next entry is dated July 31, and thus begins:—

"A strange difference between our surroundings now and those when I last wrote! Then they were ice, solitude, and the roaring of the sea, now they are barking dogs, numbers of native Greenlanders, boats, tents, and the litter of an encampment—in short, life, activity, and summer, and above all, the rocky soil of Greenland beneath our feet."

These lines were written as we were leaving the first Eskimo encampment we had come to, but before I continue from this point I had better explain how we managed to get so far.

On the evening of July 28, after having finished the entry in my diary which I have quoted above, we drifted into a fog which concealed the land from us. In the course of the afternoon the ice had several times opened considerably, though we were very near its outer edge, where one would have expected the swell to keep it packed close. It had not, however, opened to such an extent that we could safely take the boats inwards, because of the rolling. But as some of us were taking the ordinary evening walk before turning in, we were struck by the way in which the floes were separating. It looked to us as if the ice were opening even out seawards, which was an extremely unusual sight. We felt we really ought to set to work,

but we were tired and sleepy, and no one seemed at all inclined for such a proceeding. To tell the truth, too, I was now quite tired of being disappointed in the way we had been, and was very strongly disposed to put straight out to sea. We had now so often worked inwards through open ice, and the only result of all our labour had been to get driven out to sea again. This time, thought I, we will see what happens if we sit idle instead of working. And so we crept into our bags, though leaving the usual man on watch with orders to call us out in case the ice opened still more.

In the night the fog thickened and nothing was to be seen of our surroundings. Sverdrup's watch came on towards morning. He told us afterwards that as he walked up and down in the fog and after a time looked at the compass, it struck him that he must have gone clean out of his wits. Either he or the instrument must have gone mad, for the black end of the needle was pointing to what he held to be south. For if he looked along the needle with the black end away from him he had the breakers on his left. But if the end of the needle pointed to the north, as it ought, then the breakers must be on the west or land side. This could not be, so he must suppose that either he or the needle had gone crazy, and, as this is not a weakness to which compasses are liable, therefore the fault must lie with him, though it was a state of things which he had certainly never contemplated. Subsequently the phenomenon was explained in a somewhat different way, for the breakers he had heard proved to be the sea washing the shore.

In the morning I happened to be lying awake for a time. It was now Ravna who had the watch, and, as usual, he had kept at it for four hours instead of two. I lay for some time watching with amusement his bearded little face as it peeped through the opening into the tent. At first I thought he was wondering whether his two hours were not up and he might wake Kristiansen, who was to follow him. But then it struck me that to-day there was a peculiar, uneasy expression in this face, which was not at

all familiar. So at last I said: "Well, Ravna, can you see land?" And he answered eagerly in his queer, naive way: " Yes, yes, land too near." Both the Lapps habitually used *alt/or,* "too," instead of *meget,* "very." I jumped out of the bag and from the tent-door saw land much nearer than we had ever had it before The floes were scattered, and I could see open water along the shore. Ravna was indeed right; land was much too near for us to be lying idly in our bags. So I turned the others out, and it was not long before we had dressed and breakfasted. The boats were launched and loaded, and we were soon ready. Before we left this floe, which had carried us so well and was in all probability to be our last, I went up on to its highest point to choose our best course for land. Our surroundings were changed indeed. The whole field of ice seemed to have been carried away from land and outwards to the south-east. I could see nothing but ice in that direction, and there was that whiteness in the air above it which betokens large fields. Towards the south, on the contrary, and along the shore, there seemed to be nothing but open water. We were not far from the edge of this water, and it stretched northwards also for some way along the coast, ending at a point where the ice seemed to lie close into the land. We were therefore now on the inner edge of the ice-belt, and the outer edge was not distinctly visible from where I stood. It is strange how quickly one's fate changes. It was quite plain that we should now soon be on shore, and, had this been told us yesterday, not one of us would have allowed the possibility of such a thing.

So off we started and pushed quickly landwards. The water was open enough for us to row pretty well the whole way, there being only two or three places where we had to force a passage.

Some hours later we were through the ice. The feelings that possessed us as we took our boats by the last floe and saw the smooth, open water stretching away in front of us up to the very shore are scarcely to be described in words. We felt as if we had escaped from a long and weary imprisonment and now all at once saw a bright and hopeful future lying before us. Life was indeed bright and hopeful now, for when can it be brighter than when one sees the attainment of one's wishes possible, when uncertainty at last begins to pass into certainty? It is like the tremulous joy which comes with the breaking day, and when is not the dawn fairer and brighter than the full noontide?

Chapter IX.

*THE EAST COAST OF GREENLAND.*

The first thing we did when we were through the ice was to look for the nearest land. We wanted to feel the Greenland rocks beneath our feet as soon as possible, and, besides, I had long promised chocolate and a Sunday dinner for the day we first touched dry land again.

Almost opposite to us, and nearer than anything else, was the high rounded summit of Kutdlek Island. It would, however, have taken us too much out of our way to put in here, as we were going north. So we steered across the open water to the more northerly island of Kckertarsuak.

On the way we passed under a huge iceberg which lay stranded here in the open water. On its white back sat flocks of gulls, strewn like black dots about its surface. As we went by, a big piece of ice fell crashing into the vater, and crowds of seabirds rose and wheeled round us, uttering their monotonous cries. This was all new to us. To have living creatures about us again was cheering indeed, while it was even still more grateful to be able to row unhindered through all this open water.

As we advanced, however,-we found that we had still some obstacles to pass before reaching land, as there was another belt of ice stretching southwards parallel with the shore. But it was of no great breadth, and, as the ice was fairly open, we forced our way through without much trouble. At last our boats, flying the Norwegian and Danish flags, glided under a steep cliff, the dark wall of which was mirrored in the bright water, and made it nearly black. The rock echoed our voices as we spoke, and the

moment was one of extreme solemnity. Beyond the cliff we found a harbour where we could bring our boats ashore. Then we scrambled out, each striving to get first to land and feel real rocks and stones under his feet, and to climb up the cliffs to get the first look round. We were just like children, and a bit of moss, a stalk of grass, to say nothing of a flower, drew out a whole rush of feelings. All was so fresh to us, and the transition was so sudden and complete. The Lapps ran straight up the mountain side, and for a long while we saw nothing more of them.

KtTDLtK ISLAND AND CAI'E TOKUKN-SKJO1.IJ.

*(By tlu Author.)*

But as soon as the first flood of joy was over we had to turn to more prosaic things, that is to say, our promised dinner. The cooker was put up on a rock down by the boats, and the chocolate set under way. Plenty of cooks were ready to help, and meanwhile I thought I might as well follow the 1-apps' example and go for a mountain climb, to see how things looked, and how the land lay further north.

So I started up, first over some bare rock, over a drift of snow, and then across some flat, moorlike ground, grown with lichens and heather, and sprinkled with huge erratic boulders. I can still clearly and distinctly remember every stone and every stalk. How strange it was, too, to have a wider view again, to look out to sea and see the ice and water shining far below me, to see the rows of peaks round about me lying bathed in the hazy sunshine, and to see, too, the " Inland ice " stretched out before me, and, I might say, almost beneath my feet.

To the south was the high rounded summit of Kutdlek Island, and beyond it the fine outline of Cape Tordenskjold. I welcomed the latter as a fellow-countryman, as not only the name but the form recalled Norway. I sat down on a stone to take a sketch and bask in the sun. As I rested there, delighting in the view and the mere fact of existence, I heard something come singing through the air and stop in the neighbourhood of

my hand. It was a good well-known old tune it sang, and I looked down at once. It was a gnat, a real gnat, and presently others joined it. I let them sit quietly biting, and took pleasure in their attack. They gave me, these dear creatures, sensible proof that I was on land, as they sat there and sucked themselves full and red. It was long, no doubt, since they last tasted human blood. But this was a pleasure of which, as shall soon be told, we had afterwards reason to grow more than tired.

I sat a while longer, and presently heard a familiar twitter. I looked up and saw a snow-bunting perched on a stone close by, and watching the stranger's movements with his head first on one side and then on the other. Then he chirped again, hopped on to the next stone, and, after continuing his inspection for a while, flew off. At such times and places life is always welcome, and not least so when it comes in the form of a twittering little bird, and finds a response in the small bird element of one's own nature, especially if one has long been outside the regions of spring and summer. Even a spider which I came across among the lichens on a stone on my way up was enough to turn my thoughts to home and kindlier scenes.

From my point of vantage I could see a good way to the north. It looked as if we were to have open ice for the first bit, but beyond Inugsuit the floes seemed to lie closer, and clearly promised to give us trouble. But it was now time for me to go down and join the others, as the chocolate must be nearly ready. It was nothing like so, however, when I reached the shore. The water was not yet boiling, and it was plainly

I UIK I'lRST LANUINC-I'1.ACK.

*(Jrom a photograph.")*

a case of unskilful cooks. But they had certainly not had much practice while we were drifting south, as, if I remember right, we had only cooked three times in twelve days. Meanwhile I spent the time in taking a photograph of the scene—of a spot which takes a prominent place in the history of our expedition. At last the long-expected chocolate was ready, and six patient throats could at last enjoy deep draughts of the glorious nectar. Besides fuller allowances of the ordinary fare, we were treated, in honour of the day, to adjuncts in the form of oatmeal biscuits and Gruyere cheese, and our native delicacies " mysost" and "tyttebaer"-jam. It was indeed a divine repast, surpassing anything we had had hitherto; we deserved it and equally well enjoyed it, and our spirits were at the height of animation.

Balto's account of our stay on this island sets forth that " the spot was quite free of snow, grass-grown, and covered with heather and a few juniper-bushes. We had quite a little feast here, and were treated to all the best we had—cheese, biscuits, jam, and other small delicacies. The cooking-machine was put up on a rock; we made chocolate, and sat round the pot, drinking, with the sea lying at our feet. Nansen took several pictures, and the place was named GameT's Haven."

We came to the conclusion that we might for this once take our time and enjoy life to the full, but that this must be the last of such indulgence. Henceforth our orders were to sleep as little as possible, to eat as little and as quickly as possible, and to get through as much work as possible. Our food was to consist in the main of biscuits, water, and dried meat. To cook anything or to get fresh meat there would be little or no time, though there was plenty of game. The best of the season was already passed, and little of the short Greenland summer remained. But still we had time to reach the west coast, if only we used that time well. It was a question of sticking to our work, and stick to it indeed we did

Our grand dinner was at last finished, and about five o'clock in the afternoon we embarked again and started on our way north.

At first we pushed on quickly, as the water-way was good and clear, but as evening came on things changed for the worse. The ice packed closer, and often we had to break our way. From time to time, however, we came upon long leads of open water and made ground fast. The sun sank red behind the mountains, the night was still and woke all our longings, the day lay dreaming beyond the distant peaks, but there was little time for us to indulge in sympathy with Nature's moods and phases. The whole night we worked northwards through the ice. At midnight it was hard to see, but with attention we could distinguish ice from open water by the reflection from the glowing evening sky.

I was the more anxious to push on, for it was not far to the ill-famed glacier of Puisortok, where Captain Holm on his voyage along the coast in 1884 was kept by the ice seventeen days. I imagined that the reason why this spot had so evil a reputation was because the current held the floes more closely packed here than elsewhere, and it seemed to me of vital importance that we should reach this point of difficulty as soon as possible, in order to take the first opportunity caused by the opening of the ice to push by.

In the course of the night we reached the headland of Kangek or Cape Rantzau, where the ice was packed so close that we could row no longer, but had to force our way. Before our axe, long boat-hooks, and crowbars all obstacles had, however, to recede, and we worked steadily on. But the new ice formed on the water between the floes added much to our labour, as towards morning it grew thicker and hindered the boats considerably, and it even remained unmelted till well into the day. Towards morning, too, our strength began to give out; we had now worked long and were hungry, as we had eaten nothing since our great dinner of the day before. Some of us were so sleepy, too, that we could scarcely keep awake. In our zeal to push onwards, and our enjoyment of our new life, we had quite forgotten bodily needs, which now asserted themselves with greater insistence. So we landed on a floe to rest and refresh ourselves. Breakfast was a pure enjoyment, though we could scarcely allow that we had time to sit still to eat it. Then came the sun; his beams shot up through space, lighter and lighter grew the sky, the spot on the northeast horizon burned brighter and brighter, and then the globe of fire himself rose slowly above the plain of ice. We let mind and body bask in his rays; new life quickened in us, and weariness had in a moment fled away. Once more we set to work in the growing dawn.

But the ice was closer packed than ever, and inch by inch and foot by foot we had to break our way. Often things looked simply hopeless, but my indefatigable comrades lost not heart; we had to push through, and push through we did.

We passed Cape Rantzau, passed Karra akungnak, which is known from Holm and Garde's voyage in 1884, and reached Cape Adelaer, where things were bad, even to despair. The floes lay jammed together, huge and unwieldy, and refused to move. With our long boat-hooks we tried to part them, but in vain. All six as one man fell to, but they lay like rocks. Once more we put all our strength into our work, and now they gave. A gap of an inch inspirited us; we set to again, and they opened further. We now knew our strength, and perseverance was sure of its reward. Presently they had parted so.far that we could take the boats through after hacking off the projecting points of ice. Thus we pass on to the next floe, where the same performance is repeated. By united exertion pushed to its utmost limits, we force our way. It needs no little experience to take boats safely through ice like this. One must have an eye for the weak points of the floes, must know how to use to the best advantage the forces at one's disposal, must be quick to seize the opportunity and push the boats on just as the floes have parted, for they close again immediately, and if the boats are not through, and clear, they are at once unmercifully crushed. Several times, when we were not quite quick enough, Sver-drup's boat, which followed mine, was nipped between the floes till her sides writhed and bulged under the pressure; but her material was elastic, and she was finally always brought through without real mishap.

At last we passed Cape Adelaer, and

worked along the shore, through ice that still lay closely packed, to the next promontory, which I have since named Cape Garde. We reached this cape about noon, and determined to land and get something to eat, and some sleep, both of which we sorely needed after more than twenty-four hours' hard and continuous work in the ice. We had just with great difficulty dragged our boats up the steep rocks, pitched our tent, and begun our preparations for dinner, when there occurred an event which was entirely unexpected, and to our minds indeed little short of miraculous.

My diary of the next day records the occurrence thus:— " Yesterday, July 30, about noon, after an incredibly laborious struggle through the ice, we had at last put in by—let us for the moment call it Cape Garde—a promontory to the north of Karra akungnak to get some food and a few hours' sleep. The much-dreaded glacier, Puisortok, lay just in front of us, but we hoped to get by it without delay, though it had kept Holm back for no less than seventeen days. While we were having some dinner, or, more accurately, were busy getting it ready, I heard amid the screams of the gulls a cry of a different kind, which was amazingly like a human voice. I drew the others' attention to the fact, but there was so little probability of our finding human beings in these regions that for some time we were contented to attribute the noise to a 'diver' (Colymbus) or some similar bird, which was perhaps as little likely to occur up here as a human being himself. However, we answered these cries once or twice, and they came gradually nearer. Just as we were finishing our meal there came a shout so distinct and so close to us that most of us sprang to our feet, and one vowed that that could be no 'diver.' And indeed I think that even the staunchest adherent of the sea-bird theory was constrained to waver. Nor was it long before Balto, who had jumped up on a rock with a telescope, shouted to us that he could see two men. I joined him at once, and soon had the glass upon two black objects moving among the floes, now close to one another, now

apart. They seemed to be looking for a passage through, as they would advance a bit and then go back again. At last they come straight towards us, and I can see the paddles going like mill-sails—it is evidently two small men in 'kayaks.' They come nearer and nearer, and Balto begins to assume a half-astonished, half-uneasy look, saying that he is almost afraid of these strange beings. They now come on, one bending forwards in his canoe as if he vere bowing to us, though this was scarcely his meaning. With a single stroke they come alongside the rocks, crawl out of their 'kayaks,' one carrying his small craft ashore, the other leaving his in the water, and the two stand before us, the first representatives of these heathen Eskimo of the east coast, of whom we have heard so much. Our first impression of them was distinctly favourable. We saw two somewhat wild but friendly faces smiling at us. One of the men was dressed in a jacket, as well as breeches, of sealskin, the two garments leaving a broad space uncovered between them at the waist. He had on ' kamiks,' the peculiar Eskimo boots, and no covering for the head except a few strings of beads."

Here my entry describing this strange meeting is broken off, though my recollection of the scene is still as vivid as if it had all happened yesterday, and it is an easy matter for me to supply all that is wanting. The other one had, to our surprise, some garments of European origin, as his upper parts were clad in an " anorak," a sort of jacket, of blue cotton stuff with white spots, while his legs and feet were cased in sealskin trousers and "kamiks," and his waist was also to a large extent quite bare of clothing. On his head he had a peculiar broad and flat-brimmed hat, formed of a wooden ring over which blue cotton stuff had been stretched. On the crown was a large red cross covering its whole expanse. This pattern of head-dress, in various garish colours, and generally with the cross upon it, is very common among the Eskimo of the east coast. They use them when in their " kayaks," partly for the shade they afford, and

partly for the decorative effect Later they showed us some of these hats with great pride. They were little fellows, these two, evidently quite young, and of an attractive appearance, one of them, indeed—he with the beads in his hair—being actually handsome. He had a dark, almost chestnut-brown skin, long jet-black hair drawn back from the forehead by the band of beads and falling round his neck and shoulders, and a broad, round, attractive face with features almost regular. There was something soft, something almost effeminate, in his good looks, so much so indeed that we were long in doubt whether he was a man at all. Both these little fellows were of light and active build, and were graceful in all their movements.

As they approached us they began to smile, gesticulate, and talk as fast as their tongues would go, in a language of which, of course, we understood not a single word. They pointed south, they pointed north, out to the ice and in to the land, then at us, at our boats, and at themselves, and all the time chattering with voluble persistence. Their eloquence, indeed, was quite remarkable, but little did it enable us to comprehend them. We smiled in our turn and stared at them in foolish helplessness, while the Iapps showed open indications of uneasiness. They were still a little afraid of these "savages," and held themselves somewhat in the background.

Then I produced some papers on which a friend had written in Eskimo a few questions the answers to which I was likely to find serviceable. These questions I now proceeded to apply in what was meant to pass for tolerable Eskimo, but now came the Greenlanders' turn to look foolish, and they stared at me and then at each other with an extremely puzzled air. I went through the performance again, but with exactly the same result, and not a word did they understand. Persevering, I tried once or twice more, the only effect of which was to make them gesticulate and chatter volubly together, leaving us as wise as we were before. In despair I threw the papers down, for this was a performance that could only lead to premature grey hair. I wanted to find out something about the ice further north, but the only semblance of success was that I thought I heard them mention Tingmiarmiut, at the same time pointing northwards, and once, too, Umanak—or, at least, I seemed to catch some sounds which these names might be supposed to represent—but even this left us in exactly the same state of darkness. Then I had recourse to signs, and with better success, for I learned that there were more of them encamped or living to the north of Puisortok, and that it was necessary to keep close under the glacier to get by. Then they pointed to Puisortok, made a number of strange gesticulations, and assumed an inimitably grave and serious air, admonishing us the while, all of which apparently meant that this glacier was extremely dangerous, and that we must take the greatest care not to run into it, nor to look at it, nor to speak as we passed it, and so on. These East Greenlanders, it is said, have a number of superstitious notions about this particular glacier. Then we tried by means of signs to make them understand that we had not come along the land from the south, but from the open sea, which intelligence only produced a long-drawn sonorous murmur, deep as the bellow of a cow, and, as we supposed, meant to express the very extremity of astonishment. At the same time they looked at one another and at us with a very doubtful air. Either they did not believe a word we told them, or else, perhaps, they took us for supernatural beings. The latter was probably their real estimate of us.

Then they began to admire our equipment. The boats, above all, attracted their attention, and the iron fittings especially excited the greatest astonishment and admiration.

We gave them each a bit of meat-biscuit, at which they simply beamed with pleasure. Each ate a little and carefully put away the rest, evidently to take home to the encampment. All this while, however, they were shivering and quaking with the cold, which was not to be wondered at, as they had very little in the way of clothing on, and, as I have said, were completely naked about the waist, while the weather was anything but warm. So, with some expressive gestures telling us that it was too cold to stand about there in the rocks, they prepared to go down to their canoes again. By signs they asked us whether we were coming northwards, and, as we answered affirmatively, they once more warned us against the perils of Puisortok, and went down to the water. Here they put their skin-capes on, got their " kayaks " ready, and crept in with the lightness and agility of cats. Then with a few strokes they shot as swiftly and noiselessly as water-fowl over the smooth surface of the sea. Then they threw their harpoons or bird-spears, which flew swift as arrows and fell true upon the mark, to be caught up again at once by the "kayaker" as he came rushing after. Now their paddles went like mill-sails as they darted among the floes, now they stopped to force their way or push the ice aside, or to look for a better passage. Now, again, an arm was raised to throw the spear, was drawn back behind the head, held still a moment as the dart was poised, then shot out like a spring of steel as the missile flew from the throwing-stick. Meanwhile they drew further and further from us; soon they looked to us like mere black specks among the ice far away by the glacier; and in a moment more they had passed behind an iceberg and disappeared from our view. And we remained behind, reflecting on this our first meeting with the east coast Eskimo. We had never expected to fall in with people here, where, according to Holm and Garde's experience, the coast was uninhabited. These we thought must be some migrant body, and in this belief we retired to our tent, crept into our bags, and were soon fast asleep.

Balto's description of this meeting, though written a year after the occurrence, agrees so closely with the notes in my diary which were entered the day after it, but have never been accessible to him, that I think I ought to quote it in justice to his memory, if not for its own sake. " While we were sitting and eating," he writes, "we heard a sound like a human voice, but we thought it was only a raven's cry. Presently we heard the same sound again, and now some of us thought it was a loon screaming. Then I took the glasses and went up on to a point of rock, and, looking about, saw something black moving across an ice-floe. So I shouted, 'I can see two men over there on the ice,' and Nansen came running up at once and looked through the glass too. We now heard them singing their heathen psalms, and called to them. They heard us at once, and began to row towards us. It was not long before they reached us, and as they came closer one of them gave us a profound bow. Then they put in to shore, and, getting out, dragged their canoes up on to land. As they came near us they lowed like cows, which meant that they wondered what sort of folk we were. Then we tried to talk to them, but we could not understand a word of their language. So Nansen pulled out his conversation-book and tried to talk to them that way; but it was no use, because we could not make out how the letters were pronounced in their language. Then Nansen went down to the boats and fetched some biscuit, which he gave to them, and afterwards they rowed away again northwards."

About six o'clock in the afternoon I woke and went out of the tent to see what the ice was doing. A fresh breeze was blowing off the land, and the floes had parted still more than before. There seemed to be a good water-way leading north, and I called my companions out.

We were soon afloat and steering northwards for the dreaded glacier, in the best water we had had as yet. I was in constant fear, however, that things would be worse further on, and lost no time. But things became no worse, and the ice up here consisted chiefly of larger and smaller glacier-floes, which are much better than sea-floes to have to deal with in wooden boats, which are not cut by their sharp edges as skin-boats are. What hindered us most was that the water between the floes was full of small brash of the broken glacier ice. We pushed through, however, and the water proved comparatively good the whole way. Without meeting serious obstacles we passed the glacier, sometimes rowing right under the perpendicular cliffs of ice, which showed all the changing hues of glacier-blue, from the deepest azure of the rifts and chasms to the pale milky-white of the plain ice-wall, and of the upper surface, on which the snow still lay here and there in patches.

It is difficult to see what it really is that has given this glacier its evil reputation. It has very little movement indeed, and therefore seldom calves, and when it does the pieces which come away must be relatively small, for there are no large icebergs to be seen in the sea near its edge. Nor is there depth enough of water to make such possible, and, furthermore, at several points the underlying rock is visible, so that the glacier does not even reach the water throughout its whole extent.

However, Graah and even earlier writers record the excessive dread which the Eskimo have for this dangerous glacier, which is always ready to fall upon and crush the passer-by, and far away from which, out at sea, huge masses of ice may suddenly dart up from the depths and annihilate both boat and crew. The name Puisortok also points in this direction, as it means " the place where something shoots up." It occurs at more than one point on the eastern coast in connection with glaciers, though its real force and intention is not easily explicable. That the Greenlander crews employed by Holm and Garde had the same superstitious dread of this same glacier is made very plain in their interesting narrative. Garde tells us that the idea prevalent among the natives of the southern part of the west coast is that "when one passes Puisortok one has to row along under an overhanging wall of ice which may fall at any instant, and over masses of ice which lurk beneath the surface of the water, and only await a favourable moment to shoot up and destroy the passing boats."

The Eskimo of the south-west have no doubt got their superstitious notions.

from the wild natives of the east coast with whom they have come into contact. The latter even have a number of rules of conduct which should govern the behaviour of the passer-by if he wish to escape alive. There must be no speaking, no laughing, no eating, no indulgence in tobacco, neither must one look at the glacier, nor mention the name Puisortok. If he do the latter, indeed, the glacier's resentment is such that certain destruction is the result.

In spite of all this one thing is certain, that Puisortok falls far short of its reputation. As I afterwards discovered, it is not even in connection with the great sheet of " Inland ice." It is a comparatively small local glacier lying upon a mountain ridge which is separated from the " Inland ice " by a snow-covered valley on its inner side. This is, of course, the reason of its relatively slight movement, which, according to Garde's measurements, is not above two feet in the twenty-four hours. Its very form and inclination also point to the fact that it is only local

The only remarkable thing about it is that it has so long a frontage to the sea. Garde estimates its breadth at about five miles, which is apparently correct. This fact, as Garde suggests, must plainly be the reason why the Eskimo are so afraid of it, for, as it comes right out into the sea, and has no protecting belt of islands and rocks, they are forced to pass along its face in the course of their journeys up and down the coast. The Eskimo dread any passage of the kind, which is not unreasonable, as the glaciers are continually calving, or dropping masses of ice from their upper parts, and the danger to passing craft is by no means imaginary. For if a boat happen to be off a glacier at the moment of its calving, it will in most cases, no doubt, be lost beyond all hope of salvation. Even if the falling masses do not come into direct contact with it, the water is agitated to such a tremendous extent, and the floes and floating fragments of ice are thrown about so violently, that the chances of escape are very small.

All the great glaciers, however, lie far

in the recesses of narrow fjords, which in the course of ages they have themselves cut out or deepened by their powerful onward movement. But it is seldom that the Eskimo find their way into these fjords, and it is not as a rule necessary for them to pass close under these huge cliffs of ice, whose dangerous caprices they nevertheless well know. It is therefore, after all, not so much a matter for wonder that they feel anxiety when they have to pass so long a stretch of glacier as Puisortok, notwithstanding its comparatively gentle ways.

Be this as it may, we passed the glacier without mishap, and no superstitious terror prevented us from enjoying to the full the fantastic beauty of these mighty walls of ice.

The water was still comparatively favourable as we worked north, and we pushed on fast. Our courage rose and rose, and we grew more and more convinced that nothing would now hinder us from reaching our goal.

THE ESKIMO ENCAMPMENT AT CAPE BIM.E. *(fly I'. Nifltenfrom a photograph?)*

Chapter X.

*THE EAST COAST—AN ESKIMO ENCAMPMENT.*

As we drew near Cape Bille, the promontory which lies to the north of Puisortok, we heard strange sounds from shore—as it were, a mixture of human voices and the barking of dogs. As we gazed thither we now caught sight of some dark masses of moving objects, which, as we examined them more closely, we found to be groups of human beings. They were spread over the terrace of rock, were chattering in indistinguishable Babel, gesticulating, and pointing towards us as we worked our way quietly through the ice. They had evidently been watching us for some time. We now too discovered a number of skin-tents which were perched among the rocks, and at the same time became aware of a noteworthy smell of train-oil or some similar substance, which followed the off-shore breeze. Though it was still early, and though the water in front of us seemed open for some distance, we could not resist the temptation of visiting these strange and unknown beings. At the moment we turned our boats towards shore the clamour increased tenfold. They shrieked and yelled, pointed, and rushed, some down to the shore, others up on to higher rocks in order to see us better. If we were stopped by ice and took out our long boat-hooks and bamboo poles to force the floes apart and make ourselves a channel, the confusion on shore rose to an extraordinary pitch, the cries and laughter growing simply hysterical. As we got in towards land some men came darting out to us in their " kayaks," among them one of our acquaintances of the morning. Their faces one and all simply beamed with smiles, and in the most friendly way they swarmed round us in their active little craft, trying to point us out the Way, which we could quite well find ourselves, and gazing in wonder at our strong boats as they glided on regardless of ice which would have cut their fragile boats of skin in pieces.

At last we passed the last floe and drew in to shore. It was now growing dusk, and the scene that met us was one of the most fantastic to which I have ever —"-T' been witness. All about the ledges of An Eskimo Boy From rock stood long rows of strangely wildand Cape Bille. shaggy-looking creatures—-men, women, *From it fihotverabh.)* j L-ij 11 Li and children all in much the same scanty dress—staring and pointing at us, and uttering the same bovine sound which had so much struck us in the morning. Now it was just as if we had a whole herd of cows about us, lowing in chorus as the cowhouse door is opened in the morning to admit the expected fodder. Down by the water's edge were a number of men eagerly struggling and gesticulating to show us a good landing-place, which, together with other small services of the kind, is the acknowledged Eskimo welcome to strangers whom they are pleased to see. Up on the rocks were a number of yellowish-brown tents, and lower down canoes, skin-boats, and other implements, while more "kayaks" swarmed round us in the water. Add to all this the neigh-

bouring glacier, the drifting floes, and the glowing evening sky, and, lastly, our two boats and six unkempt-looking selves, and the whole formed a picture which we at least are not likely to forget The life and movement were a welcome contrast indeed to the desolation and silence which we had so long endured.

It was not long, of course, before our boats were safely moored, and we standing on shore surrounded by crowds of natives, who scanned us and our belongings with wondering eyes. Beaming smiles and kindliness met us on all sides. A smiling face is the Eskimo's greeting to a stranger, as his language has no formula of welcome.

Then we look round us for a bit Here amid the ice and snow these people seemed to be comfortable enough, and we felt indeed that we would willingly prolong our stay among them. As we stopped in front of the largest tent, at the sight of the comfortable glow that shone out through its outer opening, we were at once invited in by signs. We accepted the invitation, and as soon as we had passed the outer doorway a curtain of thin membranous skin was pushed aside for us, and, bending our heads as we entered, we found ourselves in a cosy room.

The sight and smell which now met us were, to put it mildly, at least unusual. I had certainly been given to understand that the Eskimo of the east coast of Greenland were in the habit of reducing their indoor dress to the smallest possible dimensions, and that the atmosphere of their dwellings was the reverse of pleasant. But a sight so extraordinary, and a smell so remarkable, had never come within the grasp of my imagination. The smell, which was a peculiar blending of several characteristic ingredients, was quite enough to occupy one's attention at first entrance. The most prominent of the components was due to the numerous train-oil lamps which were burning, and this powerful odour was well tempered with human exhalations of every conceivable kind, as well as the pungent effluvia of a certain fetid liquid which was stored in vessels here and there about the room,

and which, as I subsequently learned, is, from the various uses to which it is applied, one of the most important and valuable commodities of Eskimo domestic economy. Into further details I think it is scarcely advisable to go, and I must ask the reader to accept my assurance that the general effect was anything but attractive to the unaccustomed nose of the newcomer. However, familiarity soon has its wonted effect, and one's first abhorrence may even before long give way to a certain degree of pleasure. But it is not the same with every one, and one or two of our party were even constrained to retire incontinently.

For my own part, I soon found myself sufficientlyat ease to be able to use my eyes. My attention was first arrested by the number of naked forms which thronged the tent in standing, sitting, and reclining positions. All the occupants were, in fact, attired in their so-called "natit" or indoor dress, the dimensions of which ESKIMO GARMENTS, ETC., KROM THE KAST COAST OF GREKNLANU, IN THE ETHNOGRAPHICAL MUSEUM AT CHRISTIANIA.

I. Woman's breeches; II. Man's indoor dress; III. Woman's indoor dress: IV. Amulet-strap worn by men; V. " Kamik," or Eskimo boot; VI. and VII. Knives.

are so extremely small as to make it practically invisible to the stranger's inexperienced eye. The dress consists in a narrow band about the loins, which in the case of the women is reduced to the smallest possible dimensions.

Of false modesty, of course, there was no sign, but it is not to be wondered at that the unaffected ingenuousness with which all intercourse was carried on made a very strange impression upon us conventional Europeans in the first instance. Nor will the blushes which rose to the cheeks of some among us when we saw a party of young men and women who followed us into the tent at once proceed to attire themselves in their indoor dress, or, in other words, divest themselves of ev,ery particle of clothing which they wore, be laid to our discredit, when it is remembered that we had been accustomed to male society exclusively during our voyage and adventures among the ice. The Lapps especially were much embarrassed at the unwonted sight.

The natives now thronged in in numbers, and the tent was soon closely packed. We had been at once invited to sit down upon some chests which stood by the thin skin-curtain at the entrance. These are the seats which are always put at the disposal of visitors, while the occupants have their places upon the long bench or couch which fills the back part of the tent.' This couch is made of planks, is deep enough to give room for a body reclining at full length, and is as broad as the whole width of the tent. It is covered with several layers of sealskin, and upon it the occupants spend their whole indoor life, men and women alike, sitting often cross-legged as they work, and taking their meals and rest and sleep.

The tent itself is of a very peculiar construction. The framework consists of a sort of high trestle, upon which a number of poles are laid, forming a semicircle below, and converging more or less to a point at the top. Over these poles a double layer of skin is stretched, the inner coat with the hair turned inwards, and the outer generally consisting

I 5 of the old coverings of boats and "kayaks." The entrance is under the above-mentioned trestle, which is covered by the thin curtain of which I have already spoken.

This particular tent housed four or five different families. Each of them had its own partition marked off upon the common couch, and in each of the stalls so formed man, wife, and children would be closely packed, a four-foot space thus having sometimes to accommodate husband, two wives, and six or more children.

Before every family stall a train-oil lamp was burning with a broad flame. These lamps are flat, semicircular vessels of pot-stone, about a foot in length. The wick is made of dried moss, which is placed against one side of the lamp and continually fed with pieces of fresh blubber, which soon melts into oil. The lamps are in charge of the women, who have special sticks to manipulate the wicks with, to keep them both from smoking and from burning too low. Great pots of the same stone hang above, and in them the Eskimo cook all their food which they do not eat raw. Strange to say, they use neither peat nor wood for cooking purposes, though such fuel is not difficult to procure. The lamps are kept burning night and day; they serve for both heating and lighting purposes, for the Eskimo does not sleep in the dark, like other people; and they also serve to maintain a permanent odour of train oil, which, as I have said, our European senses at first found not altogether attractive, but which they soon learned not only to tolerate, but to take pleasure in.

As we sat in a row on the chests, taking stock of our strange surroundings, our hosts began to try and entertain us. The use of every object we looked at was kindly explained to us, partly by means of words, of which we understood nothing, and partly by actions, which were somewhat more within reach of our comprehension. In this way we learnt that certain wooden racks which hung from the roof were for drying clothes on, that the substance cooking in the pots was seal's-flesh, and so on. Then they showed us various things which they were evidently very proud of. Some old women opened a bag, for instance, and brought out a little bit of Dutch screw-tobacco, while a man displayed a knife with a long bone handle. These two things were, no doubt, the most notable possessions in the tent, for they were regarded by all the company with especial veneration. Then they began to explain to us the mutual relations of the various occupants of the tent. A man embraced a fat woman, and thereupon the pair with extreme complacency pointed to some younger individuals, the whole pantomime.giving us to understand that the party together formed a family of husband, wife, and children. The man then proceeded to stroke his wife down the back and pinch her here and there to show us how charming and delightful she was, and how fond he was of her, the process giving her, at the same time, evident satisfaction.

Curiously enough, none of the men in this particular tent seemed to have more than one wife, though it is a common thing among the east coast Eskimo for a man to keep two if he can afford them, though never more than two. As a rule the men are good to their wives, and a couple may even be seen to kiss each other at times, though the process is not carried out on European li nes, but by a mutual rubbing of noses. Domestic strife is, however, not unknown, and it sometimes leads to violent scenes, the end of which generally is that the woman receives either a vigorous castigation or the blade of a knife in her arm or leg, after which the relation between the two becomes as cordial as ever, especially if the woman have children.

In our tent the best of understandings seem to prevail among the many occupants. Towards us they were especially friendly, and talked incessantly, though it had long been quite clear to them that all their efforts in this direction were absolutely thrown away. One of the elders of the party, who was evidently a prominent personage among them, and probably an "angekok" or magician, an old fellow with a wily, cunning expression, and a more dignified air than the rest, managed to explain to us with a great deal of trouble that some of them had come from the north and were going south, while others had come from the south "and were bound north; that the two parties had met here by accident, that we had joined them, and that altogether they did not know when they had had such a good time before. Then he wanted to know where we had ESKIMO WOMAN FROM THE EAST COAST OF GKF.F.NLAM).

*(From a photograph taken by the Danish '' Koncbaad" expedition.)*

come from, but this was not so easily managed. We pointed out to sea, and as well as we could tried to make them understand that we had forced our way through the ice, had reached land further south, and then worked up northwards. This information made our audience look very doubtful indeed, and another chorus of lowing followed, the conclusion evidently being that there was something supernatural about us. In this way the conversation went on, and all things considered, we were thoroughly well entertained, though to an outside observer, our pantomimic efforts would, of course, have seemed extremely comical.

I will not be rash enough to assert that all the faces that surrounded us were indisputably clean. Most of them were, no doubt, naturally of a yellowish or brownish hue, but how much of the colour that we saw in these very swarthy countenances was really genuine we had no means of deciding. In some cases, and especially among the children, the dirt had accumulated to such an extent that it was already passing into the stage of a hard black crust, which here and there had begun to break away and to show the true skin beneath. Every face, too, with few exceptions, simply glistened with blubber. Among the women, especially the younger section, who here as in some other parts of the world are incontinently vain, washing is said to be not uncommon, and Holm even accuses them of being very clean. But as to the exact nature of the process which leads to this result it will perhaps be better for me to say no more.

It might be supposed that the surroundings and habits of these people, to which I have already referred, together with many other practices, which I have thought it better not to specify, would have an extremely repellant effect upon the stranger. But this is by no means the case when one has once overcome the first shock which the eccentricity of their ways is sure to cause, when one has ceased to notice such things as the irrepressible tendency of their hands to plunge into the jungle of their hair in hot pursuit, as their dirt-encrusted faces —a point on which, I may remark, we ourselves in our then condition had little right to speak—and as the strange atmosphere in which they live; and if one is careful at first not to look too closely into their methods of preparing food, the general impression received is absolutely attractive. There is a frank and

homely geniality in all their actions which is very winning, and can only make the stranger feel thoroughly comfortable in their society.

People's notions on the subject of good looks vary so much that it is difficult to come to a satisfactory determination with regard to these Eskimo. If we bind ourselves down to any established ideal of beauty, such as, for instance, the Venus of Milo, the question is soon settled. The east coast of Greenland, it must be confessed, is not rich in types of this kind. But if we can only make an effort and free our critical faculty from a standard which has been forced upon it by the influences of superstition and heredity, and can only agree to allow that the thing which attracts us, and on which we look with delight, for these very reasons possesses the quality of beauty, then the problem becomes very much more difficult of solution. I have no doubt that, were one to live with these people for a while and grow accustomed to them, one would soon find many a pretty face and many an attractive feature among them.

As it was, indeed, we saw more than one face which a European taste would allow to be pretty. There was one woman especially who reminded me vividly of an acknowledged beauty at home in Norway; and not only I, but one of my companions who happened to know the prototype, was greatly-struck by the likeness. The faces of these Eskimo are as a rule round, with broad, outstanding jaws, and are, in the case of the women especially, very fat, the cheeks being particularly exuberant. The eyes are dark and often set a little obliquely, while the nose is flat, narrow above and broad below. The whole face often looks as if it had been compressed from the front and forced to make its growth from the sides. Among the women, and more especially the children, the face is so flat that one could almost lay a ruler across from cheek to cheek without touching the nose; indeed, now and again one will see a child whose nose really forms a depression in the face rather than the reverse. It will be understood from this that many of these peo-

ple show no signs of approaching the European standard of good looks, but it is not exactly in this direction that the Eskimo's attractions, generally speaking, really lie. At the same time there is something kindly, genial, and complacent in his stubby, dumpy, oily features which is quite irresistible.

Their hands and feet alike are unusually small and well-shaped. Their hair is absolutely black, and quite straight, *f'l'l: ''*j«i

'.- ESKIMO BEAUTY, FROM THE EAST COAST, IN HER OLD AGE.

*..'ielsen/rom a photograph taken by the Danish " Koncbatui" expedition.)* resembling horse-hair. The men often tie it back from the forehead with a string of beads and leave it to fall down over the shoulders. Some who have no such band have it cut above the forehead or round the whole head with the jawbone of a shark, as their superstitions will not allow them on any account to let iron come into contact with it, even when the doubtful course of having it cut at all has been resolved upon. But, curiously enough, a man who has begun to cut his hair in his youth must necessarily continue the practice all his life. The women gather their hair up from behind and tie it with a strip of seal-skin into a cone, which must stand as perpendicularly as possible. This convention is, of course, especially stringent in the case of the young unmarried women, who, to obtain the desired result, tie their hair back from the forehead and temples so tightly that by degrees it gradually gives way, and they become bald at a very early age. A head which has felt the effects of this treatment is no attractive sight, but the victim in such cases has generally been a long time married and settled in life, and the disadvantage is therefore not so keenly felt.

After we had been sitting in the tent for a while one of the elders of the company, the old man with the unattractive expression, of whom I have already spoken, rose and went out. Presently he came in again with a long line of seal-skin, which, as he sat on the bench, he began to unroll. I regarded this performance with some wonder, as I could not imagine what was going to happen. Then he brought out a knife, cut off a long piece, and, rising, gave it to one of us. Then he cut off another piece of equal length and gave it to another, and the process was repeated till we all six were alike provided. When he had finished his distribution he smiled and beamed at us, in his abundant satisfaction with himself and the world at large. Then another of them went out, came back with a similar line, and distributed it in like manner; whereupon a third followed his example, and so the game was kept going till we were each of us provided with four or five pieces of seal-skin line. Poor things! they gave us what they could, and what they thought would be useful to us. It was the kind of line they use, when seal-catching, to connect the point of the harpoon to the bladder which prevents the seal from escaping, and it is astonishingly strong.

After this exhibition of liberality we sat for a time looking at one another, and I expected that our hosts would show by signs their desire for something in return. After a while, too, the old man did get up and produce something which he evidently kept as a possession of great price and rarity. It was nothing else than a clumsy, rusty old rifle, with the strangest contrivance in the way of a hammer that it has ever been my good luck to see. It consisted of a huge, unwieldy piece of iron, in which there was a finger-hole to enable the user to cock it. As I afterwards found, this is the ordinary form of rifle on the west coast of Greenland, and it is specially constructed for use in the "kayak." After the old man had shown us this curiosity, and we had duly displayed our admiration, he made us understand by some very unmistakable gestures that he had nothing to put in it. At first I pretended not to grasp his meaning, but, this insincerity being of no avail, I was obliged to make it plain to him that we had nothing to give him in the way of ammunition. This intimation he received with a very disappointed and dejected air, and he went at once and put his rifle away.

None of the others showed by the slightest token that they expected anything in return for their presents. They were all friendliness and hospitality, though no doubt there was a notion lurking somewhere in the background that their liberality would not prove unproductive, and, of course, we did not fail to fulfil our share of the transaction next day. The hospitality, indeed, of this desolate coast is quite unbounded. A man will receive his worst enemy, treat him well, and entertain him for months, if circumstances throw him in his way. The nature of their surroundings and the wandering life which they lead have forced them to offer and accept universal hospitality, and the habit has gradually become a law among them.

After we considered we had been long enough in the tent we went out into the fresh air again, and chose as our camping-ground for the night a flat ledge of rock close to the landing-place. We then began to bring our things ashore, but at once a crowd of natives rushed for our boats, and numbers of hands were soon busy moving our boxes and bags up on to the rocks. Every object caused an admiring outburst, and our willing helpers laughed and shouted in their glee, and altogether enjoyed themselves amazingly. The delight and admiration that greeted the big tin boxes in which much of our provender was packed were especially unmanageable, and the tins were ESKIMO, FROM THK CAMP AT CAPE BILLLi.
*(Front a f holograph.)*
each passed round from hand to hand, and every edge and corner carefully and minutely examined.

As soon as the boats were empty we proposed to drag them up, but here again all insisted on giving their help. The painter was brought ashore, manned by a long line stretching far up the rocks, and the boats hauled up each by the united efforts of twenty or thirty men. This was splendid sport, and when u one of us started the usual sailor's chorus to get them to work together, the enthusiasm reached its height.

They joined in, grown folk and children alike, and laughed till they could scarcely pull. They plainly thought us the most amusing lot of people they had ever seen. When the boats were safe ashore we proceeded to pitch our tent, an operation which engaged all their attention, for nothing can interest an Eskimo so much as any performance which belongs to his own mode of life, such as the management of tents and boats and such things. Here their astonishment does not overcome them, for they can fully understand what is going on. In this case they could thus admire to the full the speedy way in which we managed to pitch our little tent, which was so much simpler a contrivance than their great complicated wigwams, though at the same time it was not so warm.

Our clothes, too, and, above all, the Lapps' dress, came in for their share of admiration. The tall, square caps, with their four horns, and the tunics with their long, wide skirts and edging of red and yellow, struck them as most remarkable, but still more astonished were they, of course, in the evening, when the two Lapps made their appearance in their reindeer-skin pelisses. All must needs go and feel them and examine them, and stroke the hair of this wonderful skin, nothing like which they had ever seen before. It was not seal-skin, it was not bear-skin, nor was it fox-skin. "Could it be dog-skin?" they asked, pointing to their canine companions. When we explained that it was nothing of that kind they could get no further, for their powers of imagination had reached their limit Balto now began to gibber and make some very significant movements with his hands about his head, with the idea of representing reindeer horns, but this awoke no response. Evidently they had never seen reindeer, which do not occur on that part of the east coast which they frequent

Then we distributed the evening rations, and ate our supper sitting at the tent-door, and surrounded by spectators. Men, women, and children stood there in a ring many ranks deep, closely watching the passage of every morsel of biscuit to our lips and its subsequent consumption. Though their mouths watered to overflowing at the sight of these luxuries, we were constrained to take no notice. We had no more in the way of bread than we actually needed, and, had we made a distribution throughout all this hungry crowd, our store would have been much reduced. But to sit there and devour one's biscuits under the fire of all their eyes was not pleasant.

Our meal over, we went and had a look round the encampment. Down by the water were a number of " kayaks " and a few specimens of the " umiak " or large skin-boat, which especially interested me. One of the men was particularly anxious to show me everything. Whatever caught my eye, he at once proceeded to explain the use of by signs and gestures. Above all, he insisted on my examining his own "kayak," which was handsomely ornamented with bone, and all his weapons, which svere in excellent condition and profusely decorated. His great pride was his harpoon, which, as he showed me triumphantly, had a long point of narwhal tusk. He explained to me, too, very clearly the use of the throwing-stick, and how much additional force could be given to the harpoon by its help. Every Eskimo is especially proud of his weapons and "kayak," and expends a large amount of work on their adornment.

By this time the sun had set and the night fallen, and consequently the elements of weirdness and unreality which had all the time pervaded this scene, with its surroundings of snow and ice and curious human adjuncts, were now still more predominant and striking. Dark forms flitted backwards and forwards among the rocks, and the outlines of the women with their babies on their backs were especially picturesque. From every tent-door through the transparent curtain shone a red glow of light, which with its suggestions of warmth and comfort, led the fancy to very different scenes. The resemblance to coloured lamps and Chinese lanterns brought to one's mind the illuminated gardens and summer festivities away at home, but behind these curtains here lived a happy and contented race, quite as happy, perhaps, as any to which our thoughts turned across the sea.

Then bed-time drew near, and the rest we sorely needed after the scanty sleep of the last few days. So we spread our sleeping-bags upon the tent-floor and began the usual preparations. But here again our movements aroused the keenest interest, and a deep ring of onlookers soon gathered round the door. The removal of our garments was watched with attention by men and women alike, and with no sign of embarrassment, except on our part. Our disappearance one by one into the bags caused the most amusement, and when at last the expedition had no more to show than six heads the door of the tent was drawn to and the final " Good-night" said.

That night we could sleep free from care and without keeping watch, and it was a good night's rest we had in spite of barking dogs and other disturbances. It was late when we woke and heard the Eskimo moving busily about outside. Peeping through the chinks of the door, we could see them impatiently pacing up and down, and waiting for the tent to be thrown open again that they might once more feast their eyes on all the marvels hidden inside. We noticed to-day, and we supposed it was in our honour, that they were all arrayed in their best clothes. Their clean white frocks, made of the same thin membranous skin as the tent curtains, shone as brilliantly as clean linen in the distance, as their wearers walked up and down and admired their own magnificence. Down by our boats, too, we saw a whole congregation, some sitting inside and others standing round. Ever)' implement and every fitting was handled and carefully scrutinised, but nothing disturbed or injured.

AN ESKIMO FROM CAPE BILI.E. *(Frcm an instantaneous photograph.*

Then came the opening of the door, and forthwith a closely packed ring of spectators gathered round, head appearing above head, and row behind row, to see us lying in our bags, our exit thence, and gradual reinstatement in our clothes. Of all our apparel that which excited most wonder and astonishment was a coloured belt of Kristiansen's, a belt resplendent with beads and huge brass buckle. This must needs be handled and examined by each and all in turn, and of course produced the usual concerted bellow. Then our breakfast of biscuits and water was consumed in the same silence and amid the same breathless interest as our supper of the night before.

After breakfast we walked about the place, for we had determined to enjoy life for this one morning and see what we could of these people before we left them. I had tried, unnoticed, to take a photograph of the ring which thronged our tent-door, but as I brought the camera to bear upon the crowd some of them saw my manoeuvre, and a stampede began, as if they feared a discharge of missiles or other sorcery from the apparatus. I now tried to catch a group who were sitting on the rocks, but again with the same result. So the only expedient was to turn my face away, and by pretending to be otherwise engaged to distract the attention of my victims and meanwhile secure some pictures.

ESKIMO FROM CAHE BIU.K. *(FrtJin a photograph.)*

Then I took a tour round the camping-ground with my camera. Outside one little tent, which stood somewhat isolated, I found an unusually sociable woman, apparently the mistress of the establishment. She was relatively young, of an attractive appearance altogether, with a smiling face and a pair of soft, obliquely set eyes, which she made use of in a particularly arch and engaging way. Her dress was certainly not elegant, but this defect was, no doubt, due to her established position as a married woman, and must not be judged too harshly. In her "amaut," a garment which forms a kind of hood or Kskimo From Cafe BiLi.E. bag behind, she *(From a photograph.)* ,J swarthy baby, which she seemed very fond of, and which, like many of the mothers, she did her best to induce to open its black eyes and contemplate my insignificance. This was partly, no doubt, the flattery of the coquette; on the whole we got on very well together, and unperceived I secured several photographs. Then the master came out of the tent, and showed no sign of surprise at finding his wife in so close converse with a stranger. He had evidently been asleep, for he could hardly keep his eyes open in the light, and had to resort to a shade, or rather some big snow-spectacles of wood. He was a strongly-built man, with an honest, straightforward look, was very friendly, and showed me a number of his things. He was especially proud of his " kayak "-hat, which he insisted on my putting on my head, while he meantime unceremoniously arrayed himself in my cap. This performance was little to my

"OUTSIDE ONE LITTLE TENT I FOUND AN UNUSUALLY SOCIABLE WOMAN." *(By E. Nielsen, from a photograph.)* taste, as it was quite uncertain what would be the result of the exchange to me. Then he took me to sec his big boat or " umiak," as well as other of his possessions, and we parted.

I went on, and looked into some other tents. In one of them I found two girls who had just taken a big gull out of a cooking-pot, and were beginning to devour it, each at work with her teeth on one end of the body, and both beaming with delight and self-satisfaction. The bird still had most of its feathers on, but that did not seem to trouble them much. Perhaps, after the manner of the owl, they subsequently ejected them.

Some of the women had noticed that the Lapps used the peculiar grass known as " sennegraes," of which I have already spoken, in their boots, and they now brought each of us a huge supply of the commodity, smiling most coquettishly as they made their offering. We expressed our thanks, of course, by an equally lavish display of smiles. Then they began to inquire, by means of signs, whether we had no needles to give them in return. I could have gratified them, certainly, since I had brought a number of these articles of barter, which are much prized on the east coast. But my real object was to keep them in case we had to spend the winter in these parts, in which case they would have proved invaluable. So I told them that we could not let them have any needles in exchange for their grass, and gave them instead a tin which had had

" Thkn Thk Master Came Out preserved meat in. This made them simply wild with delight, and with sparkling eyes they went off to show the others their new acquisition. The grass came in very handy for the two I.apps, whose store was running short, and without this grass in his shoes a Lapp is never thoroughly comfortable. They had a deal to say, too, about this Eskimo " scnnegra?s." The fact that these people had sense enough to use the grass impressed Ravna and Ballo to a certain extent, but they declared OK THK TKNT." *(/'raw a photograph.)* it had been gathered at the wrong time of year, being winter grass taken with the frost on it, instead of being cut fresh and then dried, in accordance with the practice of rational beings. It was of little use to point out to them that it was not the habit of the Eskimo to lay up greater stores of such things than he actually needed to keep him going.

But the time of our departure drew near, and we began by degrees to make our preparations. A man now came up to us and asked whether we were going northwards. At our answer in the affirmative his face brightened amazingly, and it proved that he was bound in the same direction with his party, to whom he went at once and announced the news. The camp was now a scene of lively confusion, and, while we and the Eskimo vied with one another in our haste to strike our tents, launch our boats, and stow our goods, the dogs, who well knew what was in progress, expended their energy in a howling competition.

As the tent we had spent the preceding evening in was going southwards, it was necessary that we should go and make some return for the presents we had received. So with a number of empty meat-tins I went in and found a party of half-naked men taking a meal. I gave them one each, which delighted them hugely, and some of them at once showed their intention of using them as drinking-vessels. Outside I found the possessor of the rifle, who again urged upon me the fact that he had no ammunition for jt. But when e» ese „ to ,

A BOY FROM CAPE BI.I.I.K. *(Frew a ph*

&TM-C?L2L-

" »l '"". too ' /" "' tho "'' ''«''o 'CS-:':; .; %c *it of* u ' to n ' Practice f!,, " *ceding* evenin "ards, *go t/ie pres* souththat
return received,
meat-
Party of
eal. j -" of *I* presented him with a large tin instead he expressed perfect contentment and gratification.

The great skin-tents were soon down and packed away in the boats. It was indeed quite astonishing to see the speed with which these Eskimo made ready for a journey with all their household goods and worldly possessions, though, of course, there were a great number of helping hands. We had almost finished our preparations too, when a salt-box was pleased to discharge its contents in the middle of one of the provision-bags. This had to be seen to at once, and the Eskimo consequently started before us. Two of the boats set off on their southward journey, and two more presently disappeared behind the first point of rock to the north. The company of "kayakers," however, were still left, as they stayed behind to bid each other a more tender farewell, before they parted, perhaps, for a separation of some years. This leave-taking gave rise to one of the most comical scenes I have ever witnessed. There were altogether a dozen or more of their little canoes, and they all now ranged up side by side, dressed as evenly as a squad of soldiers. This extraordinary manoeuvre roused my attention, of course, and I could not imagine what it purported. I was not left long in ignorance, however, for the snuff-horns were presently produced, and the most extravagant excesses followed. Their horns were opened and thrust up their noses again and again, till every nostril must have been absolutely filled with snuff. Several horns were in circulation, and each came at least twice to every man, so that the quantity consumed may well be imagined. I wanted to photograph them, but lost time and could not bring my camera to bear upon them before the line was broken, and some of the canoes already speeding away southwards among the floes.

This general treating with snuff is the mode in which the Eskimo take leave of one another, and is a very similar performance to the ceremonious dram-drinking among our peasants at home. In this particular case only those who had come from the south had anything to stand treat with. They were evidently fresh from the Danish colonies beyond Cape Farewell, as their abundant supply of snuff proved, while the others were probably bound south on a similar errand. These pilgrimages occur unfortunately too often, though their emporium lies at no trifling distance—a couple of years' journey, in fact, for those who live furthest up the coast.

One would almost expect that so long a journey would

'THE LINK WAS BROKEN, AND SOME OK THE CANOKS ALREADY SPEEDING AWAY SOUTHWARDS AMONG THE FLOES." (/'row a photograph.) be followed by a long stay at the place of business. But this is not the case, and the Eskimo, in fact, spends little more time over his periodical shopping than a lady of the world over a similar, but daily, visit. In half an hour, or an hour perhaps, he has often finished, and then disappears again on his long journey home. A shopping expedition of this kind will therefore often take four years at least, and consequently a man's opportunities in this way in the course of a lifetime are very limited. These are quite enough, however, to produce a mischievous effect. One is apt to suppose that it is the want of certain useful things, otherwise unattainable, that urges them to these long journeys; but this is scarcely so, for the real incentive is without doubt a craving for tobacco. As a matter of fact they do buy some useful things, like iron, which they get chiefly in the form of old hoops, but they really have a good supply of such things already, they do not use them much, and they are not absolutely necessary. Most of their purchases are things which are either altogether valueless or else actually injurious.

Among the latter must especially be reckoned tobacco, which is the commodity of all others most desired, and which they take in the form of snuff. Smoking and chewing are unknown on this coast, but their absence is made up for by all the greater excess in snuff-taking, the indulgence in which is quite phenomenal. They buy their tobacco in the form of twist, and prepare it themselves, by drying it well, breaking it up, and grinding it fine on stone. Powdered calcspar or quartz or other rock is often added to the snuff to make it go farther, and to increase, it is said, the irritating effect upon the mucous membrane.

In addition to tobacco they buy other things which certainly have an injurious effect upon them, such as, for instance, tea. Coffee, curiously enough, these people have not learned to like, though this drink is bliss celestial to the west-coast Eskimo.

It is truly fortunate that they have no opportunity of getting spirits, as the sale is absolutely prohibited by the Danish Government. Of other European products, they buy biscuits, flour, peas, which they are particularly fond of, and similar things. Articles of clothing, too, are in great demand, such as thick jerseys from the Faroe Islands, cotton stuffs for outer tunics, and material out of which they can make hats; old European clothes are highly valued, and they have an idea that when they can dress themselves out in these worn-out, rubbishy garments they cut a far finer figure than when they content themselves with their own warm and becoming dress of seal-skin.

In exchange for such things, which are of little value to us and of still less real worth to them, they give fine large bearskins, fox-skins, and seal-skins, which they ought to keep for their own clothes and the other numerous purposes for which they can be used. It is, of course, unnecessary to remark how much better it would be if these poor Eskimo, instead of decking themselves out in European rags, would keep their skins for themselves, and confine themselves to those regions where they have their homes, instead of straying to the outskirts of European luxury and civilisation.

Many may think that this access to vegetable food is an advantage for the Eskimo, and possibly it would be if he had the chance of regularly supplying himself with flour and such things in small quantities. But, as the opportunity only occurs perhaps a few times in the course of a man's life, the value of such a change of diet is, of course, very small. The effect, indeed, may very well be the opposite of beneficial, inasmuch as these Eskimo, when they do get European victuals into their possession, impose no restraint upon their appetites, but eat like wolves as long as the supply lasts, and an unwonted indulgence of this kind may easily produce serious internal disturbances.

There is a story current which well shows the beneficent effect of European fare upon the Eskimo stomach. A boat's crew of east-coast pilgrims had paid their visit to one of the trading places near Cape Farewell, and had, among other things, bought a quantity of peas. They were already on their homeward journey, and had put in to a little island for the purpose of cooking some of their peas and enjoying their first meal. They set their peas to boil, but, with the scantiness of experience only to be expected of them, they had no idea of the time necessary for the process, and set to work upon the peas while they were yet half-cooked. Now, the Eskimo are commonly reputed to eat at times even beyond the limits of ordinary repletion, and these poor folk no doubt continued the indulgence as long as their powers allowed them. But, as every one knows, half-cooked peas have a most uncomfortable tendency to swell as moisture gradually penetrates them. These peas proved too much for the Eskimo, and the consequence was that not long afterwards the whole company of victims to European food were found dead upon the island.

This story is declared to be a matter of common knowledge, but, whether it be a fact or not, there is nothing at all improbable about it, and it is a good illustration of the benefits likely to result from access to foreign articles of food. Though the consequences need not be always so disastrous as on this occasion, still the real benefit can be but slight. When the Eskimo have at length consumed their purchases and must needs return to the old manner of life, the net result is that they have lost a number of useful possessions, and have acquired a feeling of want and longing for a number of unnecessary things. This is, in fact, the usual way that the blessings of civilisation first make themselves felt upon the uncivilised.

Chapter XI.

*THE EAST COAST—ANOTHER STAGE NORTHWARDS.*

When we were at last ready to start, all the " kayakers " had disappeared except one, who, no doubt, wished to show us the civility of escorting us. Our surroundings were now just as empty and desolate as an hour ago they had been full of life and movement. Instead of on tents and dogs and human beings, the sun now shone down upon ice and snow and barren rocks.

We embarked and set off northwards along the coast. At first the water was open, and we worked hard at our oars, for the Eskimo boats had a substantial start, and as we hoped to profit largely by their knowledge of the water and ice, we were anxious to travel in their company. It was not long before we came up with them, and found them lying under shelter of a point of land, and apparently in difficulties. Some women stood up in one of the boats and waved to us. When we came nearer we were desired by the help of signs to go on in front and force a passage through the ice. This was certainly in direct contradiction to our hopes and speculations, but of course we went to the front, and glided quietly by them in between two huge floes, which lay locked together and looked immovable. This was the obstacle which had brought the Eskimo to a standstill. But wheri we drove our first boat in between the two floes, and partly by using it as a wedge, partly by the help of our poles with all six men at work, really managed to force the two monsters apart, the admiration

of our friends knew no limit, and was expressed in the usual extraordinary way. We now pushed on, breaking through the ice, which here caused no great difficulty. The two big boats followed, with four " kayaks " in close attendance. Every movement on our part was accompanied by a sustained and vigorous bellow from behind, which was encouraging, though it was not the most melodious music we could have wished for.

We were much amused to see the " kayakers " taking snuff. One of them especially was insatiable, and I believe he stopped every ten minutes to pull out his huge snuff-horn and fill both his nostrils. He sneezed, too, sometimes so violently that it was a mystery to me how he managed to keep his canoe on an even keel during his convulsions. When he looked at us again after one of these sneezes, with his upper lip covered with snuff and the tears trickling from his eyes, his jovial face was so inestimably comical that every time we saluted him with shouts of laughter, in answer to which he nodded, smiled, and beamed with good humour. Then, too, they kept shouting from time to time the only word of their language which we managed to fix, and this, too, by the way, we fixed slightly wrong. It was "pitsakase," and meant, as we imagined, "a splendid journey! " or something of the kind, as it was ejaculated on all occasions, as well when we forced our way through the ice as when we were rowing along in open water. But when we reached the west coast we learnt of the Eskimo there —whose language is much the same—that the word really means " How clever you are! " or sometimes " How good (or kind) you are!"

The larger boats used by the Eskimo, which have often been referred to already, and are called by them " umiaks," are, as I have said, only manned by women. Among Eskimo of pure blood it is considered beneath a man's dignity to row in one of these boats. But a man— in most cases the head of the household—must do the steering; and this duty is incumbent on him, much as he would prefer to be in his "kayak." These

"umiaks" are of considerable length, extending to thirty feet or even more, though they are, as a rule, longer on the west coast of Greenland than on the east, where, owing to the prevalence of drifting ice, a short boat is, of course, not so difficult to manoeuvre as a longer one, unhandy as these boats are in any case in such circumstances.

The women who manned the two boats which followed us rowed in a most extraordinary fashion, and not to any regular stroke. They began at a moderately fast rate, but the stroke was presently quickened, and then quickened again, growing shorter and shorter, of course, at each increase. As they pulled, too, they rose from their seats and stood upright in the boat in the middle of each stroke, and the whole performance was consequently of a very spasmodic and jumpy character. Then, suddenly, just as the bucketing had reached an *allegro vivace* pitch, there was an " easy all": the rowers rested to regain their wind, and then the same performance was gone through again. One of these buckets was, of course, only of very short duration, but there was a never-failing supply of them; and in this unorthodox way they really managed to get along pretty fast. In open water they quite kept pace with us, or often even passed us; which is not, however, to be wondered at, as we had only two at the oars in each boat, while they had as many as six or seven. Once something delayed us, and our companions went on ahead. When we caught them up we found that they had again been stopped by the ice, and some of the women were making signals to bring us to their help. We then came up with our long boat-hooks, as usual, and could scarcely help laughing when we found a single Eskimo standing and pushing valiantly at a huge ice-floe with a little stick. He looked so infinitely powerless and absurd as he stood there alone, and, of course, it had not struck the other men and women in the boats to' come and help him. We now brought all hands to bear as usual, and the floes were forced to give way. We got through and pushed on, but the long boats were caught behind us, and only struggled through with some difficulty. This, indeed, happened again and again, that the longer boats were stuck in the channel which we, with our shorter boats, had just

N /1 V, *itm-* made for them. For this reason we might have pushed on a long way ahead, if we had not waited for the others. That such should be the case with these much and often praised Eskimo boats, without which Holm and Garde declare a voyage up the east coast out of the question, was a matter of no small surprise to me.

This has long been the view held by the Danes. They have had little or no actual experience in the navigation of such waters as these; and, taking it for granted that among the floes the Eskimo can have no equals, they have insisted that the peculiar Eskimo boats must be the best type for the purpose, and at the same time that they must be manned by Eskimo crews. My experience leads me to the very opposite conclusion, and I am convinced that European boats, with good European crews who are accustomed to the sort of thing, are far to be preferred for this work. Nor is there any truth in the assertion which has been made that European boats cannot carry enough to serve the purpose.

It was now getting time for us to have a meal, and we accordingly had to distribute the rations. The Eskimo, who have a remarkable power of resisting hunger, meanwhile pushed on. Two of the " kayakers," however, stayed behind to watch us eating, "e gave them some pieces of biscuit, which delighted them immensely. Then we started again and soon came within sight of the others. Two of the men we saw had climbed high up on the rocks on a point beyond Ruds Island, and were looking out northwards over the sea and ice. This was a bad sign, and meant, perhaps, that the ice was impassable. Meanwhile the others went on, and before we caught them up we had to pass the mouth of the fjord which lies between the island and the mainland. It now began to look like bad weather, the sky was darkening and rain beginning to fall. We put on our waterproofs and pushed hopefully

on, but had not gone far before we saw the Eskimo boats coming back to meet us. When they neared us all the women pointed to the sky with very grave faces, while the men explained that the ice was packed badly on ahead. They insisted that we must put back to the island and encamp there for the time being. I, however, made them understand that we wanted to go on, but they represented to me that this was impossible. I had my doubts about the impossibility, but thought it better not to proceed till I had been ashore and seen with my own eyes how things looked. So we all turned back to land, the Eskimo boats keeping inside the island, while we made for the nearest point. One of the " kayakers" who saw our design followed us to apply all his powers of persuasion, as far as signs would allow. It was not to much purpose, however, for as soon as we reached the shore. I ran up on to a rock, and when, by the help of the glasses, I saw that the water looked fairly promising on ahead, we made up our minds then and there to push on at once. When our friend found that his eloquence was of no avail he went away with a very dejected air. However, we gave him a tin for a parting gift, and this seemed to alleviate his sorrow to no little extent. No doubt the rain was the real cause of the Eskimo's retreat. They did not seem to like the idea of getting wet, especially the women, several of whom had babies on their backs. It is not to be wondered at that they tried to induce us to encamp with them, for we were of course beings of much too wonderful a nature for them to lose any opportunity of enjoying our entertaining society, and it was not at all impossible besides that a certain amount of profit of a more material kind would accrue to them from the association.

So we proceeded on our way, not a little proud, it must be confessed, of the fact that we were continuing our journey when the natives, who knew the water, had given up the attempt. For a long time, too, all went well, and our confidence increased. But when we reached the middle of the fjord which we were now crossing we discovered

that it was not all child's play. The ice was here packed rather close, and a tearing current was playing with the great floes in a very unpleasant way. These monsters were now crashing one against the other, now floating apart again, and we had to be more than usually careful to keep our boats from getting crushed. The farther we got, too, the worse things looked. Once we were just between two long floes; they were driven.violently together by the movements of their neighbours, and it was only by a very rapid retreat that we saved ourselves. Late in the evening, however, we reached the other side of

Tiik Vikw To mi; soi ni From " Thk KAGI.KS NEST.

*(I''r0tn a photograph.)* the inlet in good order, but here the shore was so steep that it was no easy matter to find a camping-place. But we presently came across a cleft in the rock, which gave us just enough room to haul up the boats by the help of the hoisting-tackle which we had with us. Higher up again in the cliff side was a ledge just big enough to hold our tent. The whole position was eminently suggestive of an eyrie, and "The Eagle's Nest" we consequently named it. The Eskimo name is Ingerkajarfik, and the place lies in lat. 62 10' N. and long. 42 12' V.

The ledge which formed our camping-ground was not the most convenient sleeping-place I have known. It sloped to such an extent that when we woke next morning, after an excellent night's rest nevertheless, we found ourselves all lying in a heap at one side of the tent.

Next day again we had glorious sunny weather. Just to the south of us a huge glacier stretched far out into the sea, and its blue masses, torn and rent by crevasses, played enchant-ingly in the sunlight. After a hearty breakfast we lowered our boats again and loaded them, and then, having taken a photograph of the view to the south, we started on our way through fairly open water. There were floes everywhere, but they did not lie close, and without any great difficulty we were able to wind in and out among them.

A little past noon we reached a small

island off Mogens Heinesens Fjord, and put in to shore in an excellent harbour to have our dinner. This little island seemed to us the loveliest spot we had ever seen on the face of the earth. All was green here; there was grass, heather, sorrel, and numbers of bright flowers. Up at the top we found the ruins of two old Eskimo houses, and here the vegetation was most luxuriant. It was a simple paradise, and wonderfully delightful we found it to lie here stretched on the greensward in the full blaze of the sun and roast ourselves to our heart's content, while we enjoyed the rare pleasure of a short rest. Then we gathered a few flowers in memory of this little Greenland idyll, and taking to the boats again resumed our northward journey.

The coast we had been passing along hitherto is not remarkable for any beauty of outline or mountain forms. It is low, monotonous, and chilling. As a rule the snow and ice of the glaciers come right down into the sea, and, as the map shows, there are comparatively few places where the low, grey rocks appear above the snow.

This afternoon, however, after we had passed the opening of Mogens Heinesens Fjord, which lies in a ring of fine, wild peaks, we came into a landscape of an entirely different character. Nowhere here did the snow-fields or glaciers stretch down to the sea; all along we found bare ground and rocks, the latter often rising out of the water to considerable heights; and inland, especially to the north, we had glorious mountain views of peak rising behind peak and range behind range; and such was the coast continuously to Igdloluarsuk, an unbroken, but ever-varying scene of wildness and beauty. Everything in this world is relative, and thus we seemed to ourselves to have now entered into a more fertile, more genial region. A warmer, kindlier sun even seemed to beam upon our existence. Even in the midst of the icefloes our minds were now open to thoughts of summer and summer moods, now that we had bare rock to look at instead of everlasting ice and snow. The change

for us would scarcely have been much more complete if we had been suddenly transported to the most fruitful regions of the earth. Far to the north, too, we now saw the blue peaks of Tingmiarmiut beckoning and enticing us, as it were, to the land of promise.

As we advanced we met more and more huge icebergs, many of which lay stranded along the shore. Towards evening we saw by some small islands off Nagtoralik some most extraordinary white peaks, or rather spires, rising above the horizon. Their form was so singular that for a long time I could not imagine what they were, but I eventually discovered that they were the pinnacles of a colossal iceberg of the most fantastic appearance that I have ever seen. I took a distant photograph of it, but this gives absolutely no idea of its overwhelming magnitude and the impression it made upon us as we passed beneath it. From its top rose two points like slender church spires high into the air. Far up on its cliff-like side was a huge hole passing like a tunnel through the whole mass of ice; and down below, the sea had hollowed grottoes so large that a small ship could readily have ridden within their shelter. In these cavities there were marvellous effects and tints of blue, ranging to the deepest ultramarine in 'their inmost recesses. The whole formed a floating fairy palace, built of sapphires, about the sides of which brooks ran and cascades fell, while the sound of dripping water echoed unceasingly from the caverns at its base. When one comes across icebergs of this kind, which happens now and again, a wealth of beauty is

A COLOSSAL ICEBERG OFF NAGTOKA-LIK.

*(From a. fhotortlf/i.)*
found in fantastic iorms and play of colour which absorbs one's whole imagination and carries one back to the wonders and mysteries of the fairy-land of childhood.

It was now dark, and after having groped about for a while in search of a camping-place, we finally chose a little island which lies in lat. 62 25' N. and long. 42 6' W. As usual the boats were

unloaded and hauled ashore. This was possibly the spot which is reputed by a tradition of the east coast to be the scene of a combat between a European and a Greenlander.

Next morning—we had now reached August 2—we set off again and purposed to cross the fjord which lay just to the north of us, passing on our way the island of Uvdlorsiutit. But we soon found ourselves among ice of the most impracticable kind, and were constrained to acknowledge the truth of the Eskimo dogma, the full force of which had indeed been made plain to us the day before, that, as a rule, the best water is to be found close under the shore. We had to turn back and try our luck nearer land and farther inside the fjord. As, however, the ice here also seemed closely packed and difficult, we were thinking of trying to pass the sound between the mainland and the island, when ve caught sight of Eskimo tents on its southernmost point. We put in to make inquiries as to the water-way farther north, and were not a little astonished to find ourselves received on the shore by a company of women and almost entirely naked children, in whom we recognised our friends of Cape Bille. They laughed at us heartily, and gave us to understand that they had gone by us while we were asleep, probably in the morning before. They had pitched their tents here in a snug little spot amid grass and heather. Only one man was to be seen, and he was standing by one of the tents, busy mending his "kayak," which had probably been crushed in the ice by some mischance or other. All the other men and " kayaks " were missing, and we supposed they must be out hunting in search of food.

We then asked about the water to the inside of the island, and we were told that no passage was possible that way, but that we must go outside. They even tried to make us believe that the channel was too narrow to allow of a passage, but this was not the fact, since Holm's expedition passed through several times. However, to make sure, we went outside the island, and got by without much difficulty. The ice certainly lay close at all the projecting points, but our united efforts forced a passage at these spots, and elsewhere we crept along under the shore.

Soon after noon we were at the northern end of the island, where we came across a remarkable cave running far into the rocks. Hence we pushed on across the mouth of the fjord in fairly open water, and by the evening reached land at Ting-miarmiut, the Eldorado of the east coast, with its mountains, its stretches of green grass, and its scattered bushes of willow THE NORTH SIDE OF THE FJORD AT TINGMIARMIUT.

*(Ftvut a pltolografh.)*

and juniper, the spot which was described to Captain Holm in such glowing colours by its quondam chief, Navfalik.

That evening, as we were passing the island of Ausivit some way out to sea, we heard from the land a distant sound of barking dogs, and inferred that there must be an Eskimo camp at hand. But we had now really no time for visits and civilities, and passing unceremoniously on, we stopped for the night on an islet near Xunarsuak, in lat. 62 43' N. and long. 41 49' V.

On the morning of the next day, August 3, there was so much wind blowing off the land that we determined to try and sail, and hastily rigged our boats, one with the tent-floor and the other with two tarpaulins sewn together. At first we got on well and fast, and it was a real pleasure now and again to feel our boats heel over as the gusts caught them in the short stretches of open water, where we had, however, to keep our eyes about us to avoid collisions with the floes. We had not sailed far, though, before the pleasure became somewhat more doubtful, as the squalls grew more and more violent and the wind worked round to the north. It soon grew so strong that sailing became out of the question. Then after we had rowed a while, and were getting near the high, precipitous island of Umanarsuak, the wind came down from the cliffs with such force that it was all we could do to push on at all. Things now grew worse and worse; sometimes we had to tow the

boats along the floes to make any headway, and once we were all but crushed by the violent movements of the ice. Hitherto we had kept fairly well together, but now our work was more serious, and each crew had no eyes but for its own boat and its own course. At the very height of the storm one of my men, in his zeal, broke the blade of his oar off short. We had no whole oars in reserve on board, for they had all been broken in the ice, but there was no time to be lost, and one with half a blade had to be substituted. Sometimes the gusts of wind are so strong that in spite of all our efforts we are forced backwards. Now a thole pin goes, which is a worse mishap than the last, for when a break like this occurs at a critical moment, and all the other thwarts are blocked, the consequences may be very awkward. However, we repaired the damage without delay, and were saved from drifting for this time. Thus slowly, but as surely as can be expected, we manage to crawl along towards shore by the exercise of all our powers. On our way we come alongside a floe, and, painter in hand, Dietrichson jumps out to tow us. In his zeal he fails to notice that he is jumping on to an overhanging edge of ice, which breaks with his weight, and lets him head first into the water. This was nothing unusual, indeed, but it could have happened at few more unfavourable moments than just now. With his usual activity and presence of mind he is soon out again, and once more at work with the tow-rope, as if nothing had happened. The exertion, no doubt, kept him warm, or else a ducking while this biting wind was blowing must have been peculiarly unpleasant. Such things as this, however, seemed never to trouble Dietrichson.

This floe we eventually passed, but the wind was still so strong that progress was scarcely possible. Very little more would have set us unmercifully drifting southwards. But my men plied their oar-stumps with surprising vigour, and we just held our own. Then, again, Dietrichson was just at work pushing us off another floe, when his boat-hook gave, and he was once more all but in

the water. Misfortune pursued us that day with unusual pitilessness.

At last, however, we found calmer water under the cliffs, and soon reached land, Sverdrup's boat being a little in front of us. We now had our dinner, as well as a short period of rest, which we thoroughly deserved. Then we went on again, but the wind was scarcely less violent, and when we had passed into more open water beyond the southern point of Umanarsuak, we found a nasty choppy sea against us, running out of the fjord to the north. So, though it was still very early for us, we put in to shore as soon as we reached Umanak. This day, and it was the only time during this part of our journey, we were able to really choose a place for our tent, and, moreover, to feel for the first and last time the pleasure of lying on the grass, and having something better than hard rock or ice to sleep upon. But we had really nothing to complain of on this score, for we always slept excellently, though we could well have wished for a little more in quantity. As soon as we were well ashore and settled, we determined to collect fuel, of which there was plenty in the form of juniper scrub, heather, and similar stuff, and then make some soup and a good hot meal. There were plenty of willing hands, the work was done with overflowing zeal, a big fire was soon blazing between some stones, and on them was cooking in a biscuit tin the most delicious soup and stew that mortals have ever seen. Our camping-place at Umanak, or Griflenfeldt's Island, will not soon be forgotten by the six who sat that evening round their fire and enjoyed at ease and at their leisure the only warm meal vouchsafed to them during the whole voyage up the coast. We were not the first to enjoy life in this spot, as we saw, among other things, by the ruins of some Eskimo huts which stood close at hand. That other events less agreeable than the mere enjoyment of life had taken place there was evident from the number of human bones that lay scattered about among the ruins, and one skull of an old Eskimo lay grinning at us in the daylight in a very uncomfortable and suggestive way. It seems not improbable that the inhabitants of this spot died of famine, that the place was deserted, and the huts left to fall to pieces.

The next day, August 4, the wind had dropped to some extent and we could proceed. But the ice was often closely packed, and we found it especially troublesome in the mouth of Sehested's Fjord. Here we had to push a long way in to find a passage, and it was only by the help of our axe and boat-hooks that we forced our way through at all. At nine o'clock in the evening we passed a delightful spot for an encampment, but as we thought it still too early to give over work for the day, we held on our way northwards. As a reward for our virtue, we had to push on till half-past one that night before we found a place where we could haul our boats ashore, on an islet off the island of Uvivak, in lat. 63 3' N. and long. 41 18' W. That day we had worked hard on the ice for seventeen hours with only halfan-hour's break for our midday meal.

On August 5, by the help of axe and boat-hook, we struggled on still farther through the packed ice which lay close along the shore the whole way northwards. A number of huge icebergs lined the coast, and in the middle of the afternoon, when we had passed the promontory of Kutsigsormiut, and had put in to a small island in order to get a sight of the water ahead and to lay our course, we saw at sixty or seventy yards' distance a huge block of ice suddenly detach itself and fall from one of these monster icebergs, which, losing its balance thereby, at once swung round in the water with a deafening roar. The sea WORK IN THE ICE ON THE WAY NORTHWARDS.

*By £. Nielsen, jrom a photoglyph.*
was set in violent agitation, the. floes were thrown hither and thither and dashed together, and a small rock which rose out of the water in front of us was completely washed by the great waves. Had we gone on instead of stopping, as we had at one time contemplated, we should have had little chance of escaping being dashed against the rocks of the shore.

After a very hard spell of work we reached, late in the evening, a small islet which lay full in the opening of Inugsuar-miutfjord. Here we had intended to stop for the day, worn and tired as we were, but to our astonishment we suddenly found ourselves passing out of the closely packed ice into an open stretch of water. The fjord lay bright and smooth before us right away to the island of Skjoldungen. We were tempted to make use of the opportunity, so after an extra ration of meat-chocolate we went on again and eventually found a good camping-place on an islet at the other side.

On the east coast of Greenland there is a considerable ebb and flow in the tide. As a rule at this time we were unfortunate enough to have low water in the evening just as we had to take our boats ashore, and we were obliged in consequence to haul them a long way up to get them out of reach of the rising tide. This particular night, too, we had, as usual, moved the boats and baggage well up, and in the morning were not a little surprised to find that our beer-keg and a piece of board which we had used to prop the boats with were gone. The sea had even washed over some of our provision tins, but as these were watertight no damage was done. But we had good reason to be thankful for having bought our experience so cheaply. For the rest of the way we were very careful about the boats. The loss of the keg, which was the one we had carried off from the *Jason,* depressed us all considerably. This was not because it had any beer in it, for that we had consumed long ago. We had taken to using it as a water-vessel. The water we would drink from the bung-hole, and as we then smelt the fragrant emanations which still came from the interior, we could easily and to our great comfort persuade ourselves that we were actually imbibing some feeble and shadowy form of the invigorating drink we so much missed.

This morning, too, we were visited by a still less welcome guest. I woke to find myself scratching my face vigorously, and to see the whole tent full of mos-

quitoes. We had begun by taking great pleasure in the company of these creatures on the occasion of our first landing on the Greenland coast, but this day cured us completely of any predilections in that way, and if there is a morning of my life on which I look back with unmitigated horror, it is the morning which I now record. I have not ceased to wonder indeed that we retained our reason. As soon as I woke I put on my clothes with all speed, and rushed out into the open air to escape my tormentors. But this was but transferring myself from the frying-pan to the fire. Whole clouds of these bloodthirsty demons swooped upon my face and hands, the latter being at once covered with what might well have passed for rough woollen gloves.

But breakfast was our greatest trial, for when one cannot get a scrap of food into one's mouth except it be wrapped in a mantle of mosquitoes, things are come to a pretty pass indeed. We fled to the highest point of rock which was at hand, where a bitter wind was blowing, and where we hoped to be allowed to eat our breakfast in peace, and enjoy the only pleasure of the life we led. We ran from one rock to another, hung our handkerchiefs before our faces, pulled down our caps over our necks and ears, struck out and beat the air like lunatics, and in short fought a most desperate encounter against these overwhelming odds, but all in vain. Wherever we stood, wherever we walked or ran, we carried with us, as the sun his planets, each our own little world of satellites, until at last in our despair we gave ourselves over to the tormentors, and falling prostrate where we stood suffered our martyrdom unresistingly, while we devoured food and mosquitoes with all possible despatch. Then we launched our boats and fled out to sea. Even here our pursuers followed us, but by whirling round us in mad frenzy tarpaulins and coats and all that came to hand, and eventually by getting the wind in our favour, we at last succeeded in beating off, or at least escaping from, our enemy. But the loss of blood on our side was nevertheless very considerable. Never have I in my life fallen among such hungry mosquitoes. But, I may add, Greenland is one of the countries of the world which is most visited by this plague.

Chapter XII.

*THE EAST COAST—FURTHER DEALINGS WITH*

*THE ESKIMO.*

This day, August 6, we passed on the outside of Skjoldungen through closely packed ice. North of the island we were obliged to push a good way into the fjord, and here passed along a coast equalling in beauty anything which we had yet seen. On all sides the glaciers thrust into the sea their precipitous walls of ice, the faces of which were here and there hollowed into deep dark blue caves. A passage along such cliffs of ice is not quite free from danger. Several times that day, as well as on others, it happened that huge blocks from glaciers and icebergs, too, fell into the water not far from us, under any of which a boat would have been crushed to fragments.

When we had crossed the fjord, which is known as Akorninap-kangerdlua, the ice still being tight and obstructive, and were off a little island by Singiartuarfik, we suddenly heard the sound of human voices, and at the same time became aware of a smell of train-oil. Looking towards land we saw a tent and a party of natives, the latter in an unusual state of commotion. As the spot lay almost in our course, we steered thither, but the shrieking and general agitation now gave way to a headlong stampede. With all their possessions of value, skins, clothes, and what not, one figure after the other disappeared up the mountain-side. We could see them running as fast as their best legs would take them, and winding in and out in a long line among the ledges and projecting rocks. The party seemed to be almost exclusively women and children. The last we saw was a woman who dived into the only visible tent, but soon reappeared with 9 O an armful of skins and then fled like a rabbit after the rest up the slope. Their figures grew smaller and smaller as they increased the dis-

tance between themselves and us, though a few women stopped in their curiosity a long way up and observed our proceedings from a projecting ledge. Meanwhile we moved on towards the tent, but no living creature was to be seen save a dog, which, curiously enough, lay quietly before the door. Though we had no business to transact with these people and had no time to stop, we did not like to leave them without assuring them of our harmlessness. We made signs to them, we shouted to them the best Eskimo we could, but all to no purpose, as they simply stood and stared at us. But at last one woman seemed unable to withstand the attractions of our demonstration, and quietly and hesitatingly she came nearer and nearer, with another following a little way behind. By degrees they came within hearing, though this did not make things much better, since we had nothing to say to them. But at least they now had the chance of distinctly seeing our friendly faces and reassuring looks and gestures, as well as the empty tins we displayed as prospective presents. The tins proved irresistible. The women assumed looks of extreme embarrassment and hesitation, though their appearance scarcely justified any apprehension that their beauty could lead them into trouble. But at this moment a man appeared suddenly upon the scene, and inspired them with so much courage that they came almost to the water's edge and stood there as we sat a little way out in our boats. We now looked one at the other, while the Eskimo, the man acting as precentor, intoned the usual chorus of wonder and admiration. He indeed looked, as he stood there, for all the world like a mad bull, though no doubt there could have been nothing milder or more peaceable than the train of his thought at the moment. On his back he had a jacket of some cotton stuff, and on his head a " kayak " hat of the usual broad, flat form worn on the east coast of Greenland, made of a wooden hoop covered with calico and marked with a cross in red and white, his whole get-up showing unmistakable signs of a connection

with the trading stations of the west coast. We now pulled farther in, and one of us jumped ashore with the painter. At this manoeuvre the natives at first fled incontinently, but then returning to within a few paces and seeing we made no further sign of hostility, they became reassured once more and again came nearer. We now magnificently presented them with an empty tin, friendship was at once established, and their faces beamed with joy and with their admiration for the generous strangers. By this time more of them had gathered round, and it seemed that the men had been out in their canoes, but had been called back by the women's screams.

The newcomers were all shown the precious gift, and were given to understand that our intentions were not hostile. The most noteworthy among them was a little hunchbacked fellow, with a pleasant oldish face and particularly smart attire. We now made our boats fast and walked up the slope, finding, to our surprise, a whole encampment of tents which lay behind a low ridge and had not been visible before. More astonished still were we to see a "Danebrog" flag waving on a little staff beside one of the tents. This, we supposed, must have been obtained from Captain Holm some years ago, as he describes having distributed Danish flags here and there among the Eskimo. It was very strange that they should have been so afraid of us, since, if this were the case, they must have come into contact with Europeans before. But there must have been something uncanny about us, as we came in our own boats and our own company, while Holm had boats like those they used, and was rowed and steered by their own countrymen. Nor is it unlikely that the traditions which they have received from the west Greenlanders of the destruction of the "kavdlunak," or Europeans, at the hands of their forefathers, and the dread that the latter will come one day out of the sea in ships and avenge the deed, are still predominant in their minds. In a little bay below the encampment was a big family boat, which had evidently been just launched in readiness for flight.

As I wanted to taste dried seal's flesh and thought besides that it would be a wise measure to cache some, if we could get it, with the boats, I proceeded to ask for some by the help of the appropriate word from my vocabulary, but with the usual unproductive result. But when I went and took hold of a piece of meat which was hanging up to dry in front of one of the tents, they understood me at once and brought out several joints. In return for this I gave them a large darning needle, which magnificent scale of payment produced a lively exchange, and our friends came out with one huge piece of seal's flesh after the other, for which they received more needles. Each of us, too, was presented with a piece, so in addition to the needles we gave them some more tins. Ravna, however, absolutely refused to take any present, and in spite of pressure persisted in his determination. I afterwards heard that this was because he thought these poor people would have need of their meat themselves, and besides, he considered a needle altogether insufficient payment, and would be no party to such nefarious dealings.

Balto in his account of this meeting says: " When we had rowed across the mouth of a fjord, we again smelt a smell of rank seal-blubber, but the heathens had taken to flight with their women and children, and were up on the rocks far above the tents. When we had come into the bay where the tents stood, we lay there looking at these poor creatures who had run away. Then Nansen shouted to them, ' Nogut piteagag!' which should mean ' We are friends,' but is shocking bad Eskimo. But they took no notice of this, and stood waving their hands to us as if to say, 'Go away! go away!' Then two men came out from behind a knoll. They came down to the water, and when they got close to us, they bellowed like the other heathens. One man did not seem to be more than three feet high. Then we went ashore, and asked them to let us have some dried seal's flesh, for we saw some hanging up round about, and we had read in Captain Holm's book that dried seal's flesh is very good to eat. We gave them some needles for the meat, and then went on."

As Balto says, we soon embarked again, and we had not got far before we saw some of the men come paddling after us and towing enormous pieces of seal-meat which they wished to exchange for more needles. Just as we were getting into our boats, too, we had seen the little dwarf in the distance, coming along dragging a great piece with him, as he wanted to have his share too in the general exchange. He did not reach us in time, and we were now surprised to see a little fellow paddling along far away in our wake, and to recognise in him the same little hunchback. He certainly made a most comical figure, as he sat in his "kayak," with his little bent back scarcely showing above the gunwale. He was evidently exerting himself prodigiously to overtake us and effect a deal with his piece of meat; but in spite of all his efforts, the poor little fellow never reached us, and had to turn back disappointed.

As we advanced we met one "kayak" after the other, the occupants of which all followed us, and were particularly friendly and communicative. At last we had an escort of no less than seven of them, who, paddling round and round the boats, expressed the most unqualified admiration for us and our belongings.

When they had escorted us a long way and darkness was just coming on, they fell off little by little, and then lay still on the water for a while to watch us before they turned homewards. Just as the four last of them had dropped behind and were having their last look, I caught sight of a seal on a floe in front of us. Though this might have provided us with some very welcome fresh meat, I could not resist signalling to the four " kayaks," for we all wanted to see an Eskimo catch his seal. They came to us at once, but could not understand what we wanted, as from their low canoes they could not see the seal over the edge of the ice. I pointed, they looked and looked again, and then suddenly caught sight of him. It was a treat to see the " kayaks " get under way and the pad-

dles fly round, as the four started in pursuit, crouching as they went, in order to get near under cover of the ice. Two of the men outstripped the others and were fast drawing within distance. The seal now seemed a bit uneasy, but every time he lifted his head and looked towards them, the " kayakers " stopped dead, and did not stir till he turned away again. Then came a few more powerful strokes and another halt, and by this means they had got so near that we were expecting to see them every moment throw their harpoons, when suddenly the seal plunged into the water. They waited a while longer with their harpoons raised, ready to throw in case their prey showed himself again, but no seal appeared, so they turned homewards empty-handed.

We, too, a little disappointed, went on our way northwards, and finding the water open reached the island on which Sav-sivik lies, and encamped for the night on an islet off its east side in lat. 63 20 N., long. 41 W. This island is known from the fact that Graah passed the winter of 1829-30 on its inner side at Imarsivik.

Next day, August 7, we again found the ice awkward and difficult, but by dint of energy and perseverance we pushed through, and were rewarded again by finding more open water farther north. This day, too, we fell in with difficulties of another kind. Hitherto we had got on excellently with Holm and Garde's map of the coast, but here there was something altogether wrong. There seemed to be a number of islets, islands, and fjords which were not marked upon the map at all, or if so, then wrongly, and things came to such a pass at last that I determined to navigate after my own head and trust to luck. What was the matter with this part of the map was a mystery to me, till I got home again and found that Holm had not been able to survey this section of the coast in the short time at his disposal, and had consequently been obliged to work from Graah's map instead. Nevertheless one would have supposed that Graah knew this particular neighbourhood well, seeing that he spent one winter there.

The coast to the north of this was prolific in sea-fowl, and there were several bird-rocks. Of gulls and guillemots we shot all that came in our way, but we had no time to stop for the purpose. On one rock, where numbers of guillemots nested, we climbed up to get some of the young ones, but our spoil consisted of only two. These birds, as a rule, manage to lay their eggs in such inaccessible places that fellow-creatures who have no wings cannot often reach them, except at the risk of breaking their necks. But the young guillemots are at the same time fat and rich, and are a real delicacy.

As we were shooting gulls and guillemots off a rock beyond Cape Moltke, we suddenly heard the whirr of wings and saw a flock of eider-duck rushing by us. There was just time to bring the gun round and have a shot at them, and two birds fell. These were the first eider-duck we met with on the coast. The same day, later in the evening, another big flock came flying north. I heard Sverdrup from the other boat tell me to look out, and I also heard the whirr of their wings, but there was not light enough for a shot, as I could only get a glimpse of them against the dark background of the shore.

Meanwhile, we pushed on steadily northwards, and the misgivings of the I-apps became more visible every day, and were more openly expressed. Balto, the spokesman, had several times confided to me that they had felt more comfortable since they came across the Eskimo and had seen that they were decent folk and not cannibals, as he had been told at home in Finmarken, and that it would be possible to pass a winter with them in case of need. But now that we had seen the last of the natives, as they supposed, and were still going northwards, the two had begun to get very uneasy, and to complain of the hard work and short commons, and because we had had to come so far north, and yet had found no place from which to get up on to the ice, for there could be no question of such a thing on a coast like this, and they were sure it could never be any better. I always consoled Balto by telling him that farther on by Umivik, or a little way beyond that, the coast was much better, as indeed he must have seen himself as we drifted by in the ice on our way south. But he always declared that he had seen nothing of the kind, and this particular day his complaints were so vociferous and high-pitched that I grew quite tired of them, and gave him a good sound lecture on his miserable cowardice, enforced by the strongest language at my command. This brought matters to a head, and Balto now resolved to speak his mind, and tell me all that he had been nursing up for the last few days. I had told them in Christiania, he declared, that they should have their coffee every day, and just as much food as they liked. But they had only had coffee once in three weeks, and as for the food, why, they had miserable rations served out to them. There was one thing he would tell me, that not a single one of them had eaten his fill since they reached the coast. They were starved, and besides were treated like dogs, were ordered about, and had to work from early morning till late at night, and harder than beasts. This was too much; for his part he would gladly give hundreds of pounds to be safe back at home again.

I now explained to him that they had had no coffee, first, because no promise had been made to them on this point or any other; secondly, because there had been no time to make coffee; and thirdly, because it was not good for them. Then I represented to him what the consequences would be if we were all allowed to eat as much as we liked. The provisions might perhaps last us to the middle of Greenland, when it would be rather too late to repent. We must all share and share alike with the food, and as for the ordering about, he must understand that on such an expedition there must be one will and only one. But no, he refused to understand anything of the kind, refused to be comforted, and never ceased to deplore that he had fallen among people " who had such strange ways," as he expressed it. It was the Lappish nomadic tendency and the want of a spirit of submission which came out on these occasions, and it continued to do so in spite of Balto's good-nature and amiability. It was scarcely to be wondered at, indeed, and, as a matter of fact, I saw less and less of it as time went on.

There is no denying that it was hard upon us to go through the heavy work we did along the coast, and that upon a limited ration of dried food. We had been accustomed to eat our fill more or less, and our stomachs found it difficult to reconcile themselves to this strong but concentrated and compact form of food. By degrees we got used to it, and then things went better. It was, as Kristiansen said, the consciousness that what we got was enough for us which kept us going. When he got home he was asked whether he had had a good meal all the time. " No," he said, "he had never eaten as much as he was good for." "Well," was the answer, "you did not like that, did you? " " No, not at first," said he, " when we were not used to it; but then Nanscn told us that what he gave us was enough, and that did the trick. And so it was enough, you see."

The coast now began to get less abrupt, and the mountains lower and more rounded in form. We had in fact reached a section of the coast at which we could begin to contemplate our ascent, and to which I had long been anxious to attain, since if any mishap were to befall us and make our farther advance by boat impossible, we could nevertheless take to the " Inland ice." Our confidence now almost reached the limits of presumption, and our hearts grew very light To this contributed not a little the fact that we had this evening an excellent water-way and brilliant weather, and made rapid progress.

As on the previous night, too, there was a glorious show of northern lights in the southern sky. The great billows of light rolled backwards and forwards in long, undulating streams. The flickering of the rays and their restless chase to and fro suggested crowds of combatants, armed with flaming spears, now retiring and now rushing to the onset, while suddenly as if at given signals huge volleys or missiles were discharged. These flew like a shower of fiery darts, and all were directed at the same point, the centre of the system, which lay near the zenith. The whole display would then be extinguished, though only to begin and follow the same fantastic course again. The Eskimo have a pretty legend of the northern lights, and believe them to be the souls of dead children playing at ball in heaven.

We encamped for the night on the inner side of the island of Kekertarsuak. We had no sooner pitched our tent than we were startled by a thundering report from the south, from the direction of Cape Moltke. We seemed to feel the air itself vibrate and the very earth tremble. We rushed up to the nearest crag and looked southwards, but it was all too far off, and we could see nothing. The noise lasted some ten minutes, and the sound was as if a whole mountain side had fallen into the sea, and set the water in violent agitation, so that the waves reached almost to where we stood, and broke against the shore and rocks. Probably it was some enormous iceberg which had dissolved into fragments or changed its position in the water, though it is not at all impossible that it was an avalanche of rocks. At several places along the coast we had seen traces of such.

The next day, August 8, we proceeded in open water and splendid weather, and made an attempt to pass inside the Islands at Igdloluarsuk and across Kangerdlugsuak or Bern-storffsfjord, but were much surprised to find the fjord simply full of glacier and other ice, which lay close in shore and barred all progress. So after I had been up on the innermost point of the island of Sagiarusek, and convinced myself of the impossibility of this route, we turned back to go outside the island. On the top of this point I found what I at first took to be a fallen cairn, the stones being laid some across others, and forming a kind of oblong chamber. Though the Eskimo fox-traps are not generally built exactly in this way, I nevertheless think that it must have been an old arrange-

ment of the kind. Again, on the south side of the island, we noticed at the end of a small inlet some tall stones standing upright We rowed in to see what they were, and came upon the most charming spot we had yet seen in Greenland, a little flat green meadow, and in front of it a big tarn of fresh water, with small fish swimming in it of a species which I could not determine. On one side of the meadow were ruins of Eskimo houses, one of them very large, and the rest smaller. There were many skeletons in and outside the large house, including a particularly well-preserved Eskimo skull, which we carried off. These bones pointed to the conclusion that this settlement, too, had been depopulated by famine.

Here we resolved upon a little self-indulgence and enjoyment

"Tllli MOST (HARMING SPOT VK HAD Y1CT SEEN IN GREENLAND.
*From a / Wtj,fvr///.*)
of life, and, though it was not yet dinner-time, to lie in the long grass and rest and bask in the sunshine, while we ate the sorrel which, with other plants, grew here in luxuriance.

The Eskimo certainly knew what they were about when they settled in this spot, for there was an excellent and well-protected harbour with a good piece of beach for their skin-boats, and, as I have said, the situation was charming. The five flat stones which were standing upright and first drew our attention to the place were long a riddle to me, but after I had had some conversation with Captain Holm on the subject, I was inclined to the view that they were stocks for the " umiaks," or large skin-boats, that is to say, supports on which the boats are raised to be dried, and to which they are fastened when laid up for the winter.

There are besides many other traces of human occupation on these islands, which are, as a matter of fact, not one island, as they are given on Holm's map, but two, divided by a narrow sound, and the outer being the smaller. On several of the points also I found similar cairns of stones, or, as I suppose, remains of old fox-traps.

By the outermost islet off Igdloluarsuk we found the mouth of the fjord so full of huge icebergs that we had to go seawards to find a practicable passage. On our way we tried to push between the icebergs, but were soon stopped. The floes get jammed so fast in between these monsters by the furious current that there is no possibility of moving them. So we had to return once more and go further out to sea.

If in ordinary ice it is necessary to get a look ahead from some high-lying point, it is no less necessary to take the same measures among icebergs such as these. So whenever we came across one that was easily accessible we naturally mounted it at once. Imposing as these floating monsters look from below, when one rows beneath them, the effect, as far as regards their magnitude, is nothing to that produced when one sees them from above. One we ascended at this particular moment was fairly flat and even on its upper surface, which in fact formed a plateau of considerable extent, an entry in Dietrichson's diary declaring that it was a quarter of an hour's walk across at its narrowest part. The surface was hard snow, and there were slopes which would have suited us and our " ski " to perfection. Its highest point was certainly more than two hundred feet above the water. If the reader will now bear in mind that the portion below the water is in all probability six or seven times as thick, he will be able to reckon a total of at least 1400 feet. And when he adds to this a breadth of 1000 or 1300 yards, or even more, he will be able to realise sufficiently distinctly what the lumps of ice are actually like which float in these seas, and of which there are hundreds and thousands along this coast. Off this one fjord alone there were incalculable numbers of them. From that we were on there was a fine view, and the masses of icebergs looked like an alpine landscape of pure ice. Between them were chasms at the bottom of which one saw the sea. One of these lay at our feet, and we could see a narrow strip of dark blue water winding in its channel between two precipitous walls of ice, each nearly two hundred feet in height The beauty of the whole landscape in this world of ice with its blue cliffs and strange outlines is very striking.

Icebergs are generally of two types, and nowhere could we have seen better how well these two types are distinguished than here where so many lay in view. One is at once inclined to think that they have had two quite different origins. Some of the icebergs have a very broken and riven surface, full of rents and irregularities. Such a surface is exactly that of a glacier which descends into the sea. These icebergs always have a very irregular outline, and by this and their blue tint one can tell them at great distances. Their origin is plain enough, and they must be the product of sea-glaciers.

But there is also a much more prosaic type of iceberg, such as that on which we were now mounted. These have the form of an immense cube of ice with a comparatively smooth and polished upper surface, sharply-cut precipitous sides, and no blue crevasses. They are much whiter than the other kind and give an impression of far greater solidity. One can row beneath them with much more confidence, for they are not nearly so ready to drop fragments upon the head of the passer-by. Though owing to their smooth surface they are altogether unlike glacier-ice, they are without comparison the more numerous of the two forms. There are certainly five times as many of these square icebergs as of the more irregular *type*.

Now whence do these other icebergs come, and how are they formed? This is a question over which I have long puzzled without arriving at any certain conclusion. It is a simple impossibility that there should be glaciers anywhere in these regions which flow so quietly into the sea that their surface is smooth and quite devoid of crevasses. Besides these very icebergs may be seen floating in the fjords just off" glaciers of the ordinary torn and ragged form. They must consequently have their origin in these glaciers, from which the icebergs of the former type certainly come.

The only satisfactory explanation which occurs to me is that the irregular icebergs have, since their detachment from the glacier, happened to retain their original position, that is to say. with the rent and fissured surface uppermost, while the regular or cubical forms have, either in the act of calving or subsequently, turned over, and now show either the worn and smooth surface of the bottom or side of the glacier or else the plane of fracture, which would naturally also be comparatively level and free from fissures.

We saw, to our joy, that beyond the stretches of icebergs, which nevertheless themselves extended a long way to the north, there was good navigable water, apparently as far as we could see. So after having laid down a course which would take us' without difficulty to this open water, and then having chanted a pasan in honour of the occasion, we went down to the boats again prepared to work at high pressure in order to get through the doubtful part before the ice packed. This soon happens among these changing currents, and the prospect of being wedged fast for the night among these capricious icebergs was not to be thought of. So, as rapidly as our oars would take us, we pushed on through the narrow channels, in which we could see nothing but the deep blue water below us, with here and there a floe on its surface, the cliffs of ice on either hand, and high above our heads a slender strip of sky.

Though several times huge icebergs fell in pieces or turned over round about us, setting the sea in violent motion and making the air resound, we passed without mishap through the whole mass of them, which extended a long way north of the opening of the fjord. Once we had to seek a passage through a tunnel which ran through a great iceberg, and from which the dripping water showered heavily down upon us. Whether all this congregation of icebergs conies from BernstorfFs Fjord, it is hard to say, but it seems scarcely likely, though this fjord is one of those of the east coast which provides icebergs in the largest quantity.

Having passed Cape Mosting and the worst of the ice in good order, we spent the night on a small islet or rock lying OPEN WATKR AMONG THE 1CKHKKGS ON AUGUST 9. *(By A. Block, from an instantaneous plwttigraph, taken that titty from a Jloe.)* in lat. 63 44' N., long. 40' 32' W. As there was no flat ground of sufficient extent to accommodate our tent, which, besides, we had found too warm to sleep in the last few nights, we stretched our sleeping-bags upon the rocks. Just opposite us on the mainland was a sea-bird cliff thronged with gulls, which made such a disturbance the whole night long that we heard them as we slept and wove them into our dreams. In order to be level with them, I paid them a visit next morning, which cost a certain number of them their lives, and provided us with a pleasant addition to our larder, which was already stocked with a fair quantity of game. These young gulls, which were just now ready to fly, are excellent meat for hungry folk like us.

We could plainly see that an ascent of the " Inland ice " would be fairly easy from any point of the coast along which we were now passing. There were some numbers of what the Eskimo call "nunataks," that is to say, peaks or masses of rock projecting above the surface of the ice. The ordinary belief among Greenland travellers is that the ice round these is always rough and fissured. But this is certainly only the case when the ice has a comparatively rapid movement and the rocks form obstacles which divert the stream, as it were, and lead to irregularities. In many cases, I am inclined to believe, these "nunataks" tend on the other hand to make the ice smooth and even, as they check the onward movement, which would otherwise be more rapid and give rise to the ordinary fissures and dislocations.

However, there was no need for us to take to the ice yet, as the water seemed to be open right away to Umivik, whence the distance to Kristianshaab would be considerably less. So we continued on our way north in water which grew more and more open, and amid continual crashes from the icebergs and glaciers around us.

This particular evening we had a strange experience. We were between two icebergs, and just engaged in forcing two floes apart, when we heard a crash and saw a huge piece fall from the berg on our larboard side on to one of the floes on which we were standing, and which it partly crushed, and thereby made us a good passage through. Had we started to force our way through here a few minutes sooner, which indeed we were very nearly doing, we should undoubtedly have been annihilated. Curiously enough, this was the third incident of the kind which had happened to us.

On Kekertarsuatsiak, a little island lying at the mouth of Krumpcnsfjord, where we had our dinner, I climbed to the summit, which was very high, and gave me an excellent view to the north. The water seemed to be open and clear offices as far as I could see in the direction of Umivik. There were a great many icebergs and glacier-fragments, especially off Gyldenlove's Fjord and Colberger Heide. Seawards, too, I had a fine view, and here the ice seemed very much scattered. The high mountains by Umivik, and especially the conical peak of Kiatak, which marks our eventual destination, seem THK VIEW TO THE NORTH FROM (IUK CAMl'ING-Pl. ACK AT KANGF.KAJUK. (f" 'rtm a fh otograph.) quite near, and yet, according to the map, they are still thirty miles away. This fact I conceal from the others, who think the mountain is so close that we shall reach it to-night, and who, therefore, row with increased energy.

That evening we reached Kangerajuk, a point by Colberger Heide, where there was a strip of bare land between two enormous glaciers. It was all we could do to draw our boats high enough up, and we could find no ground at all to pitch p our tent upon, so, as on the preceding night, we slept in our bags in the open air, on two slabs of rock which would just lodge us. As the dew was very heavy, we passed a moist night, and amid a continual cannonade from the glaciers and the numberless icebergs which lay round about us.

Early next morning I was woke by a raven which sat and croaked a greeting from a crag opposite us. I found the ' - -/T.-.;------ THE LAST DAY OF OUR COAST VOYAGE (AUGUST lo). *(Ry A. nix'i.Jrain an instantaneous phttosrapli, taken thai jay from n flat.)* glorious sunshine too tempting, and, slipping unnoticed out of my bag, I took a photograph of the view to the north, with a huge arm of the glacier on Colberger Heide in the background, and in the foreground my two bedfellows, Svcrdrup and Dietrichson, who were still deep in their morning sleep, and will, I hope, forgive the liberty of this unceremonious presentation. In the distance is the peak of Kiatak. which is our goal for the day.

We now had the most splendid weather and the openest water that had hitherto fallen to our lot, and we pushed on fast. Dinner was particularly enjoyable, as a gentle breeze sprang up from the south, and we were able to hoist our sails and make good progress while we ate at leisure. I do not think I have rowed towards a mountain so obstinately distant as this Kiatak, a peak of some 2500 feet. We had now had it in sight for two days, and it seemed as far off as ever. At last, however, by the help of sails and oars, we began to draw in upon it. Now came a sea-fog to intercept us, but before the shore was quite enwrapped, we had come near enough to choose a landing-place and take our bearings accordingly.

Chapter XIII.

*OUR LAST ENCAMPMENT ON THE EAST COAST.*

About eight o'clock on the evening of August 10 we landed in a thick fog at our last camping-place on the east coast of Greenland. Just as I stepped ashore a flock of birds of the snipe kind, possibly dunlins, rose and settled again on a rock close by. A shot brought down four of them, and the acquisition of these dainty birds was a good beginning. We had gradually learnt the art of unloading our boats with wonderful celerity, but the speed of this evening surpassed all previous records. All the work was done with keenness and despatch, and the zeal was not lessened by my promise to make some coffee. Balto was especially to the fore and reckless beyond measure. No sooner was he up on the rocks before he began to entertain us with an extract from the service after one of the clergymen away in Finmarken. His representation was excellent from an artistic point of view, but the performance was a sin which he never ventured to commit unless he were quite sure of his life. To-day, too, he indulged in an oath or two, which was the first time for a long while. He even went so far as to give back to Ravna the 1.appish Testament which he had borrowed and had in his possession for a long time, his idea being that he had no further use for it now. But when Sverdrup advised him not to be too cocksure, and warned him that there might be many a slip yet before the west coast was reached, he became a little more doubtful, and we had at least no more swearing.

In my diary for this day I wrote among other notes: "While the boats were being unloaded I set about making coffee, this being the second warm meal we had had during the twelve days of our voyage up the coast. Supper and the coffee were enjoyed on the rocks down by the boat amid general satisfaction, and even the Lapps seemed contented. We' were conscious of having reached one of our destinations and of having overcome one of our difficulties. Certainly the worst part of the journey still remained, but we should have firmer ground to go upon, more trustworthy ice to deal with, no drifting floes, and no boats liable to be crushed every moment. The Lapps especially would be much more at home on the snow-fields of the ' Inland ice' than among the capricious floes "

"The landscape round about us would certainly not attract every one in the same degree as it did us. We sat on grey gneiss rocks and had on either hand a glacier running into the sea. The fog had lifted to some extent, and now and again we could see parts of the mountain Kiatak. In the water floated scattered fragments of glacier-ice. The whole scene was a study in grey and white, touched here and there with blue, a sky of grey, a leaden sea with white spots of floating ice, grey rocks with patches of white snow, and blue in the crevasses of the glaciers and in the icebergs out at sea. But the dulness of the landscape found no reflection within us. This evening we retired to rest in a singular state of elation, after having secured a comfortable site for our tent high up on the rocks."

The next day, August n, rose gloriously bright and fine. From our tent we could see the blue sea stretching away to the horizon, its surface broken here and there by the wandering blocks of ice, and its waves, raised by the gentle morning breeze, dancing and glittering in the sunshine. To the south we saw Colberger Heide rise out of the water with its mantle of snow and ice and protruding crags. In front of us, or to the east, was the huge conical mass of Kiatak, stretching from the blue sea at its foot to the pale, cloudless August sky above. Beyond this and to the north lay the white snowfields of the " Inland ice," which grew bluer and bluer and more and more rent and scarred as it fell towards the sea, and ending in lofty cliffs of seamed and fissured ice. From these great blue walls come all the icebergs and smaller blocks that are floating in the water round. Above, the snowfield is a simple white expanse, broken only now and again by the blue streak which marks a wide crevasse; slowly it passes away inwards and out of sight, ending in a white ridge which shows almost warm against the green-blue sky.

OL'K LAST ENCAMPMENT ON THE KAST COAST ON THE MORNING OF AUGUST II. l"ro)n it photograph.)

Nature has not many sounds in these parts. Only the petulant screams of the terns pierce the ear as one stands and gazes at the grand and simple beauty of this desolate landscape. From time to time, too, one hears from the glaciers, whenever a new fissure forms or some mass of ice is jerked suddenly forwards, a sullen rumble which has the most striking likeness to a cannon shot. If for a moment one forgets one's surroundings, or hears these reports in one's early morning sleep, the deception is singularly complete.

But we have, in fact, no time to spend in the contemplation of Nature's wonders. The sun has long been calling us to work, so we must get our breakfast over with all speed. Most of the party have to go to work at once to scrape the rust off our sledge-runners and then off the steel-shod "ski." In their present state, after the ravages of salt-water and damp, they are all absolutely useless. Dietrichson's business is to make a map of the bay, the point and the adjacent glaciers, while Sverdrup and I are to set out upon our first journey on the " Inland ice." We must needs discover if an ascent is possible just here, and which will be the best course to take. We were indeed consumed with impatience for Ihe first sight of this undiscovered country, in which, as we imagine, the human foot has as yet never trodden. But there are certain things to be done before we start. We must take some astronomical observations, now that we have the sun, and some photographs too. as the weather is so favourable.

At last, now that the sun has passed the meridian and we have taken the altitude, we are ready to set off. With our bag of victuals, our glacier-rope, and ice-axes we start up the stretch of mountain-side on which our tent stands, and which lies like an island between two streams of ice. We were soon at the head of it, and there found a small moraine, from which we got a good view over the ice in front of us. We could now see that it was not so level as it had looked from the sea, as the white surface was seamed with numerous crevasses on every side. They were especially plentiful in the two streams of ice which lay on either side of us, one to the north and the other to the south. After we had tried the northern branch and found it altogether impossible, we could see that our only course was along the ridge which lay between the two arms. Here we advanced a good way over solid ice. At first it was hard and rough, with a rugged surface which crunched beneath our feet and cut the soles of our boots unmercifully. Then we reached softer and wetter coarse-grained snow in which we sank to some extent. But it was not long before we came to crevasses, though at first they were narrow and harmless and easily covered in the stride. Then they grew broader and opened a view to depths unfathomable. These were not even to be jumped, and we must needs skirt them either to the right-hand or to the left.

As most of my readers doubtless know, the crevasses generally run across the current of the ice-stream. They are due to the passage of the ice over ridges and changes of level in the glacier-bed. The lower layers are compressed, while the upper are parted by the strain and show a long, continuous rent which reaches nearly to the bottom of the whole mass of ice, and lies parallel to the ridge which has caused the fracture. The numerous inequalities in the bed and the downward movement of the mass of ice give rise to fissures corresponding in number and size, all of them, as a rule, running in about the same direction. Again, if the glacier, after passing a cross-ridge, sinks into a trough or hollow, where the course of the ground thus becomes concave instead of convex, all the fissures are closed up and filled with snow and water, which freezing together gradually efface them.

For a long while we got on fairly well, partly because we could keep along the crevasses northwards, which did not take us much out of our course, and partly because they were in themselves not very long, and soon narrowed sufficiently to let us jump over them. Often, too, we crossed them on snow-bridges or on narrow strips of ice, left by the incomplete severance of the mass, and forming diagonal bridges across the chasms, the bottomless blue depths of which we could see on either side as we passed over. As long as the covering layer of snow was thin, there was no danger for us, as we could see when we had firm ground beneath our feet, and when it was necessary to be careful or quicken our steps. We had the rope round our waists, of course, and kept it tight between us in Alpine fashion in order to minimise the consequences of a fall.

But as we get farther up the snow increases in depth, we sink to our ankles, progress grows heavy, treacherous cornices overhang the crevasses, and sometimes the fissures are completely covered. We have to grope and poke before us with our staffs, or we soon find ourselves only separated from the uttermost depths by a few inches of wind-driven snow through which the pole falls almost by its own weight. We neither of us had bad falls, though it was nasty enough now and again when one or other of us sank to the armpits and felt his legs dangling in space. This was a performance of which ve soon got tired, KAI.L INTO A CRKYASSE.

*(By E. Nielsen, from a sketch by the Author.)*

and as soon as we could we changed our line and moved farther south, where there was less snow and not so many crevasses. Here we could push on with less care and made fair progress. In time the crevasses ceased almost entirely, but to make up for this the coarse, wet snow was here deeper than ever, and it was unconscionably heavy work to plod along, sinking far above the ankles at every step. We now bitterly regretted that we had not brought our " ski" or Canadian snowshoes with us. We had the Norwegian " truger " on our backs certainly, but they were of no use, as the bearing-surface was too small for this kind of snow.

We had ascended pretty gradually since we left the bare rock at a height of about 400 feet. In front of us to the north-west was a ridge, which we thought would give us the view we wanted into the interior could we only get there. We looked wistfully towards it, but the way was long, and the snow, as I have said, in a villainous state. We are hungry, too, and as the sun is still high enough to let us think of bodily enjoyment, we put our "truger" on the snow, stamp holes in front of them, and thus make ourselves warm and comfortable seats in the sunshine. It was a true relief to get a little rest like this. We set vigorously to work on our pemmican and biscuits, scanning the landscape meanwhile, and enjoying the brilliant weather and cloudless sky. The reflec-

tion of the sun from the white surface of the snow troubles our eyes to some extent, and unfortunately we have left our spectacles behind in the camp and have no protection against the glare.

To the south in front of us the furrowed and riven surface of the broad ice-stream falls away seawards. We know that there are peaks and rocks below, but they are hidden from us as we sit here, and we see the blue sea stretching from the edge of the ice right away to the horizon. There is no real floe-ice in sight, nothing but a few scattered fragments here and there which come from the glaciers. How different things were a few weeks ago when we drifted by. Then the ice lay in a broad belt stretching from the shore some twenty or thirty miles out to sea, and so closely packed that not even our little boats could find a passage through. Now a whole fleet could make its way to land at any point it pleased, and without touching a single floe. Later in the day, when we had mounted higher, we could see right away to the mountains by Cape Dan. The surface of the sea was everywhere smooth and bright, and. there was no drifting ice in view.

But our dinner is over, and we have no time to lose if we are to reach the ridge before sundown, which is the time one gets the clearest distant views over the surface of the snow. So we trudge off again with the renewed vigour which only food and rest can give one. The snow gets worse and worse. There was now a thin crust upon it, the result of the last few days' frost, and this took it out of us terribly. It let us through pitilessly every time we trod upon it, and hung about our ankles as we tried to draw our feet out again. This kind of thing will beat the strongest; and dead-beat we certainly were, more especially because our legs were altogether untrained. It was many months since they had had any exercise, except for a little hauling of the boats about the floes.

But there was no mercy for us. We must push on in order to reach the ridge as soon as possible, as it looked as if we should have rain and thick weather up there if we put it off till too late. The

sky already seemed uncomfortably grey and dull along the upper edge. So we redoubled our efforts, and determined not to be beaten. It would be too absurd to arrive up there just late enough to see nothing, and be obliged to wait there till we could get a view, or else come up again next day. So the pace was increased and the stride lengthened till Sverdrup—who is short in the leg—came near to straining himself in his efforts to keep up with me and make use of the foot-holes which my long legs made in the snow. I could hear him cursing my seven-league boots till he must have been blue in the face with the exertion. At last, after we had thought again and again that we were there, but found the ground still rising in front of us, we reached the top of the long-sought ridge. But, alas! alas! life is full of disappointments: as one reaches one ridge there is always another and a higher one beyond which blocks the view. So it was here, and we must go on; we must inspect the ice farther in, for that is the object of our expedition. No doubt we are justified in supposing that we have already passed the worst ice in the ten miles or so we have gone to-day, but it may well be that there is still difficult ground beyond. So we start off again as fast as our legs will take us towards the highest point of the ridge in front. There seem to be a number of crevasses, but they are not of a kind to stop us. It now began to rain a little as we were climbing the rather steep slope in front of us. The going is heavier than ever, and we sink in the snow above our knees. Rain and fog may threaten as they please; we have to stop now and again to get our breath, exhausted as we are. This time, as far as we can see, we are not to be fooled; if only the rain will let us, we seem likely to get a good view inwards. Already we can see some way, and I even get a glimpse of a projecting peak that has not been visible before. So we stride on with greater eagerness than ever.

At last we are on the top, and are richly rewarded for all our toil and tribulations. The great white snowfield lies before us in all its majesty. The rain is still falling in the form of fine dust-like spray, but it is not enough to hinder us from seeing all necessary detail even at a considerable distance. The whole surface seemed smooth and crevasse-less quite to the horizon. This we had expected, indeed, but what we had not expected was the number of "nunataks," or peaks, small and large, which pro-truded from the great field of snow for a long distance inwards. Many of them were covered and quite white, but many others showed cliffs and crags of bare rock which stood out in sharp contrast to the monotonous white ground, and served as welcome resting-places for the eye.

We reckoned the distance to the far-thest of these peaks to be some twenty-five or thirty miles, and we did not sup-pose that we should be able to reach them for many days. The gradient was even and slight as far as we could see; but the going was anything but good, as we had already learnt; and the last bit especially had been desperately heavy. If the nights were not likely to be frosty, our prospects were not brilliant. But the barometer showed that we were now some 3000 feet above the sea, and at an-other couple of thousand feet or so we felt sure of frost, at least at night. Poor unsophisticated wretches, who wished for cold in the interior of Greenland '

But our object was attained. In spite of " nunataks," and in spite of our be-ginning the ascent from the very sea-level, we had found the passage of the ice quite as simple and straightforward a business as we had ever ventured to hope. By this time we are hungry again; the evening is far gone; the sun must have set long since, though the rain clouds have hidden it from view, and it is not too early for us to sit down upon our " truger " and bring out our provi-sion-bag once more.

Supper being over, ve have to con-template our return. We are at least ten, if not fifteen miles from camp. There is no sense in going back the way we came; we came out for a reconnais-sance, so we must try and discover whether there is not an easier route by some other line. Especially we thought

it possible that a mountain which lay to the south of us would give good access to the snow. We should be able to get up to a good height with firm ground still beneath our feet, and we should avoid the worst of the glacier-ice. It was cer-tainly late in the evening for exploring purposes, but there was no help for it; we must explore and put up with the night meanwhile.

As the snow up here was at its worst and loosest, we put our " truger" on, to see whether they would not be of a lit-tle use to us, and they really were. So we set off refreshed upon our homeward way, steering for the mountain that lay to the south. But darkness came on quickly, and we had not gone far before it grew uncomfortably difficult to see the crevasses at a satisfactory distance. As yet, indeed, there were not many of them, but we must be prepared to meet with more than enough of them before long. We have to keep along the top of the ridge, which just here runs between two depressions which we have on ei-ther side. By this means we keep fairly clear of them. For a while all goes well; the snow is better, so good indeed that Sverdrup takes his "truger" off. We al-ready see our mountain at no great dis-tance, and here we hope to find water, and mean to have a good rest and stretch our weary limbs on the bare rock. We longed indescribably for this firm ground, and we were sure it could not be far off now. But how often are one's reckonings altogether upset when one has to do with ice, whether it be in the form of floe or glacier. We had not gone many steps before we began to suspect that our " not far *off"* might prove to be quite far off enough, and even more too. We were now met in fact by longer and nastier crevasses than any we had yet seen. At first we managed pretty well, and with my " truger " I found I could jump with greater certainty than I had done before without their help, and could venture more boldly on to the snow-bridges, as they did not let me through so readily. When these bridges were too weak to tread upon, we had re-course to a more cautious method, and crawled over flat on our stomachs.

"WHEN THK BRIDGES WKHR TOO WEAK WE CKAWI.KI) OVKR FLAT ON OUR STOMACHS."
*(By E. Nielsen, from a sketch ly the Author.)*

But presently the crevasses became so broad that bridges were not to be ex-pected, and we had to go round them. Round them we went too with a vengeance, following them often by the half-hour, sometimes upwards, some-times downwards, but they grew longer and longer still. At last we reached one broader than all its predecessors, and longer too, as we were destined to learn. This we determined to follow upwards, as we thought that there was most chance above of finding its end. This had been the case with most of them, but this time we were thoroughly sold. We went on and on, and on again, far-ther and farther from our goal; the peak of our mountain grew fainter and fainter in the darkness, but the crevasse re-mained as broad as ever. There were no bridges, and it was so dark that we could see no sign of change ahead. There was nothing for it but patience, which is a jewel indeed on such occasions. But it is a long lane that has no turning, and though we still went on and on we came to the end at last. We now promised ourselves that this was the last time we would follow a crevasse upwards. The other way at least brought us nearer to the mountain, where we were certain to find water for our parched throats.

By this change of tactics we made greater progress, and we now had the pleasure of seeing our goal loom nearer in the darkness. We had not many more steps to go when we saw in front of us a dark stripe or band in the snow. At first we thought it was another crevasse, even now separating us from the rock, but to our indescribable joy we discov-ered that it was water, glorious running water. We soon had our cup out, and drank, and drank, and drank again, and revelled in it, as only those can who have waded the whole day long through deep, wet snow without a drop of any kind to wet their lips. I scarcely think there is a greater enjoyment in life than plenty of good cold water when one is ready to perish of thirst. If it is ice-water, as it was here, one drinks till the numbness of one's teeth and forehead bids one stop, then one rests a bit and drinks again, slowly and solemnly drawing the water in, so that one may not have to stop again too soon—the enjoyment is in fact divine. When on this occasion we had drunk as much as we were good for, we filled our cup and flask, went on the few paces that remained to the cliffs, and finding a comfortable seat on a jutting rock, where we could stretch our limbs at will and get a good support for our weary backs, we turned to the provision-bag again. What delight we found here too! A tramp all day in the snow like this produces both hunger and fatigue, and we had more than enough of both to make existence supremely delightful as we lay there and devoured our pemmican, chocolate, and biscuits.

But presently it began to rain, which was not quite so delightful, and the darkness had increased so much that we could now not see more than two or three paces in front of us. But we had a good way to go to the tent, so we had to start off again. We kept to the ice along the edge of the mountain side, where the surface was tolerably smooth, as it often is along the rocks, where the ice has not much movement, or is even fro/en fast. For a time progress was easy, but then the incline grew so steep and slippery that it was all we could do to find and keep our footing. Still more uncomfortable did things become when we found more huge crevasses lying in our path. In the darkness we could just see the great chasms which lay ready to receive us as soon as we made a false step or allowed our feet to slip. The rocks by our side were so precipitous that there was no escape that way, and we had to follow the line we were now taking. Without mishap we reached a rock which jutted out into the ice. Here below us, and between the main mass of the mountain and the glacier, was an enormous " bergschrund," or chasm, some thirty or forty yards across and abysmally deep; in the ice in front we could just see a number of crevasses,

the width of which we could not determine, but they were evidently more than big enough to stop our progress. There was nothing for it but to take to the rocks up a gully which came down just by us, by this means skirt the projecting point and "bergschrund," and see if there were a more practicable course down below. It was a true satisfaction to have the firm rock beneath our feet again, and to feel the pleasure of a good foothold. In spite of the heavy rain which wetted us to the skin, we sat down for a long rest upon some boulders. We were now inclined to wait till dawn for a further attempt upon the glacier, as we felt sure that it would be full of crevasses further down, and in the darkness we might easily get completely fixed or even come to grief for good and all. At last came daybreak, red and glowing in the east, and spreading a warm flush over the sky and landscape. Beneath us lay the glacier, which now looked more practicable than we had expected. We chose the line which seemed easiest, and set off once more. Though we now crossed the glacier not far from the edge which falls precipitously into the sea, the ice was not so full of crevasses and impassable as it had been higher up. It was rough and rugged enough in its way, full of upstanding pinnacles and sharp ridges divided by clefts and hollows. It was often quite sufficiently hard work to cross these latter, though they were not deep: but the real long, bottomless crevasses, which we had found up above, were not abundant here, and occurred only in certain parts. The reason why there are so few of these down here must be that they are filled with water, which freezes and turns them into mere furrows and irregularities in the ice.

Our difficulties were now soon at an end, and after a couple of hours' walking we came within sight of the camp. It was five o'clock in the morning, and, as we expected, all our comrades were sound asleep. Our first business was to get hold of some food and make the most of what our larder provided. This was an indulgence which we thought we had fully deserved after our tramp

of eighteen or twenty miles. Then we crawled into the sleeping-bags, stretched our tired limbs, and soon floated into dreamland, well satisfied with this our first excursion on the much discussed and much dreaded " Inland ice " of Greenland, which we had always heard was so impossible of access, and still more impossible to traverse. As we had expected, we had not met with these impossibilities, but the world would no doubt say that we had had the devil's own luck with us, and had reached our goal with much more ease than we deserved.

Before we were ready for our final start, however, we had certain preparations to make which would take a considerable amount of time. Our boots especially needed thorough overhauling and repair, as the excursion of the day before had taught us in the most emphatic way that the " Inland ice" demanded no common strength and substance of sole. The

Q steel runners of the sledges and "ski," too, had to be still further scraped and polished; all our baggage had to be repacked, and everything that we were going to cache here set apart. So for the next two or three days all the members of the party might have been seen sitting about on the rocks outside the tent, busily occupied in the various arts of peace, that of the cobbler taking a particularly prominent place. It was a strange sight to see these figures, which outwardly had very little in them to remind an observer of the cobbler's stall, sitting here amid these wild surroundings with boots between their knees, and plying meantime the awl, thread, and bristle with as much apparent dexterity as if they had done nothing else all their lives.

A Corrler's Stall On The East Coast.
*(From a fhatoginfl:.)*

Chapter XIV.
*OUR START FOR THE WEST COAST—THE ASCENT OF THE ICE.*

As I have already said, we spent the first day or two after our expedition on the ice in a thorough overhauling and rearrangement of our equipment. The weather meanwhile was dull, rainy, and mild, and we were therefore in no hurry to start, as we hoped for bright weather with frost at night. We lived during these days almost entirely on sea-birds, which we had shot during our voyage up the coast, but had hitherto had no time to eat. We enjoyed this fare ama/ingly, and it must have been a fine sight to see the party sitting on the rocks round the camp-kettle, which consisted of a tin box previously devoted to biscuits, and each member fishing out his own bird with his fingers, and proceeding forthwith to tear it in pieces and devour it by the help of hands and teeth. Modern adjuncts of the table such as forks, I need scarcely say, were not to be found among us, and I can vouch from my own experience that such things are not at all necessary, seeing that the forks with which nature has provided us are exceedingly practical instruments, as long as one does not plunge them into inordinately hot cooking vessels; a discretion which is, of course, the outcome of a very short experience.

On August 14 the weather improved, and we resolved upon a start. Sverdrup and I considered that the best route was up the mountain side on which he and I spent the night of our glacier excursion, provided at least that it proved easily accessible from the sea.

So we launched our boats once more, loaded them with all our baggage, and set off with the intention of beginning our climb there and then. But we had hitherto had no view of this mountain from the water, and we now found its base so precipitous that an ascent with our heavy loads would have been much too laborious an undertaking. Our only course therefore was to return to our old camping-ground and start from there. So our boats were unloaded at this spot once HAULING THE BOATS ASHORK ON AUfH'ST 15.

(/Vtw *a fîlwlegrafth.*)

again, and it was late at night before the day's work was finished.

On the morning of August 15 the boats were hauled up to their last resting-place, a little cleft in the rocks, which promised them a tolerable degree

of shelter and protection. Ve placed them carefully with their keels uppermost, blocked them with stones to keep them steady in a wind, and it is to be hoped they are still there just as we left them. But it is quite possible, of course, that the Eskimo have already found them, and appropriated the iron parts and fittings of the boats and many other wonderful things. If this be so, it is not easy to imagine what kind of supernatural beings they have taken us for, who have thus abandoned our valuable possessions and so mysteriously disappeared. Under them we stored a small supply of ammunition, dried seal's flesh, and a few other things.

THE LAST RESTING-PLACE OF THE BOATS.

*. (Front a photograph.)*

A curiosity among the latter was the Eskimo skull which we carried off from Igdloluarsuk, and here deposited in the locker of one of the boats. If the natives have come across our cache, the discovery of this skull has no doubt scared them not a little. A number of tools, chiefly belonging to the boats, were also left there, and among them a sail-maker's palm, the want of which we afterwards felt acutely. As I have said already, I had intended to leave one of our guns here, too, but when the time of parting came, we were so overcome by its charms that we had not the heart to abandon it to this desolate fate.

On a small piece of paper, too, I wrote a short account of the progress of the expedition so far, packed it carefully in a little tin, and enclosed this in the bread-box which had belonged to our sealing-boat. In my account I wrote that we were quite hopeful of reaching the west coast, if we were only favoured with sufficient frost; as it turned out, we were favoured with a good deal more than enough.

The Lapps maintained that we might just as well leave one of the big sleeping-bags behind, as we could easily put four men into one of them, while they could sleep in their fur coats, Balto even declaring that they could put up with seventy degrees of frost. However, I considered it better to see how things

were before I consented to such a step, and I told them it was not unlikely that they might be glad of the bags to sleep in after all. Balto still insisted that that would never be, and that the extra bag would be only so much dead weight. It was not long, however, before he had good reason to change his opinion.

As it was now too warm in the daytime, and the snow consequently soft, we determined to do our hauling work at night. So at nine in the evening the sledges were finally loaded and we started on our way for Christianshaab.

At first our progress was slow. The snow came nearly down to the sea, so we could begin hauling at once; but the gradient was steep, and we had to put three men to each sledge. Our loads were heavy, too, each sledge weighing somewhat more than two hundred-weight. When we had got so high that we could think of dragging them singly, we redistributed the weight, so that four of them were about two hundred pounds; and the fifth, which had two to pull it, weighed about double as much. This first night we had fine weather and just enough frost to make the snow hard. The ground was favourable except for the steepness of the incline, and of crevasses we as yet found none. Towards morning, however, we reached some unpleasant ice, which was full of depressions and irregularities, but had at the same time a harclish surface on which the sledges travelled well. After a first stage of some two or three miles we pitched our tent at a height of about five hundred feet. It was a pleasure almost divine to get half a dozen cups of good hot tea with condensed milk and then to creep into our sleeping-bags after this OUK CAMPING-PLACK ON THE MORNING OK AUGUST 17.

*By A. Hlich,from a photograph.)*

our first spell of sledge-hauling. I have no doubt there was a pretty general consensus of opinion among us that we had had pleasanter work in the course of our lives, but these opinions we kept each to himself. Just as we were proposing to go off to sleep it was discovered that we had left our only piece of Gruyere cheese at the place where we had halted

for our midnight dinner. To leave this cheese behind was scarcely to be thought of, and yet to fetch it, tired as we were, was also too much to be expected. But then Dietrichson came forward and offered to go and get it, declaring that there was nothing he should like so much, as it would give him a little morning walk before he went to bed, and a look round besides, which would be to the advantage of his map. I remember that it was with a feeling of simple admiration that I saw him start gaily off on his errand, and that I could not myself conceive that any one f.ND- KR WAY ON AUGUST 17.
*(By tht Author.)*
could find pleasure in such an expedition after the work we had had already.

On the evening of the day we broke up again and went on over ice of the same rough kind. Towards midnight it grew so dark that we could no longer see, so at eleven o'clock we encamped, made some chocolate, and waited for daylight. Before we started off again we took a photograph of-the tent and the ice to the south stretching downwards towards the sea.

We now got on to some smoother ice, but the snow grew looser and crevasses began to appear, thougli the first were negotiable without any great difficulty. Towards morning it began to rain; as the hours passed things grew worse and worse, and existence to us less joyous. We all got into our waterproofs, of course, but waterproof these garments were certainly not, and the rain poured down upon us till every rag we had on was wet through. There was no chance of our getting chilled or frozen, though there was a moderately sharp wind blowing, as our work kept us warm, and we had to put forth all our strength. But to feel one's clothes cling to one's limbs and hinder every movement is not a state of things to make hard work pleasanter. We kept on till past noon; the ascent was not too steep to allow of the sledges being brought up with tolerable ease, but we had to put two men to each of them. Crevasses were plentiful, so we had to go warily. We could not rope ourselves together, as that made

the hauling work too difficult, so we had to be content with attaching ourselves to the sledges by our strong towropes, which were again made fast to the stout hauling-strap and belt we each wore. If we went through the snowbridges which crossed the fissures, we were left hanging securely, as long as the sledge did not follow us, which, owing to its length, was not very likely to happen. As a matter of fact, we fell through rarely, and then only to the armpits, so that by the help of our staffs we were able to get out again without other assistance.

Now and again, however, one or other of us experienced the strange abdominal sensation of having the ground suddenly go beneath his feet and his body left swinging in the air from the chest downwards. At these times we generally managed to recover ourselves without any further invitation from outside. It was, as a rule, an easy business to bring our long sledges over these crevasses. They had so large a bearing-surface that they would run well over with their own impetus, though from time to time it happened that the snow gave way slightly beneath them.

This day we did not stop till nearly noon, when we encamped on a flat ledge between two huge crevasses, the weather being now altogether impracticable. We found unspeakable consolation this particular day in dry clothes and hot tea, and the number of cups which we consumed passed the limits of calculation. After having laid our staffs and " ski" under the tent-floor in order to keep our bed reasonably dry, and having taken all possible measures to exclude the rain, we retired to our bags. The smokers, too, were allowed a pipe of tobacco, THKKIC DAYS IN THK TKNT. (/ *E. Nielsen, from a rough sketch by the Author.* and altogether we made ourselves exceedingly comfortable under cover while the elements raged in all their fury without. For three whole days, from noon oti August 17 to the morning of August 20, we were now confined to the tent by a violent storm and uninterrupted rain. The whole time we only left our sleeping-bags for the purpose of

getting food and for other small errands. The greater part of the time we spent in sleep, beginning with an unbroken spell of twenty-four hours. Rations were reduced to a minimum, the idea being that as there was no work to do, there was no need for much food, though we had to take just enough to keep ourselves alive, the whole consumption amounting to about one full meal a day. Some of the party found the allowance unreasonably short, and piteously urged the clamorous demands of their inner organs. When not eating or sleeping, we filled the gaps in our diaries, told stories in turn, and read a paper by Professor Helland on the "icefjords" of Greenland, besides our "Nautical Almanac," our "Table of Logarithms," and the other equally interesting books of which our modest library consisted. Ravna and Balto read their New Testament as usual on such occasions. Our waking moments were, however, perhaps chiefly spent in gazing at the tent roof and listening to the rain splashing overhead ancl the wind tearing and shrieking round the walls and among the guyropes. It is pleasant, no doubt, to lie snugly housed while tempests rave outside, but there is also no gainsaying that we longed to hear the rain beat a little less pitilessly and the wind howl a little more gently round our tent.

At last, on the morning of August 20, the weather so far improved that we could resume our journey, and in preparation we fortified ourselves with a supply of hot lentil soup, to make up for the famine rations of the three preceding days.

The ice was still much fissured, and as we were about to attempt the ascent of a ridge which lay in front of us, we found the crevasses so numerous and formidable that there was no possibility of passing them. Here they ran not only parallel, but also across each other, a combination before which one is completely powerless. We had to turn back and try more to the north, and sitting on the sledges we slid down the slope again between the crevasses. Below we found the ice less broken and the gradient less steep. Progress was here comparatively easy, and at places we could even haul our sledges singly, Sverdrup and I going on in front with the heaviest to choose the route. The rain had here evidently contributed to make the going better for us, as it had made the snow firmer in places and often washed it away altogether. At times, however, we still sank deep, but could we only have got a little frost, things would have been excellent. Yet on the whole the surface was very rough, and Balto writes in his narrative:—

"On August 20"—(he probably means August 22)—"the ice was terribly rough, like the great waves of the sea. It was awful work to drag the sledges up these waves, and when we went down the other side the lumps of ice came rolling after us." (This is a circumstance I do not myself remember. ) "The ropes we pulled with cut our shoulders, till they felt as if they were being burnt." VIEW OVER THE "INLAND ICK " TOWARDS KIATAK (ACUUbT 20). *(Ry Hie A ill liar.)*

Towards eight o'clock that evening the sky looked as if it would clear, and as we felt sure that this would bring us frost, we stopped and camped at once to wait till the snow got harder. Next morning, August 21, we turned out at four. The sky was clear, and though the thermometer showed that there was still a certain amount of warmth in the air, the crust on the snow was nevertheless sufficiently hard to bear us. The gradient was still steep, and the crevasses large and numerous, but we pushed on fast and without mishap in the most glorious weather, keeping at work till well into the morning, when the blazing sun began to make the snow softer and softer. This work under such conditions is terribly exhausting, and we suffered from an unquenchable thirst. We had already passed the limit of drinking-water, and were destined to find no more till we reached the west side. All we get is what we can melt by the warmth of our own bodies in the tin flasks which we carry at the breast inside our clothes and sometimes next the very skin. Few of us are long-suffering enough to wait till the AX1K1TSOK, JOIINSTKl.-P'S AND

KOKNKRUl-'S " NUXATAKS " (AL'Gl'ST 2l). *he Author, from a. photograph.)* snow is turned to water, but as it grows a little moist we suck out the few drops which it produces.

About eleven we had reached the top of a ridge which we had set as our goal for the day's march, a distance of some three or four miles. Reyond, the ice sloped gently inwards, and was particularly free from crevasses. So we thought we must have already overcome the first difficulty of our ascent, and felt justified in marking the occasion by a festal meal, distinguished by extra rations of cheese, jam, and oatmeal biscuits. We were now all but 3000 feet above the sea, and could see "nun-ataks" here and there in front of us, while we already had a whole row of them alongside us to the north.

At two o'clock on the morning of August 22 we went on again. There had been nine degrees of frost in the night and the snow-was as hard as iron, but the surface was exceedingly rough, so rough indeed that a sledge occasionally upset. By nine oclock the sun had such power that we were obliged to halt after having again accomplished a stage of three or four miles.

We began to feel the want of water more and more keenly, and were very glad to get a good drink of tea. With a view to making this beverage still more refreshing, I hit upon the brilliant notion of putting citric acid into it, for we had all heard, of course, that lemon juice was a most delicate addition. It never struck us that we already had condensed milk in our tea, and our disappointment when we saw the milk slowly curdle and sink to the bottom in lumps was indescribable. We drank the mixture, however,and I, who, as the inventor and patentee, was bound to set the others a good example, could say no less than that I found the refreshing qualities of the tea increased by the addition of citric acid in spiteof the unwelcome lumps of curd. But this dictum did not meet with general acceptance, and the experiment was never repeated.

We started off again the same evening about nine o'clock. The ice was still very rough; we had now to haul our sledges up on to the crests of the steep waves, now to let them rush down into the hollows. The strain on the upper part of the body was very trying, and Balto was quite right in saying that our shoulders felt as if they were burnt by the rope.

But if we often suffered a good deal in the way of work, we had full compensation during these nights in the wonderful features of the sky, for even this tract of the earth has its own beauty. When the ever-changing northern lights filled the heavens to the south with their fairy-like display—a display, perhaps, more brilliant in these regions than elsewhere —our toils and pains were, I think, for the most part forgotten. Or when the moon rose and set off upon her silent journey through the fields of stars, her rays glittering on the crest of every ridge of ice, and bathing the whole of the dead fro/en desert in a flood of silver light, the spirit of peace reigned supreme and life itself became beauty. I am convinced that these night marches of ours over the "Inland ice" left a deep

O

O and ineffaceable impression upon the minds of all who took part in them.

We presently reached a steep incline and our work was worse than ever. We had to put several men to each sledge, but even then the labour was cruelly exhausting. Consequently our astonishment and joy knew no bounds when we had climbed some hundred feet higher and then found the surface stretching flat in front of us as far as we could see in the moonlight, and the snow as hard and level as the ice on a frozen lake. This glorious state of things made us very triumphant. Anything better was beyond our imagination, and we began to reckon how soon we should reach the west coast, if we had such snow to deal with all the way.

The question had arisen whether it would not be as well to reduce the weight of our loads without abandoning any of our provisions. Balto gave it as his opinion that we could safely leave the Indian snow-shoes behind, as they

could be of no use to us. I agreed that this might be so as long as we had snow of this kind to cross, but it was impossible to tell how long this would last. Then Balto broke out: " Good heavens! just hear what Ravna says then. He is an old Lapp; he has lived forty-five years on the mountains, and he says that he has never used anything of the sort, and that no one is going to teach an old man like him. And I say just the same myself: I am a Lapp, OPEN AIR COOKERY.
*(From a photograph.)*
too, and there is no one who can teach us Lapps anything about the snow." I laughed and answered: " You Lapps think yourselves so precious clever, but you are not unlikely to learn a thing or two before.you get home again. Do you remember, Balto, those snow-spectacles I showed you in

R

Christiania? Didn't you want to know what was the good of those rubbishy things? Didn't you say that you Lapps never used anything of the kind, and yet you had good eyes? But who was it whose eyes first wanted snow-spectacles, and found them excellent things? Wasn't it you two Iapps? Take care it doesn't turn out just the same with these snow-shoes. Not one of them shall be left behind "

Balto maintained that it was a very different thing with the spectacles, and acknowledged that he had found them, not only useful, but necessary. But as for these snow-shoes, he swore by all his gods that he would never put them on his feet. Just at this time he was so confident and pleased with himself that he often indulged in the sin of swearing very emphatically. This was a state of mind very encouraging to the rest of us. to whom it served as an index of his valorous state of mind.

Unluckily, our good fortune with the hard, icy surface did not last long, though we had it all that day. There are probably not many who have had such an experience on the " Inland ice." If it had been thoroughly levelled with a plane, the surface could scarcely have been smoother. The ascent was very gradual, and there was a gentle, almost imperceptible undulation. About eleven o'clock on the morning of August 23 we stopped and pitched our tent, after having done a stage of nine or ten miles. This day, as had also been the case a day or two before, the sun beat down so fiercely on the tent-walls that the air inside was rather too warm for us, and one of the party was even constrained to go outside and lie on a tarpaulin in the shade of the tent in order to get some sleep.

At half-past six we were on the move once more. As we advanced things altered for the worse again, and the hard, icy surface was covered with a coat of freshly fallen snow.

We already began to see that we should have more frost at night than we cared about, for on the dusty new snow and in the fifteen degrees of frost which we now had the steel runners of the sledges slid no better than upon sand. So seeing the folly of now doing our work in the night instead of the daytime when the friction of the snow was likely to be less, we halted again about ten o'clock.

We were still speculating whether it were not advisable to lighten our loads by abandoning one thing or another. The first things to sacrifice were the oilcloth covers of our sleeping-bags, as, now that we had advanced so far, there was no moisture to be afraid of except in the form of snow, which was not likely to do them any damage. But it would have been too stupid simply to leave them behind without making any use of them. Oilcloth was combustible, and we might use them, of course, for cooking purposes. This was a happy thought, which found immediate favour.

A cooking-pot was the next thing necessary. But all the biscuit-tins leaked more or less on account of the rough treatment to which they had been exposed on the sledges. At last we found one which seemed moderately watertight, and operations were started in the tent. The tin was filled with snow as usual, and set up on a stand made of the steel bars which had originally been under the runners of the sledges, but had succumbed to the rough work among the ice. The oilcloth was torn up into strips, placed in a steel snow-shovel, which was made to do duty as a firebasket, and duly lighted. The fuel burned bravely; the flames rose high round the tin and shed a fine red glow on the tent-walls and the six figures, which were grouped around and sat gazing at the blaze and enjoying the real solid comfort of a visible fire.

It was the first time we had had a fire of this sort inside the tent, which wanted something of the kind to make it really cosy. But all the joys of this life are fleeting, and none have I ever known more fleeting than that which comes from burning oilcloth in a tent which has no outlet in the roof. Our fuel smoked to such an extent that in the course of a few minutes our little habitation was so full that we should scarcely have been able to see one another if we could have kept our eyes open, which we could not do, as the pain caused by the fumes was simply unendurable. If there be a mortal who has seen the inside of a barrel in which herrings are being converted into bloaters, he will be able to form some idea of the atmosphere of our tent. It was to no purpose that we opened the door, for if a little smoke did find its way out, there came more to take its place, and the cloud grew persistently denser and denser. Our pleasure at the sight of the fire had long died out; the eye that managed to open could only see a faint light glimmering far away in the fog. Most of the party followed the sensible plan of burying themselves in the sleeping-bags, and drawing the covers tight over their heads. One or two, however, had to sit out the infliction in order to look after the fire and get the water for our tea boiled. By dint of opening first one eye and then the other, and now and again thrusting the head out of the door for a little fresh air, they got through their task tolerably well. The snow began to melt, but now, by way of filling the cup of our discomfort, the tin proved deplorably leaky, and we were obliged to have recourse to something else. The cover of the tin box which formed our medicine-chest was sound enough, but it held only half the necessary amount of water. It was the only vessel available, however, and by using it in conjunction with the original tin, which was placed on edge so that its soundest side only was taken into use, we managed fairly well. Then, by firing up unremittingly, and turning the tent into a veritable " inferno," we eventually succeeded in obtaining some tea of a certain kind; but I am bound to confess that it was the worst tea-making at which I ever had the luck to assist, and I emphatically warn all whom it may concern against following our example.

Next morning, nevertheless, we had another oilcloth fire: but this time we were prudent enough to arrange the fireplace outside. We now managed to get so much snow melted that, over and above a good supply of hot soup, we were able for once in a way to get thoroughly the better of our thirst, the addition of citric acid, oil of lemon, and sugar turning the water into the most delicious lemonade. But this was the last real satisfying drink we had before we found water on the other side. Our small supply of fuel would not allow us any indulgence in this way.

We were a remarkable sight by daylight next morning. Our complexions, hitherto comparatively fair, and washed moderately clean by wind and weather, had undergone a complete transformation. In places the incrustations of soot were so thick that they could be scraped off with a knife. All wrinkles and depressions were full of this foreign substance, and great masses had settled on all outstanding points, such as the eyebrows, cheek-bones, under-lip and chin, and the fair hair with which nature had provided some among us had been dyed to a raven black. The only parts still clean were the eye-balls and teeth, and these now shone out quite uncomfortably white in contrast.

This state of things did not trouble us very much, both because soot is a relatively clean dirt, and because, as a general principle, most people, no doubt, wash themselves for altruistic reasons, and we had no chance of meeting others of our fellow-creatures for some time

to come. The tooth of time was left to work upon our faces, and the soot by slow degrees was worn away; slow, indeed, for there was, in truth, enough to withstand time's ravages for many a day.

Possibly when my readers learn that in spite of such disasters we did not wash ourselves from the day we left the *Jason* till we reached the west coast, the more narrow-minded among them will straightway class us with the least cleanly of four-footed beasts. This fate we must be content to risk, and to share in the company of many who have not even the crossing of Greenland for their excuse; and, besides, if we go a little farther back in time, there will be few among our forefathers who will not stand upon our side.

But perhaps it will be as well if I explain that washing was in ordinary circumstances one of the habits of our daily life, and that if we omitted the practice during this whole period, the omission was not without its reasons.

In the first place, while we were in the interior we had no other water than the small quantity we melted every morning and evening over our cooker, and the still smaller quantity that we could melt by the warmth of our bodies in the course of the day. But when a man is, as we were, the victim of a perpetual and intense thirst, and has the choice whether he will use his limited portion of water for washing or drinking, or, as a third alternative, for the two purposes combined, washing first and drinking afterwards, I think there is little doubt that, however conventionally minded he might be, he would devote it simply and solely to the assuaging of his thirst.

In the second place, the pleasure of washing in a temperature in which the water turns to ice if it is allowed to stand a couple of minutes, in which the fingers grow hard and stiff during their passage from the vessel to the face, and in which the face itself freezes as soon as water is put upon it, is, to say the least of it, highly questionable. I think there cannot be many whose love for cleanliness would in such circumstances lead

them beyond theory and eloquence.

In the third place, we were absolutely forbidden to wash even if we had a superfluity of water, and this at a comfortable temperature, the reason being that in this sunshine, when the glare comes not only from above, but also back from the snow below, it is as well to have as little to do with water as possible. At such times the sun attacks the skin mercilessly; it cracks it and peels it off, and will even cause sores, which will lead to a good deal of inconvenience as well as undeniable pain. I am convinced that here again, when the choice must lie between this and uncleanliness, the defenders of cleanliness will be found few and far between.

Lastly, though it might be more becoming in us and more in harmony with the conventions of the day to confess that we found it unpleasant to go so long without a wash or change of clothes, it is better to acknowledge the truth and to say openly that in these respects we felt entirely comfortable, and had, besides, too much work to do to leave us time even to think of the condition we were in.

On August 24 we had things against us all day, as the snow grew heavier and heavier to pull upon, was so loose that we sank several inches, and we had, besides, a considerable gradient to ascend. In order to keep our spirits up, every mile covered was rewarded with a cake of meat-chocolate per man. At dinner-time we cooked our meal again with oilcloth in the open air, but this time we also used a spare theodolite-stand of ash, which was condemned as superfluous. We further consigned to the flames a number of splints, which we had brought for possible broken limbs, but most of which we did not care to carry farther now that we had passed the crevassed ice without mishap. Some we kept, nevertheless, in case any of us might come to grief during the descent on the other side.

After sunset this evening we again found it distinctly cold, the friction grew worse than ever, and we came to a halt. Our march had been scarcely more than five miles. As we had had our dinner not long before, we were fain to be content with a supper of oatmeal biscuits, together with snow over which our lemonade mixture had been poured. This makes the most refreshing and exhilarating dish I know, and is much like the preparation used in,Italy and known as "granita." Indeed, if one can get really fine fresh snow, the Greenland form is even better. We were all in excellent spirits as we sat outside the tent eating our lemon-snow and biscuits, and by careful economy prolonging the enjoyment to the utmost, while we watched the rays of the moon playing over the endless stretch of white desert. My thoughts went back to the last time I had "granita." This was also by moonlight, but it was a hot summer night by the Bay of Naples, and the moon was shining on the dark waters of the Mediterranean.

On August 25 the rise was still steep, and the snow even worse, as it was loose and lay to a depth of six or eight inches. To make things complete, there was also a wind blowing full in our faces.

It had struck us that our halts for dinner took up a good deal -a 5 of time, and to-day we evolved the very happy idea of cooking as we went, and thus saving the long time we otherwise had to wait while a meal was being prepared. So the cooker was put at the back of one of the sledges, was lighted, and as the snow gradually melted into water, the cakes of soup were added, and we meantime went on our way rejoicing, and very proud of our brilliant invention. When the soup was on the boil, we halted, pitched the tent, and carried the pot carefully in. But, as luck would have it, just as we were sitting down to the enjoyment of this grand dish, I made some clumsy movement, upset the rickety erection, and all the precious soup was running over the tent-floor mixed with burning spirit, water, and lumps of snow from the upper vessel of the cooker. We were all on our legs at once, all loose objects were ejected from the tent, and by seizing the corners of the floor we gathered the liquid into the central depression. Hence it was conveyed into

the pot and set to boil again, scarcely a drop having been lost In these cases it is an excellent thing to have a waterproof tent-floor. Balto maintains that this day's soup "was not altogether pure and clean, as the floor of the tent was somewhat dirty. But we could not help that; the soup tasted just as good, for our insides were rather empty." He does not mention the fact that there was some methylated spirit in it too, but it was not much, and no doubt he thought it improved the flavour.

While we were now sitting and enjoying our dinner in the warmth and comfort of the tent, a snowstorm was getting up outside. It was only the drifting of already fallen snow, but it met us full in the face when we went on again, and through the afternoon the wind grew stronger and stronger, which in from fifteen to twenty degrees of frost is distinctly unpleasant. However, we plodded on as well as we could up a steep slope with our heads bent down and wrapped in our monkish hoods, while the fine, dusty snow did its best to find a way into all the pores and chinks of our waterproof clothes. It was late before we camped and crept into our bags, and there enjoyed our frugal supper, while the moon shed its peaceful light through a cranny in the tent-door, and we comfortably felt that we had shut out the wind and driving snow.

The storm lasted all night, and next morning, August 26, when I was about to turn out to make some coffee, I was not a little surprised to find myself, the sleeping-bags, and our clothes all buried under the snow, which had forced its way in through every crevice and had filled the tent. My boots were full of snow; when we went out to look at the sledges they had half disappeared, and great drifts lay high against the tent-walls. Nevertheless we spent a very pleasant Sunday morning with coffee and breakfast in bed.

All this day, too, the storm continued, and our work grew heavier and heavier as the snow grew deeper. I felt much inclined to tie the sledges together, make them into two rafts, as it were, and try, by the help of sails, to beat up against

the wind. If we go on at our present rate, it will be a long while before we reach Christianshaab. We hope to get a change for the better, but it does not come to-day, and we have to tramp along as best we can. A couple of miles farther on we reach a ridge which has to be climbed. We had to put three men to each sledge, and even then it was heartbreaking work to get them up, the gradient proving to be as much as one foot in four. As we were coming down after one haul, Kristiansen, who seldom said anything, turned to Dietrichson and exclaimed, "What fools people must be to let themselves in for work like this!"

Chapter XV.

*THE CROSSING OF THE "INLAND ICE"—WE CHANGE OUR COURSE FOR GODTHAAB—SOME FEATURES OF THE CLIMATE AND THE SNOW.*

We had reached a height of some 6000 feet above the sea when ve halted that evening, August 26. Taught by our experiences of the night before, we took measures to protect ourselves better against the storm and penetrating, dust-like snow. We dug a hole which gave us a bank on the weather side, and we furthermore turned one of the sledges over and covered it with tarpaulins. We thus obtained fairly good shelter, and were in excellent spirits as we sat round the singing tea-kettle and lamp, which threw a faint light about the tent and its strange group of occupants, and showed us the fine snow, which, in spite of all our precautions, settled upon everything and filled the air. When the tea was ready we lighted one of the five candles I had brought for photographic purposes, and altogether spent a most comfortable evening in defiance of the storm which shrieked outside.

There was no abatement in the wind when we woke next morning, but the tent was not so full of snow as it had been the day before. I was by this time tired of plodding along against the wind in this deep loose snow, and resolved this morning to rig the sledges and try a sail. The proposal, however, met with a good deal of opposition, especially from the Lapps. Ravna put on a most dejected look, and Balto simply unbridled his tongue He had never seen such a lot of lunatics, he said. W'anting to sail on the snow, indeed! Very likely we could teach him sailing on the sea and one or two other things perhaps, but on land and on the snow, no, never. Such infernal nonsense he had never heard. He spoke more than plainly, but to little purpose, as he had to put up with the absurdity. The sledges were placed side by side and lashed together, two going to make one vessel, and three to the other. On the first the tent-floor did duty for a sail; on the latter, which was manned by Dietrichson, Ravna, and Balto, the two tarpaulins.

I had contemplated using the tent-walls too, but when it came to the point I dared not, as they seemed too thin, and to have our tent torn in pieces in a country like this would have been a good deal worse than unpleasant. When the tarpaulins were hoisted to the wind, they came apart at once and proved unmanageable, which made it necessary to sew them together. To sit and sew with bare fingers in the cold wind and drifting snow was miserable work, but by dint of keeping our hands well rubbed and knocked about, and after toils and tribulations of all kinds and six or seven hours' work, we eventually got under way in the course of the afternoon.

We soon found that there was no question of tacking up against the wind, as we could not get within less than eight or nine points of the wind at best. But I had not really been very hopeful on this score, and had, as a matter of fact, other ends in view. I now saw plainly that with this heavy going and this persistent foul wind there was no chance of our reaching Christianshaab by the middle of September, when the last ship for Copenhagen would sail, and with it vanish our last chance of getting home this year. At the time I looked upon this eventuality as most unfortunate, seeing that we should have to waste a whole winter in Greenland, while the men would no doubt all be consumed with home-sickness. I had, too, very vague ideas as to the traffic of the west coast, and I argued that the last boat which sailed from Christianshaab

would also call at the more southerly ports, and that therefore we should have a better chance of catching her if we made for one of these, for preference Godthaab. In favour of this particular line there were other reasons, and above all the fact that an exploration of the ice along this route would be particularly interesting, seeing that it was absolutely unknown, while Nordenskiold's two expeditions had already obtained much valuable information about the tract to the south-east of Christianshaab through which we should otherwise pass. Again, it was now late in the year, and the autumn of the "Inland ice" was not likely to prove a gentle season, so the fact that it was a considerably shorter crossing to the head of one of the fjords in the neighbourhood of Godthaab than to Christianshaab was another argument which had its weight. We should thus be able to reckon upon sooner reaching more hospitable surroundings, even though we knew nothing of the condition of the ice just there and whether a descent was likely to be practicable, and even though we might not actually get to the colony of Godthaab any earlier than to that of Christianshaab by the longer route. For in the former case the land journey after one leaves the ice is much longer than in the latter, and indeed it was (mite possible that we should find this part of the route very difficult. However, we had no doubt that by one means or another we should be able to find our way to the colony, and if there were no other access, then in the last resort by sea.

All these considerations filled my head this particular morning. I consulted the map again and again, made the calculations to myself, and finally determined upon the Godthaab route. I was quite prepared to find the ice difficult to deal with just here, since there are so many glaciers converging at this point, but I felt sure we should be able to compass the descent somehow.

The point where I thought of getting down was that which we actually hit, and which lies at about lat. 64" 10' N. I aimed at this particular spot because there seemed to be no glacier just here,

while according to the map—which I may say, in passing, was absolutely wrong—there were huge ones both to the north and the south. My notion was that we should find between these two great streams of falling ice a kind of back-eddy, so to say, or belt in which the surface lay comparatively calm and level. My experience, so far as it went, had led me to this conclusion.

The rest of the party hailed my change of plan with acclamation. They seemed to have already had more than enough of the " Inland ice," were longing for kindlier scenes, and gave their unqualified approval to the new route. So the sails were hoisted, and about three in the afternoon we got under way, keeping as well up to the wind as we could. We could not do much in this way, as I have said, and as it blew about N.W., our course necessarily lay a good deal to the south of Godthaab; but since the wind was now on our side, we all preferred this deviation to unassisted hauling. By putting two men in front to pull, and keeping a third behind to steer, we got on moderately well, and though we started late and knocked off work early we did a good five miles before we stopped for the night.

I now began to consider what would really be our best route when we got off the ice on the other side. According to the map it was rather a rough country, much cut up by mountains, valleys, and fjords. Things looked most promising near Narsak, a settlement at the mouth of Ameralikfjord and to the south of Godthaab. But it seemed very likely that ve should have a good deal of trouble here, too, and I felt more and more inclined for the sea-route. Here we had obviously plenty of materials for boat-building in our waterproofs, tarpaulins, and tent-floor; we had wood for the ribs, oars, and other parts in our " ski," sledges, staffs, and bamboo poles. So far we were excellently provided, and if all hands went to work at once the job could not take us long. As soon as I had come to this conclusion, I confided in Sverdrup, who, after some consideration, quite agreed with me. And now, as it is always a good thing to have something to give definite occupation to one's thoughts, we began to discuss, as we went along, hov we had better build our boat in case such a course were advisable.

For the next two days the weather remained unchanged: there was the same storm and driving snow. At night I often feared the tent would be torn in pieces; in the morning, when we proposed to start, the sledges had to be dug out of the drifts and unloaded to have their runners scraped clean of snow and ice. Then they had to be lashed together and rigged again, and the whole was a task which we found anything but grateful in the biting wind. The lashing especially, which had to be done with the bare hand, if it was to be any good, was particularly detestable work. Then when we at last managed to get under way, it was a case of tramping the whole day in the deep snow—a heavy and exhausting business, whether one was in front with the rope or walking behind to steer. But the cruellest work of the whole day was getting the tent up in the evening, for we had to begin by lacing the floor and walls together, and as this had to be done with the unprotected fingers, we had to take good care not to get them seriously frozen. One evening when I was at this work I suddenly discovered that the fingers of both my hands were white up to the palms. I felt them and found they were as hard and senseless as wood. By rubbing and beating them, however, I soon set the blood in circulation again and brought their colour back, and so escaped any further consequences that time.

On August 28 Kristiansen had been unlucky enough to tread unwarily on the edge of a hard drift and strain his knee. For several days he was so lame that he could only walk with difficulty, which kept us back to some extent, but a persistent use of " massage " soon restored him. It was a curious sight to see him sitting with his leg bare, while Dietrichson rubbed him, in the drifting snow and bitter wind. The same day, too, the Lapps' eyes were not quite right. They, strangely enough, as I have already said, were the first to suffer from snow-blindness, and, in fact, the only ones among us who did so at all. I even had to treat Balto with cocaine, but the attack was of short duration and little consequence, and by the help of snow-, spectacles and red silk veils they both soon recovered. The rest of us went scot-free from this complaint, which many Arctic travellers have considered inevitable. If dark spectacles or veils are used, there is no doubt that it can be avoided.

Though we only had the sun in the daytime, it was the cause of a good deal of trouble to us, and in the middle of the day its action was simply intense. This was largely due to the want of density in the air at this altitude, 6500 feet; but partly also, of course, to the reflection of the rays from the huge level expanse of snow. Our faces were all more or less affected; we were burnt brown, of course, and none of us escaped losing a certain amount of skin from the nose and other prominent points. Kristiansen's face was very severely handled; his cheeks swelled and blistered, as if they had been badly frostbitten, and caused him a good deal of pain. After this we were more careful in the use of our veils, and thus escaped any serious inconvenience.

It was an odd sight to see these fine red veils fluttering against the blue sky. They led one's thoughts instinctively to the life and fashion of our promenades at home, to smart carriages, graceful figures, and bright eyes, while here were six men with grimy, weather-worn faces, and figures anything but graceful, dragging carriages of a certain sort, but which were scarcely open to the reproach of smartness.

On the afternoon of August 29 the wind so far dropped that it no longer paid to sail, and we therefore unrigged our vessels and set to work in the old way, taking a course straight for Godthaab.

This day too the snow was so loose and deep that Sverdrup, Dietrichson, and I took to the Indian snow-shoes. These implements caused us a good deal of trouble at first, as we had, in fact, had no practice with them previously. Our preliminary attempts brought us time after time headlong. At first we did not keep our feet wide enough apart: one snow-shoe caught against the other leg and over we went. Then, though for a time we managed to avoid this fault, we would put one shoe down on the top of the other, and the next attempt at a step brought us flat on our faces again. Then we learnt to straddle sufficiently and keep them clear of each other, and got on admirably for a time. But presently we would catch the nose of one of the shoes in some hard snow, and again come to utter grief. In this way we went on, time after time plunging into the snow, and then struggling on for a while with more or less success. But we soon got accustomed to the peculiarities of these snow-shoes, and then we found them of great practical HAULING ON INDIAN SNOW-SHOES.
*(Frjin ti photograph.)*
use. They bore us well up in the snow and gave us good and firm foothold, and we now regretted that we had not taken to them before.

Kristiansen tried the snow-shoes, too, but failed utterly to get upon satisfactory terms with them, and after he had fallen on his face a score or so of times, he grew so disgusted that he threw them upon his sledge and would have no more to say to s them. He then tried the Norwegian " truger " instead, but they proved very inferior, as they sank deep in the snow and made walking much heavier work. The Lapps, who had already vowed by all that they held holy that they would never use these "idiotic things," would not, of course, condescend to try them now, and it was with much contempt and disapprobation that they saw us make our first experiments with them. Consequently it was with unconcealed satisfaction that they watched us dive head first into the snow no sooner than we had started. But when things began to go better, and it was obvious that we had a great advantage over them, Balto could contain himself no longer, and cautiously ventured the inquiry whether the snow-shoes were really good to walk with, a question which he subsequently repeated several times. It was evident that he was on the point of giving way and making the experiment, in spite of his previous condemnation of them. But on the morning of August 30 the snow was in a condition to allow of "ski" being used, and he took to them instead. Ravna waited a while, but presently upon Balto's recommendation he put on his "ski," and Kristianscn soon followed them. I considered, however, that the snow-shoes were better as long as we had the rise of the ground much against us, and' so Sverdrup and I kept to them till September *2,* while Dietrichson gave them up for his " ski" the day before us. Henceforth till we reached the west coast we all used our " ski" invariably.

All this time, or for more than three weeks on the whole, our life was simply inordinately monotonous, with not a trace of any important occurrence. It is no wonder, therefore, that the veriest trifles were magnified into circumstances of consideration and were made to pad our diaries during the period. Our last sight of land, of course, came in for mention, and was recorded by Dietrichson as follows: " About ten in the morning of August 31 we saw land for the last time. We were upon the crest of one of the great waves, or gentle undulations in the surface, and had our final glimpse of a little point of rock which protruded from the snow. It lay, of course, far in the interior, and for many days had been the only dark point, save ourselves and the sledges, on which our eyes could rest. Now it, too, disappeared." We christened this last point of rock " Camel's Nunatak."

Nor could so notable an incident as the sight of a snow-bunting be passed over. My diary says: " An hour or so after we had lost sight of our last rock we were no little astonished to hear the twitter of a bird in the air and suddenly to see a snow-bunting come flying towards us. After having circled round us two or three times it settled down close by, put its head on one side, regarded us for a moment, hopped a little way on the snow, and then with a chirp flew off again northwards and was soon lost in the distance. This was our last greeting from land."

At the end of August we were still ascending. We were always hoping to reach the uppermost plateau, and that the ascent we were just then making would prove our last; but when we came to the top we always found a level stretch and then another rise beyond.

On the evening of September i we reached the top of one of these long slopes and saw before us a huge flat plain with an almost imperceptible rise westwards. There was a very marked change in the weather and appearance of the sky. Far away in the west, and almost at the level of the horizon, were closely packed banks of cloud of the round cumulus form, which we had hitherto not seen lying above the snow. I thought they must be formed by currents of moist air which rose from the sea and had followed the western slope of the continent up into the interior, and I therefore supposed that we must have got far enough to have this long-looked-for slope in view.

To the south and east there were also clouds, while the sky was clear overhead and to the north. In the latter direction the snowfield showed a distinct rise, while it fell away to the east and south. Everything seemed to point to the conclusion that we had reached the high plateau of the interior. The announcement of this to the party produced general rejoicing, for we were all heartily tired of the long slopes we had to climb, and which just lately had been especially trying. Sanguine as we were, we hoped soon to reach the westward slope, when it would all be downward travelling and pure delight, and it was in the most triumphant mood that we saw the sun sink that evening in all his glory behind the banks of clouds and transform the western sky into one scheme of glowing colour. All that we knew of beauty in this desert was contained in the evening and setting of the sun; our hopes lay in the same direction, but it was destined to be long before we saw the goal we sought.

We thought it no more than reasonable to keep this evening as "a festival, and we marked it as usual by extra rations of oatmeal biscuits, cheese, and

jam. The smokers, too, were allowed a pipe, and on the whole we had a thoroughly cheerful night.

The height to which we had now mounted had brought us to the end of the millimetre scale of our aneroid barometers. They marked a pressure of 550 mm., the elevation we had reached being about 7930 feet, and if we were to ascend still higher it would be difficult to continue our observations. By the help of the movable scale, however, we managed fairly well.

But the long-expected change of level would not come. For days—I might almost say weeks—we toiled across an interminable flat desert of snow; one day began and ended like another, and all were characterised by nothing but a wearisome, wearing uniformity which no one who has not experienced the like will easily realise. Flatness and whiteness were the two features of this ocean of snow; in the day we could see three things only—the sun, the snowfield, and ourselves. We looked like a diminutive black line feebly traced upon an infinite expanse of white. There was no break or change in our horizon, no object to rest the eye upon, and no point by which to direct the course. We had to steer by a diligent use of the compass, and keep our line as well as possible by careful watching of the sun and repeated glances i i

U *o z* back at the four men following and the long track which the caravan left in the snow. We passed from one horizon to another, but our advance brought us no change. We knew to a certain extent where we were, and that we must endure the monotony for a long time to come.

The surface over which we were passing all this time was almost absolutely level, though the tract from one slope to the other was marked throughout by long, gentle undulations scarcely discernible to the eye, the ridges and furrows of which ran nearly due north and south.

An entry in my diary for August 30 says: " The loose fresh snow which lies upon the old hard frozen surface is scarcely more than four or five inches thick to-day. It lies smooth and level, whereas for the last few days there has been a layer a foot thick, which was blown into drifts, upon which the sledges dragged heavily." From this day onwards the surface was smooth and even as a mirror, with no disturbance in its uniformity save the tracks we made ourselves.

Our day's marches were, as a rule, short, and varied between five and ten miles. The reason of this was the persistently heavy going. Had we come earlier in the season, say about rnidsummertime, we should have found an excellent, hard, and slippery surface, such as that we had during the first day or two of our ascent. On such a surface both " ski" and sledges would have run well, and the crossing could not have taken us long.

Now, however, the old hard frozen layer was covered with a loose coat of freshly fallen snow, which was as fine and dry as dust, or else packed by the wind in drifts, on the cloth-like surface of which both " ski " and sledge-runners are very hard to move. The severe cold we experienced made things, in this respect, unusually bad; the snow, as we were fond of saying, was as heavy as sand to pull upon, and the farther we got into the interior the worse it became. If, as was often the case, the upper layer were fresh and loose, then perhaps it was worst of all. On the whole, the going was so unconscionably heavy that it was only by the exertion of all our strength that we were able to make any progress at all. At every stride we had to do everything we knew, and work at this high pressure is of course very wearying in the long run.

A few extracts from my diary at this time will show what we actually thought of the state of the snow at the moment. On September i I wrote: "To-day it was unusually hard work; about eight or nine inches of freshly drifted snow as fine as dust and heavy as sand lay on the top of the older crust. This was about two inches thick and covered another layer of loose snow. At noon the effect of the sun made things worse than ever. In our despair Sverdrup and I

unscrewed the steel plates from the runners of our sledge, as we thought the wood was likely to move better. The gain was, however, questionable; the sledge still went heavily. It seems to us that it goes worse every day."

A day or two later I wrote: " Now and again things are certainly a little better, but the improvement never lasts long and seems to be followed by a period which is worse than ever. At night there is often a little fall of fresh snow, which is even heavier than the older drifts to haul upon. Though the sun shines hot upon us it has not power even at noon to melt the surface and so give us an icy crust afterwards. The whole way the snow is loose and dusty or sticky like cloth."

As a matter of fact we had a thin crust like this on August 30. My diary records my opinion that this must have been formed by the powerful effect of the sun at noon and the subsequent frost. This crust was not thick enough to bear the sledges, but it helped to make them move easier. We only had it, however, for that one day.

On September 8 again: " The snow was incredibly heavy going to-day, heavier than it has ever been before, though the surface was hard and firm. The wind-packed snow is no better than sand. We had the wind to pull against too." The next day I wrote: " It began to snow in the middle of the day, and our work was heavier than ever. It was worse even than yesterday, and to say that it was like hauling in blue clay will scarcely give an idea of it. At every step we had to use all our force to get the heavy sledges along, and in the evening Sverdrup and I, who had had to go first and plough a way for ourselves, were pretty well done up. The others who followed us were a little better off, and besides, their steel runners moved easier. The evening in the tent, however, with a savoury stew, helped us to forget the toils of the day."

These notes will be sufficient to show the difficulties and labour the state of the snow entailed upon us. I ought, however, to add that the sledge which Sverdrup and I pulled together always

travelled much worse than any of the others, so much so, indeed, that we were ultimately constrained to abandon it altogether. On September 11 I wrote in my diary: "To-day Sverdrup and I found our sledge heavy to pull beyond all toleration, and it was really as much as we could do to make it move at all. We could not quite understand what was wrong with it; it had always been worse than all the others, and Sverdrup declared that we must have had the Evil One himself for a passenger behind. This morning we therefore decided to abandon it, and take Balto's instead, while he put his load on Ravna's sledge, and the two Lapps for the future pulled together. This change caused a new sun, as it were, to rise upon our existence; Sverdrup and I, with our new sledge, pushed on so fast that the others had hard work to keep up with us. We now found life almost enjoyable."

Nor were we the only two who found the work heavy. The Lapps never ceased to complain, and one day Balto stopped and said to me: " When you asked us two Lapps in Christiania how much we could pull we said that we could manage a hundredweight. But now we have two hundredweight apiece, and all I can say is, that if we drag these loads across to the west coast we are stronger than horses."

Lest any reader should be led to believe, by what I have here said about the state of the snow and the difficulties we met with, that our " ski" were of little or no use to us, I ought perhaps to state once and for all that they were an absolute necessity, that without their help we should have advanced very little way, and even then died miserably or have been compelled to return. I have already said that " ski" are considerably better than Indian snowshoes, even for hauling purposes. They tire one less both because they have not to be lifted, but merely driven forwards, and because the legs are kept no wider apart than in ordinary walking. For nineteen days continuously we used our " ski" from early morning till late in the evening, and the distance we thus covered was not much less than 240 miles.

The weather during almost the whole time of our crossing was so far clear that we could see the sun, and there were not many days on which the sky was completely overcast. Even when there was snow falling, which often happened, it was not thick enough to prevent the sun showing through. The snow which fell was always fine, and was more like frozen mist, so to say, than the snow we are generally accustomed to in Europe. It was exactly the same as is known in certain parts of Norway as "frost-snow," which is due to the fact that the moisture of the air falls directly to the earth without going through the intermediate cloud-stage.

When the sun shone through the fine falling snow there was always a ring round it, which, together with mock-suns and the intersecting axes, were phenomena which occurred almost daily during our journey across the interior. When the sun sank so low that the halo partially disappeared below the horizon, there were generally bright mock-suns at the points of section, as well as another one immediately under the sun itself.

As we came farther and farther in the cold increased in proportion. The sun had, however, a powerful effect when the weather was clear, and at noon the heat was, for a while, even oppressive. In,my diary for August 31 I noted that just about that time the sun had been so hot that it made the snow wet and sticky, so that the sledges ran badly, and our feet got rather wet. When the sun began to sink, and it froze again, the sledges went better certainly, but it was a bad business for our feet, and we had to take care not to get them frost-bitten. It happened not infrequently that when we took our shoes off at night, they, our thick, rough socks and ordinary stockings were all frozen together into a solid mass.

After this time the sun was not sufficiently powerful to melt the snow, but it had a great effect, owing to the height at which we were, and the fact that the air was so thin and absorbed comparatively little of the warmth of the rays. On September i, for instance, a spirit thermometer marked in the sunshine 85

Fahr. (29.5 Cent.), while the real temperature of the air as obtained by a sling thermometer was very little more than 25 Fahr. (-3.6 Cent.). In the night we had had nearly twenty-nine degrees of frost (-16 Cent.). On September 3, again, a spirit thermometer laid in the sun on one of the sledges at noon showed as much as 88 Fahr. (31.5 Cent. ), while a sling thermometer gave the real temperature of the air at the same time as 12 Fahr. (-11 Cent.).

This great difference between sun- and shade-temperature is plainly due to the excessive radiation in the dry, thin air of this high plateau. A similar phenomenon was observed many years ago in Siberia by our celebrated countryman, the astronomer Hansteen. In a letter from Irkutsk, dated April n, 1829, he writes: "The considerable elevation of the country, together with its distance from the sea, makes the air exceedingly dry and causes a strong radiation, which is one reason of the low temperature of this place. The power of the sun is so great here in the spring, that at midday, when the temperature in the shade is as low as-20 R. (-13" F.) or-30 R. (-35 F. ), the water drips from the roofs of the houses on the sunny side."

As the afternoon advanced and the sun began to draw near the horizon, the temperature fell in an astonishing way, though the change was most marked at sunset.

The scale of our sling thermometers only read as low as-22 Fahr. (-30 Cent.), as no one had expected such cold at this time of year in the interior of Greenland. But after September 8 the mercury quickly retired below the scale as soon as the sun disappeared in the evening. The lowest temperature we experienced could not therefore, unfortunately, be determined with accuracy. But when I went to bed on the night of September 11 I put a minimum thermometer under my pillow. In the morning the spirit was a good way below the scale, which marked-35 Fahr. (-37 Cent.). The *Astronom Nachrichten*, vol. vii. p. 327. A HALT FOK KEFKESHMENTS. *(By A. Block, from afholograph.')* temperature was, no doubt, below —40

Fahr. (-40 Cent.), and this was in the tent, in which six men were sleeping, and in which we had cooked our food with the spirit-lamp.

The most remarkable fact in connection with the temperature was the great difference between night and day limits. It was more than 40 Fahr. (20 Cent. ), a difference which cannot occur in many parts of the globe. Something corresponding to this state of things has been observed in the Sahara, where in January it may be intolerably hot in the day and so cold that water left in the open air will freeze at night.

It is remarkable that this extraordinarily rapid fall of the temperature in the course of the night on the " Inland ice " of Greenland has not been observed before. The reason, no doubt, is that those of our predecessors who have penetrated any appreciable distance have done so at higher latitudes and at a time of year when the sun has been above the horizon the whole, or nearly the whole, night. Nor have these expeditions as a matter of fact published any full meteorological records.

Reckoning from the way the temperature sank at the approach of evening, Professor Mohn, of Christiania, has calculated that our lowest records must have reached something like-50 Fahr. (-45 Cent.). On these days the temperature of the air at noon rose to between- 4 Fahr. (-20 Cent.) and + 5 Fahr. (-15 Cent.). This was in the middle of September, and these temperatures are without any comparison the lowest that have ever been recorded at the time of year anywhere on the face of the globe. What the minimum reached in midwinter can be it is impossible as yet to form any idea.

As to the question of the highest temperature attained in the middle of summer in these regions, and whether there is any considerable melting of snow, we can form some estimate by examining the strata of the upper surface of the snowfield and finding whether the older layers show signs of having melted. This was done by us as often as we had time and opportunity.

Up to August 30, when we had

reached a height of 6530 feet, we found the old snow consistently frozen hard, and often transformed into a kind of loose, granular snow. This had evidently been exposed to violent thaws and subsequently frost. Over this old layer there was generally a coat of from five to ten inches, or even a foot, of loose, dry snow, which must have fallen after the hot season was over.

On the evening of August 31 we found, to our astonishment, when we were ramming our staffs in, preparatory to the pitching of the tent, that, though there was certainly a solid crust under the upper layer of fresh snow, yet when we had passed through this we could drive the poles down to an indefinite depth. This was a clear proof that we had already reached a height—it was then all but 7500 feet—at which the sun even at midsummer has only power enough to make a thin layer of snow wet and sticky, and that this freezes afterwards as the sun gets low again. At this height, therefore, melting can do absolutely nothing to reduce the quantity of snow, for the insignificant amount of water thus formed can get no way, as it is at once intercepted by the following night-frost.

We found a similar state of things throughout the upper plateau, there being practically no melting of the snow. On the whole the stratification was very remarkable. An entry in my diary for September 3 shows me that I tried the snow several times that day and found, as a rule, uppermost about three inches of fresh snow, then a crust about half an inch in thickness, then seven inches of loose snow again, then another crust which could only be bored with difficulty, and that after this the staff could be driven down for a foot or more through a mass which grew gradually harder and harder, till about two feet from the surface it came to a standstill altogether.

I had tried at another place somewhat earlier the same day. Here the upper layers were much the same as I have just described, but in this case the staff could be rammed down some four feet altogether, though with increasing difficulty, while it finally stopped against an absolutely solid mass.

This stratification we also found throughout the highest tract, but as a rule we could drive our staffs down as far as we would. Everything shows that in the very interior the only melting that goes on is the moistening of the upper surface just at the warmest period of the year, while this layer is solidified again immediately.

Chapter XVI.

THE CROSSING OF THE "INLAND ICE"—A STORM IN THE INTERIOR—OUR DOMESTIC LIFE.

Constant exposure to the cold which I have described in my last chapter was, as may be imagined, by no means pleasant. The ice often formed so heavily on our faces that our beards and hair froze fast to the coverings of our heads, and it was then difficult enough to open the lips to speak. This inconvenience can of course best be prevented by shaving, but this was a task for which we had neither time nor inclination.

There was less pleasure still at these altitudes when we had the wind in our faces, as an entry in my diary will best show: " On the morning of September 4 the weather was glorious and the air still. There had been a light fall of snow in the night. The sun shone over the infinitely monotonous snowfield, which, rising almost imperceptibly, stretched away and away in front of us like one huge white carpet, glittering with diamonds, soft and fine in texture as down, and laid in long, gentle undulations which the eye could scarcely follow. But in the afternoon the aspect of our landscape changed entirely. A biting wind got up from the north-west, which drove the snow before it in one huge, overwhelming whirlwind.

"The sky above then cleared completely and it grew colder and colder, the thermometer falling a degree or two below zero. The wind increased in strength; it was bitter work toiling along against it, and we had to be careful not to get badly frozen. First my nose hardened, but I discovered this in time to save it by rubbing it well with snow. I thought myself safe now, but then I felt a queer, chilly feeling under my chin,

where I found that my throat was quite numb and stiff. By more rubbing, and wrapping some mittens and other things round my neck, I put matters straight here. But then came the worst attack of all, as the wind found its way in through my clothes to the region of my stomach and gave rise to horrid pains. This was met by the insertion of a soft felt hat, and I was now armed at all points against the enemy. Sverdrup suffered pretty much as I did; how the others behind fared I do not know, but they can scarcely have been much better off. The bodily comforts of our tent were more welcome than usual that evening."

Next morning things were quiet again, but in the afternoon we had another storm of drifting snow from the south-west. This went on all night, the wind working round more and more to the south, and I rejoiced in the hope of a sail, but in the morning again, September 6, it had so far fallen that we did not think it worth while to rig up the sledges. A little later, however, it freshened up and at noon blew due south. I was for sailing, therefore, but the proposal was met with so many objections on the part of the others, who were little inclined for the necessary rigging and lashing in this bitter weather, that I unfortunately gave way. This we all had reason to regret, for as we went on the wind worked round behind us more and more and at the same time increased in force.

We had soon a full snowstorm blowing from east-southeast or east. It was therefore behind us, and carried both the sledges and ourselves on our "ski" along well, and as the ground was also slightly in our favour we made good progress. The driving snow soon grew so dense that Sverdrup and I could not see the others at twenty paces' distance, and we had to wait for them repeatedly in order not to part company. It was no easy matter to get the tent up that evening when we stopped at about eight o'clock, and those unlucky ones among us who had clad themselves insufficiently in the morning and now had to take off their outer clothes to put something extra on beneath had a terrible time. The wind blew in to the very skin; the snow drove through all the pores of shirt and jersey; one felt completely naked, in fact; and I myself nearly sacrificed my left hand to the frost in the process, while it was with the greatest difficulty that I could get all buttoned up snug again. The tent we did eventually manage to get up, but we could cook nothing that evening, as the snow drove in much too thick at all crevices and apertures. A few biscuits and some dried meat had to suffice, and we were glad enough to crawl as soon as possible into the sleeping-bags, draw the covers well over our heads, devour our food there, and as we slept leave the storm in undisputed possession outside. We had pushed on a long way that day, not much less than twenty miles, as we supposed.

The storm raged all night through, veering gradually round to due east. Next morning, the yth of September, as I woke and was still lying half-unconscious, I heard something go outside. It was one of the guy-ropes on the east side, where the wind was now blowing with such violence that every moment I expected the tent-wall to give way, more especially as there was now a great bulge in it owing to the broken rope. By the help of some bags we made the weak side somewhat stiffer, but I still expected it to split, and was wondering what we should do when we had the snow driving straight into the tent upon us. The only course could be to creep deep into the bags and leave ourselves to be buried.

We hoped, however, that the wind would drop, and meanwhile I set the lamp going and cooked some stew and tea, which comforted us greatly. Then the weather began to look a little better, and I thought we might prepare to start. So we got ourselves up in our best storm-gear and were about to go out to rig the sledges, as we meant to sail to some purpose that day. Balto was ready first and crawled out of the tent-door— which was not an easy job, as the way was barred by a snowdrift It was not many seconds before he came plunging in again, absolutely breathless, and with his face and clothes covered with snow.

The wind had completely taken his breath away, and the first words he said when he had recovered him-

T self were, " There is no going on to-day! " I put my head out and at once saw that he was right, as the whole place was a sea of drifting snow.

So we had to stay where we were, though the tent had to be supported and victuals fetched in from the sledges before we were quite snowed up. This work Balto and Kristiansen were set to do. They rigged themselves out for the purpose, and tied themselves up at every possible point to prevent the snow blowing in. Balto was ready first, and I looked out after him as he went, but he had not taken more than a few steps before he fairly disappeared in the mist of whirling snow. The sledges had almost entirely vanished, and he had to grope about for them before he found them, and it was then no easy matter to get hold of the food we wanted. When Kristiansen went out to put some storm-guys on the weather side of the tent, the wind fell upon him with such force that he had to go on all fours.

In spite of all obstacles we managed to put things fairly straight By the help of some "ski" we braced the tent-wall up from the inside, some poles along the ridge of the roof stiffened the whole structure, and we now felt moderately safe. Then we stopped all openings and crevices as well as we could with reserve clothes and such things. We never could get the tent quite snow-tight, and great drifts by degrees collected inside. Of space we had none to spare already, but it gradually grew less and less under the encroachment of the drifts within and pressure of the snow on the walls without. We were snug and comfortable enough, however. The ever-gathering drifts outside, which threatened to completely bury the tent in time, protected us well against the wind and kept us nice and warm.

Then suddenly, a little after midday, the wind dropped all at once as abruptly as if the current had been cut off short with a knife. There was an absolute calm outside, and an uncomfortable silence came upon us too, for we all knew

that the wind would presently fall upon us with still greater violence from the opposite quarter. We sat listening intently, but the attack did not come at once, and some of us thought that the storm was possibly over. But presently there came a gentle gust from the northwest, the door side of our tent, and this was soon followed by blast upon blast, each more furious than its predecessor. The storm overwhelmed us with greater fury than before, and the inside of the tent even was a mist of flying snow. Balto had taken advantage of the interval of calm to go out and fill the cooking tins, and it was all he could do to find his way back again. We were now in great straits, as the door side, against which the storm now blew, was the weakest part of the tent, and we always made a point of turning it away from the wind. By the help of " ski" poles, snowshoes, and articles of clothing we managed to strengthen this side of the tent just sufficiently and to make the doorway tolerably snow-tight, but we were now caged as fast as mice in a trap, and there was no getting out for us, however much we wished it. Meantime we made life as pleasant as possible; the smokers were allowed the consolation of a pipe; we made some coffee, which had by this time been discontinued as a daily drink, crawled into our bags, and amused ourselves as best we could.

Ravna alone, in spite of the coffee, was inconsolable, though, as a nomad Lapp, he ought to have been quite accustomed to this kind of thing. I tried to cheer him up, but he said, " I am an old Lapp; I know what a snowstorm is upon the mountains in September; you won't see the end of it yet awhile." In spite of all encouragements he refused to be comforted, and persistently maintained that he was "an old Lapp, who had lived in the snow for forty-five years."

When we woke next morning the wind had dropped so much that we found we could move on again. But it. was no easy matter to get out of our prison; the tent was buried so deep that only the ridge of the roof remained above the snow, and we had to dig our way through the drift that blocked the door. Of the sledges there was practically nothing to be seen, and we had a good deal of work to do before we got them out and were ready to start. When we did get off we found the going as usual heavier than ever.

In Balto's description of this day in the tent, he says: "One day we had terrible weather, storm and driving snow, but we pushed on all the same till the evening. At first the wind came from the north" (he means south, by the way) " and then it went round to the east. Next morning after we had made some coffee" (this is a doubtful statement, but it may pass) " one of us was going out for some purpose or other, but as soon as he opened the tent-door, he was driven back again, as the weather was so frightful outside that it seemed impossible to get out. Then I put a coat over my head, covering it so that I only left a peep-hole for my eyes, and ventured out. I went a few steps away from the tent to look for the sledges, but there was not one of them to be seen, as they were all buried in the snow. I could not see the tent either now, so that I had to take to shouting, and it was only when they answered me from inside that I could find my way back. The tent, too, was nearly covered by the snow. Next day the weather was fine again, and we had enough to do to dig all our things out of the snow again."

During this, the middle period of the crossing, our daily life went its monotonous round, unrelieved by any really noteworthy event.

The worst work of the day was turning out in the morning an hour earlier than the others in order to do the cooking. This was generally my pleasant lot, for the efforts of the others usually ended in a loss of time or spirit, of neither of which things we had a superfluity. When I woke I generally found my head completely surrounded with ice and rime. This was inside the sleeping-bag, where the breath had frozen and settled upon the hair of the reindeer-skin. Once awake and conscious one found one's self sitting in a room, the temperature of which was something like -40 Fahr., and the walls, except that on the wind

side, covered with inch-long fringes of hoar-frost, which gave one an uncomfortable shower-bath if one were unfortunate enough to knock up against them. Then followed the lighting-up of the cooking apparatus. The mere touching of the metal in this temperature was unpleasant enough, and no less so the filling of the lamp and arrangement of the wicks. The latter, if they were to burn well, had to be thoroughly soaked with spirit, which one of course got upon one's fingers, to one's great pain and infinite regret. To keep the wicks nice and dry, and thus save as much trouble in this way as I could, I generally carried them in my trousers' pocket. The lamp being eventually lighted and the cooker placed upon it, the wicks had to be attended to further, or the flame would get too high, make the lamp too hot, and cause a very undesirable explosion. The lamp often did get too hot, and it then had to be cooled down by the application of snow. Nor could the flames be allowed to burn too low, or much time was wasted in the cooking. Towards the end of our journey Balto became so skilled in the management of the cooker that he was quite equal to the work single-handed. He was very proud of the trust, and I gladly handed the task over to him, as one does not readily surrender an hour of one's morning sleep without dire necessity.

When the tea or chocolate was at last ready, the others were called, but breakfast was as a rule enjoyed in bed. Breakfast over, the next thing was to get ready for the day's march with the least possible waste of time. The sledge-runners had to be scraped clean, the baggage well packed and lashed fast, and the tent struck. Often again an observation was taken with the boiling-point thermometer before we broke up camp. Two or three times, too, samples of air were secured in the way I have already described.

When all this was done we put our " ski " on, harnessed ourselves to the sledges, and got under way, but after a couple of hours' march we generally halted, and a cake of meat-chocolate was served out to each man. Then we

went on till dinnertime came, the meal being eaten as we sat on the sledges and as quickly as possible. After another two hours or so we stopped for another cake of meat-chocolate apiece, and then two or three hours' more marching brought us to afternoon tea at about five o'clock. We now kept at work till night, the period being only broken by a third halt for the chocolate distribution.

In this extreme cold the taking of astronomical observations was often anything but agreeable. It was difficult to handle the instruments in heavy gloves and mittens, and if it was necessary to have the readings really accurate, the bare hands had to be used, and good care taken that the fingers were not frozen fast to the metal. Hut in spite of obstacles our observations both with theodolite and sextant were quite as good as one could expect to get them with such instruments. In the driving snow it was almost an impossibility to use the sextant and artificial horizon, for the latter was at once obscured, and we had to be very sharp to see anything at all. If this were out of the question the theodolite had to be used. This gave us twice the trouble, but equally good results.

When we stopped for the night, most of the party set to work at once to clear the ground for the tent, put it up and support and strengthen it with tarpaulins on the wind side. Ravna's evening task, and, I really think, the only regular work he had besides hauling during the whole journey, was to fill the cooking vessels with snow. As an old Lapp who every winter used snow for his cooking-pot instead of water, he knew well what was the best kind for melting. So as soon as we stopped, he would steal silently off with the cooker, dig himself a hole down to the old coarse snow, which melts into far more water than the newer, bring his pot back to the tent, and then, if it were already up, crawl in and sit with his legs crossed under him, not to move again till supper was ready. It was not till I had set him to this work for many days in succession that Ravna showed himself possessed of sufficient enterprise to undertake even this little job of his own accord. But little as it was, it completely satisfied him, and therewith he considered his mission in this world far more than accomplished.

The evenings in the tent, when all the party were seated round on their clothes-bags, after having carefully brushed themselves of snow, in order to bring as little of it as possible inside, were without comparison the bright spots in our existence at this particular time. However hard the day had been, however exhausted we were, and however deadly the cold, all was forgotten as we sat round our cooker, gazing at the faint rays of light which shone from the lamp, and waiting patiently KVKNIXG IN TIIK TKNT. "TUK SUIT IS KKAllY. "

*(By E. Nielsen, fiviu n sketch ly the Aitt/ wr.)*

for our supper. Indeed I do not know many hours in my life on which I look back with greater pleasure than on these.

And when the soup, or stew, or whatever the preparation might be, was cooked, when the rations were served round, and the little candle-stump lighted that we might see to eat, then rose our happiness to its zenith, and I am sure all agreed with me that life was more than worth living.

Then after supper there were various small preparations for the coming day—the cooker to be filled with snow, or the chocolate to be broken up. When all this was done we crawled into our sleeping-bags, shut the hoods close over our heads, and slept as sound a sleep as the best of European beds could have given us.

It is not unnatural that food was the axis on which our whole life revolved, and that our ideal of enjoyment was

St ».."t WEIGHING OUT THE RATIONS. *Front a photograph.)*

enough to eat in one form or another. It was to fatty food that our fancy especially turned, for, as I have said, our supply of fat was far too short. We were reduced in the end to an absolute famine, and could have looked forward to no greater treat than the full and unrestricted possession of a pound or two

of butter, or lard, or something of the kind apiece to work our hungry wills upon. The remnants after the first assault would certainly have been small. Each man had half a pound of butter served out to him a week, and as long as the ration lasted one of our favourite enjoyments was to eat our butter in large lumps, and the tin box in which we kept it once open, it was difficult indeed to put the lid on again. To some of us this enjoyment was of short duration. Kristiansen was the worst of all in this way, as he used to devour his half-pound the first day, which was of course very crude economy. To such an extent did the craving for fat go that Sverdrup asked me one day whether I thought our boot-grease, which was old boiled linseed oil, was likely to disagree with him.

As a rule, of course, the rations for each meal were all carefully weighed out, for which purpose we used a small letter-scale. The amount which I considered fully sufficient was about one kilogramme, or 2 -Ibs., per man per day. When we approached the west coast, however, all were allowed to eat as much as they liked of the dried meat, of which we had an abundance. But even then it seemed impossible to attain to a feeling of repletion.

Our daily bill of fare was as follows:—*Breakfast.*—Chocolate made with water—and when we had come to the end of the chocolate, tea—biscuits, liver pate", and pemmican. *Dinner.*—Pemmican, liver pate, and biscuits, this followed by oatmeal biscuits, and by lemonade to pour over some snow. *Afternoon tea.*—Biscuits, liver pate', and pemmican. *Supper.*—Pemmican, biscuits, and pea-, bean-, or lentil-soup. Instead of plain soup we sometimes had a stew or concoction of pemmican, biscuits, and pea-soup, all of which together made an exceptionally grateful dish. Sometimes, too, tea took the place of soup or stew.

The weekly ration of butter we were of course free to use at whatever meal we pleased. Generally we had it at dinner-time, as we found that butter eaten alone quenched the thirst well, which is

a somewhat noteworthy fact, seeing that it was salted.

As to our method of cooking, I must allow that I have seen food prepared more cleanly. I have already had occasion to point out that we had no superabundance of water. There was therefore nothing to wash the cooking-pot with, nor would such washing have been at all pleasant work if we had had water. So after we had made our peasoup or stew in the evening, the pot was handed over to be cleaned, as a special grace, by some one who had helped in the cooking. Balto was generally the lucky man, and his mode of performing the task was by licking and scraping the vessel as clean as tongue and ringers could make it. This was well enough as far as it went, but not very much can be done in this way in a deep, narrow pot, as any one who has tried will allow. The bottom of our cooker was in fact all but inaccessible.

Next morning chocolate or tea was made in the same vessel, and when after this it was emptied it was not an uncommon sight to see on the bottom a wonderful conglomeration of the remains of soup or stew mixed with half-dissolved lumps of chocolate or obtrusive tea-leaves. On the top of all this the soup was cooked in the evening again.

At these ways of ours no doubt many a housekeeper will turn up her nose, but I must assure her with all respect that never in the course of her career and with all her cleanliness has she prepared food which gave its consumers such supreme satisfaction as ours did us. Many will perhaps accuse us of simple piggishness; but it is a piggishness which in the circumstances is no more than inevitable. At the same time our methods suited us; we had no time to do more than simply eat for eating's sake; and the interior of Greenland is certainly not the place for the fastidious or the epicurean.

The high place held by butter in our regard was disputed only by the olaims of tobacco. I had taken but a small supply, as I considered the indulgence harmful at times of severe exertion. So the Sunday pipe was economised to the last degree; the tobacco was smoked first, and then the ash and wood the bowl as long as they could be induced to burn, would not of course last the whole week ou next filled with tarred yarn as the best procu was Balto who felt the want of tobacco in was nothing which the promise of a pipe would not extract from him. Of chewing tobacco we had none; but several of the party chewed great bits of tarred rope instead. I thought the same practice might relieve one's burning thirst, and made the experiment one day myself; but the rope was no sooner in my mouth than out, for a viler taste have I rarely known.

A thing I did find good to chew as we went along was a chip or shaving of wood, as it kept the mouth moist and diminished one's thirst. I made a great use of a piece of bamboo in this way, but there was nothing that came up to a shaving off one of our " truger," or Norwegian snow-shoes. These were partly made of bird-cherry wood, and the bark of this was excellent. Sverdrup and I in fact went at the " truger " so persistently that there was very little left of them when we reached the west coast. But luckily this was the only use we had to put them to.

Chapter XVII.

*THE CROSSING OF THE "INLAND ICE"— THE FIRST SIGHT OF LAND AND FIRST DRINK OF WATER.*

As the middle of September approached, we hoped every day to arrive at the beginning of the western slope. To judge from our reckoning it could not be far off, though I had a suspicion that this reckoning was some way ahead of our observations. These, however, I purposely omitted to work out, as the announcement that we had not advanced as far as we supposed would have been a bitter disappointment to most of the party. Their expectations of soon getting the first sight of land on the western side were at their height, and they pushed on confidently, while I kept my doubts to myself and left the reckoning as it was.

On September n the fall of the ground was just appreciable, the theodolite showing it to be about a third of a degree. On September 12 I entered in my diary that " we are all in capital spirits, and hope for a speedy change for the better, Balto and Dietrichson being even confident that we shall see land to-day. They will need some patience, however, as we are still 9000 feet above the sea" (we were really about 8250 feet that day), " but they will not have to wait very long. This morning our reckoning made us out to be about seventy-five miles from bare land, and the ground is falling well and continuously." The next day or two the slope grew more and more distinct, but the incline was not regular, as the ground fell in great undulations, like those we had had to climb in the course of our ascent.

On September 14 the reckoning showed that it was only about thirty-five miles to land. But even now we could see nothing, which the Lapps thought was very suspicious. Ravna's face began to get longer and longer, and one evening about this time he said, " I am an old Lapp, and a silly old fool, too; I don't believe we shall ever get to the coast." I only answered, " That's quite true, Ravna; you are a silly old fool." Whereupon he burst out laughing: " So it's quite true, is it—Ravna is a silly old fool? " and he evidently felt quite consoled by this doubtful compliment. These expressions of anxiety on Ravna's part were very common.

Another day Balto suddenly broke out: " But how on earth can any one tell how far it is from one side to the other, when no one has been across?" It was, of course, difficult to make him understand the mode of calculation; but, with his usual intelligence, he seemed to form some idea of the truth one day when I showed him the process on the map. The best consolation we could give Balto and Ravna was to laugh at them well for their cowardice.

The very pronounced fall of the ground on September 17 certainly was a comfort to us all, and when the thermometer that evening just failed to reach zero we found the temperature quite mild, and felt that we had entered the abodes of summer again. It was now only nine miles or so to land by our reckoning.

It was this very day two months that we had left the *Jason*. This happened to be one of our butter-mornings, the very gladdest mornings of our existence at the time, and breakfast in bed with a good cup of tea brought the whole party into an excellent humour. It was the first time, too, for a long while that the walls of our tent had not been decorated with fringes of hoar-frost. As we were at breakfast we were no little astonished to hear, as we thought, the twittering of a bird outside; but the sound soon stopped, and we were not at all certain of its reality. But as we were starting again after our one o'clock dinner that day ve suddenly became aware of twitterings in the air, and, as we stopped, sure enough we saw a snow-bunting come flying after us. It wandered round us two or three times, and plainly showed signs of a wish to sit upon one of our sledges. But the necessary audacity was not forthcoming, and it finally settled on the snow in front for a few moments, before it flew away for good with another encouraging little twitter.

Welcome, indeed, this little bird was. It gave us a friendly greeting from the land we were sure must now be near. The believers in good angels and their doings must inevitably have seen such in the forms of these two snow-buntings, the one which bid us farewell on the eastern side, and that which offered us a welcome to the western coast. We blessed it for its cheering song, and with warmer hearts and renewed strength we confidently went on our way, in spite of the uncomfortable knowledge that the ground was not falling by any means so rapidly as it should have done. In this way, however, things were much better next day, September 18: the cold consistently decreased, and life grew brighter and brighter. In the evening, too, the wind sprang up from the south-east, and I hoped we should really get a fair sailing breeze at last. We had waited for it long enough, and sighed for it, too, in spite of Balto's assurances that this sailing on the snow would never come to anything.

In the course of the night the wind freshened, and in the morning there was a full breeze blowing. Though, as usual, there was no great keenness to undertake the rigging and lashing together of the sledges in the cold wind, we determined, of course, to set about the business at once. Kristiansen joined Sverdrup and me with his sledge, and we rigged the two with the tent-floor, while the other three put their two sledges together.

All this work, especially the lashing, was anything but delightful, but the cruellest part of it all was that while we were in the middle of it the wind showed signs of dropping. It did not carry out its threat, however, and at last both vessels were ready to start. I was immensely excited to see how our boat would turn out, and whether the one sail was enough to move both the sledges. It was duly hoisted and made fast, and there followed a violent wrenching of the whole machine, but during the operations it had got somewhat buried in the snow and proved immovable. There was enough wrenching and straining of the mast and tackle to pull the whole to pieces, so we harnessed ourselves in front with all speed. We tugged with a will and got our boat off, but no sooner had she begun to move than the wind brought her right on to us, and over we all went into the snow. We were soon up again for another try, but with the same result; no sooner are we on our legs than we are carried off them again by the shock from behind.

0 FIKST ATTEM1TS AT SAILING.
*(By A. Btocll.)*

This process having been gone through a certain number of times, we saw plainly that all was not right. So we arranged that one of us should stand in front on his " ski" and steer by means of a staff fixed between the two sledges, like the pole of a carriage, leaving himself to be pushed along by his vessel, and only keeping it at a respectful distance from his heels. The other two members of the crew were to come behind on their " ski," either holding on to the sledges or following as best they could.

We now finally got under way, and Sverdrup, who was to u take the first turn at steering, had no sooner got the pole under his arm than our vessel rushed furiously off before the wind. I attached myself behind at the side, riding on my " ski" and holding on by the back of one of the sledges as well as I could. Kristiansen thought this looked much too risky work, and came dragging along behind on his "ski " alone.

Our ship flew over the waves and drifts of snow with a speed that almost took one's breath away. The sledges struggled and groaned, and were strained in every joint as they were whirled over the rough surface, and often indeed they simply jumped from the crest of one wave on to another. I had quite enough to do to hang on behind and keep myself upright on the "ski. " Then the ground began to fall at a sharper angle than any we had had yet. The pace grew hotter and hotter, and the sledges scarcely seemed to touch the snow. Right in front of me was sticking out the end of a "ski," which was lashed fast across the two sledges for the purpose of keeping them together. I could not do anything to get this "ski"-end out of the way, and it caused me a great deal of trouble, as it stuck out across the points of my own " ski," and was always coming into collision with them. It was worst of all when we ran along the edge of a drift, for my "ski" would then get completely jammed, and I lost all control over them. For a long time I went on thus in a continual struggle with this hopeless " ski "-end, while Sverdrup stood in front gaily steering and thinking we were both sitting comfortably on behind. Our ship rushed on faster and faster; the snow flew round us and behind us in a cloud, which gradually hid the others from our view.

Then an ice-axe which lay on the top of our cargo began to get loose and promised to fall off. So I worked myself carefully forward, and was just engaged in making the axe fast when we rode on to a nasty drift. This brought the projecting " ski "-end just across my legs, and there I lay at once gazing after the ship and its sail, which were flying on

down the slope, and already showing dimly through the drifting snow. It made one quite uncomfortable to see how quickly they diminished in size. I felt very foolish to be left lying there, but at last 1 recovered myself and set off bravely in the wake of the vessel, which was by this time all but out of sight. To my great delight I found that, thanks to the wind, I could get on at a very decent pace alone. 1 had not gone far before I found the ice-axe, in trying to secure which I had come to grief. A little way further on 1 caught sight of another dark object, this time something square, lying in the snow. This was a box which contained some of our precious meat-chocolate, and which of course was not to be abandoned in this way. After this I strode gaily on for a .

'AND TIIEKIi I LAY GAZING AFTKK Tilt SHU' AND ITS SAIL."
*(By A. Bloc/i.)*

long time in the sledge-track, with the chocolate-box under one arm and the ice-axe and my staff under the other. Then I rame upon several more dark objects lying straight in my path. These proved to be a fur jacket belonging to me, and no less than three pemmican boxes. I had now much more than 1 could carry, so the only thing to be done was to sit down and wait for succour from the others who were following behind. All that could now be seen of our proud ship and its sail was a little square patch far away across the snowfield. She was going ahead in the same direction as before, but as I watched I suddenly saw her brought up to the wind, the tin boxes of her cargo glitter in the sun, and her sail fall. Just then Kristiansen came up with me, followed not long after by the other vessel. To them we handed over some of our loose boxes, but just as we were stowing them away Balto discovered that they had lost no less than three pemmican tins. These were much too valuable to be left behind, so the crew had to go back and look for them.

Meanwhile Kristiansen and I started off again, each with a tin box under his arm, and soon overtook Sverdrup. We now sat down to wait for the others, which was not an agreeable job in this bitter wind.

Sverdrup told us that he had sailed merrily off from the very start, had found the whole thing go admirably, and thought all the time that we two were sitting comfortably on behind. He could not see behind him for the sail, but after a long while he began to wonder why there was not more noise among the passengers in the stern. So he made an approach to a conversation, but got no answer. A little further on he tried again and louder, but with the same result. Then he called louder still, and lastly began to shout at the top of his voice, but still there was no response. This state of things needed further investigation; so he brought his boat up to the wind, went round behind the sail to see what was the matter, and was not a little concerned to find that both his passengers had disappeared. He tried to look back along his course through the drifting snow, and he thought he could see a black spot far away behind. This must have been my insignificant figure sitting upon the lost tin boxes. Then he lowered his sail, which was not an easy matter in the wind that was blowing, and contented himself to wait for us.

We had to sit a long time before the others caught us up again. We could just see the vessel through the snow, but her sail was evidently not up, and of her crew there was not a sign. At last we caught sight of three small specks far away up the slope, and the glitter of the sun on the tins they were carrying. Presently the sail was hoisted, and it was not long before they joined us.

We now lashed the sledges better together and made the cargo thoroughly fast, in order to escape a repetition of this performance. Then we rigged up some ropes behind, to which the crew could hold or tie themselves, and thus be towed comfortably along. In this way we got on splendidly, and never in my life have I had a more glorious run on " ski."

A while later Sverdrup declared that he had had enough of

"SAII.1NO (IN THK INLAND ICE." *(By*

A. *IltKh,/rvm plialp* steering, and I therefore took his place. We had now one good slope after another and a strong wind behind us. We travelled as we should on the best of "ski "-hills at home, and this for hour after hour. The steering is exciting work. One has to keep one's tongue straight in one's mouth, as we say at home, and, whatever one does, take care not to fall. If one did, the whole conveyance would be upon one, and once under the runners and driven along by the impetus, one would fare badly indeed, and be lucky to get off without a complete smash up. This was not to be thought of, so it was necessary to keep one's wits about one, to hold the " ski" well together, grip the pole tight, watch the ground incessantly, so as to steer clear of the worst drifts, and for the rest take things as they came, while one's " ski " flew on from the crest of one snow-wave to another.

Our meals were not pleasant intervals that day, and we therefore got through them as quickly as we could. We stopped and crept under shelter of the sails, which were only half lowered on purpose. The snow drifted over us as we sat there, but the wind at least was not so piercing as in the open. We scarcely halted for the usual chocolate distributions, and took our refreshment as we went along.

In the middle of the afternoon—this notable day by the way was September 19—just as we were sailing our best and fastest, we heard a cry of joy from the party behind, Balto's voice being prominent as he shouted " Land ahead! "

And so there was; through the mist of snow, which was just now a little less dense, we could see away to the west a long, dark mountain ridge, and to the south of it a smaller peak. Rejoicings were loud and general, for the goal towards which we had so long struggled was at last in sight.

Balto's own account of the occurrence runs as follows: "While we were sailing that afternoon I caught sight of a black spot a long way off to the west. I stared and stared at it till I saw that it really was bare ground. Then I called to

Dietrichson, ' I can see land!' Dietrichson at once shouted to the others that Balto could see land away to the west. And then we rejoiced to see this sight, which we had so often longed to see, and new courage came into our hearts, and hope that we should now happily and without disaster cross over this ice-mountain, which is the greatest of all ice-mountains. If we had spent many more days upon the ice, I fear that some of us would have fared badly. As soon as Nansen heard this he stopped and gave us two pieces of meat-chocolate each. It was always our custom, when we reached a spot which we had long wished to reach, to treat ourselves to the best food we had. So when we came to land after drifting in the ice, when we reached Umivik, when we had climbed to the highest point of Greenland, when we now first saw land on the west side, and lastly, when we first set foot upon bare ground again, we were treated to our very best—which was jam, American biscuits, and butter."

Though this first land we saw lay a little to the north of the line we had hitherto been following, I steered for it nevertheless, because the ice in this direction seemed to fall away more rapidly. However, the point was soon hidden in the snow again, and we went on with the wind straight behind us for the rest of the afternoon without getting any further sight of land. The wind grew stronger and stronger, we flew down slope after slope, and everything went famously.

A while later both the gradient and the wind slackened off for a time, but as evening began the breeze freshened and the slope grew steeper, and we rushed along through the dense driving snow more furiously than ever. It was already growing dusk, when I suddenly saw in the general obscurity something dark lying right in our path. I took it for some ordinary irregularity in the snow, and unconcernedly steered straight ahead. The next moment, when I was within no more than a few yards, I found it to be something very different, and in an instant swung round sharp and brought the vessel up to the wind. It was high time, too, for we were on the very edge of a chasm broad enough to swallow comfortably sledges, steersman, and passengers. Another second and we should have disappeared for good and all. We now shouted with all our might to the others, who were coming gaily on behind, and they managed to luff in time.

Here also Balto has something to say: " The same evening while we were still sailing along—it may have been about half-past seven and it was rather dark— we saw Nansen, who was in front on his 'ski,' signalling wildly to us, while he shouted ' Don't come here; it is dangerous!' We, who were tearing along at full speed, found it difficult to stop, and had to swing round and throw ourselves on our sides. At the same time we saw in front of us an awful crack in the ice, which was many hundred feet deep."

As to the rest of the day's sail my diary says: " This was the first crevasse, but was not likely to be the' only one, and we must now go warily. It was suggested that it was hardly advisable to sail any further that evening, but I thought it too early to stop yet, as we must take advantage of the wind. So SAILING IN MOONLIGHT. "WHEN THK SNOW LOOKED TREACHEROUS I HAD TO GO CAUTIOUSLY AND USE MY STAFF." *(fly A. Black, from a sktlch by the Author.)*

I left the sledges and went on in front to reconnoitre, while Sverdrup undertook the steering of our boat, and the sails of both of them were taken in a bit. The wind was strong enough even to blow me along, and I could run long stretches without moving a muscle, and so covered the ground fast

" When the snow looked treacherous I had to go cautiously and use my staff to see whether I had solid ground under foot, and, if not, to signal to the others to wait till I had found a safer route. In spite of all precautions, Sverdrup and Kristiansen all but came to grief once, as the snow fell in behind them just as they had passed over an unsuspected crevasse. Meantime the wind was steadily increasing, and the sails had to be taken in more and more to prevent

the sledges overrunning me. As we were all getting hungry biscuits were served out, but no halt was made to eat them.

" It was rapidly getting dark, but the full moon was now rising, and she gave us light enough to see and avoid the worst crevasses. It was a curious sight for me to see the two vessels coming rushing along behind me, with their square viking-like sails showing dark against the white snowfield and the big round disc of the moon behind.

" Faster and faster I go flying on, while the ice gets more and more difficult. There is worse.still ahead, I can see, and in another moment I am into it. The ground is here seamed with crevasses, but they are full of snow and not dangerous. Every now and then I feel my staff go through into space, but the cracks are narrow and the sledges glide easily over. Presently I cross a broader one, and see just in front of me a huge black abyss. I creep cautiously to its edge on the slippery ice, which here is covered by scarcely any snow, and look down into the deep, dark chasm. Beyond it I can see crevasse after crevasse, running parallel with one another, and showing dark blue in the moonlight. I now tell the others to stop, as this is no ground to traverse in the dark, and we must halt for the night.

" In the west we could now see land again against the evening sky, which still shows a faint trace of day. They were the same mountains we had first seen, but they now tower high above the horizon, and to the south of these peaks again there is a long ridge of rock protruding from the snow.

" It was a difficult business to get the tent up in this strong wind, and on the hard, slippery ice, which gave no hold for our guy-ropes, and we had to cut deep holes before we could make our staffs do duty as pegs. At last, after having fared worse than usual with the cold, we got the tent up and were able to crawl into a partial shelter. No one was inclined to do any cooking that evening, as even inside the tent the wind was much too aggressive, and the little feast which was to do honour to the day, and

which we had much looked forward to, was put off till next morning. So we were content to divide our last piece of Gruyere cheese, and then, well pleased with ourselves and our day's work, creep into our sleeping-bags. I now discovered for the first time that I had got the fingers of both my hands frozen during the afternoon's sail. It was too late now to rub them with snow, as they had begun to thaw on their own account, but that night the pain they gave me was almost unendurable, till I fell asleep in spite of it."

Early next morning, September 20, I started up with the consciousness that I had forgotten to wind my watch up overnight Unluckily Sverdrup had done exactly the same, and though we wound them both up at once it was now too late. This was, of course, rather unfortunate for our longitude observations, but we were now so near land that we could reckon our position with tolerable exactitude nevertheless.

When we looked out of the tent we could see the whole country to the south of Godthaabsfjord lying spread out before us, a rough mountainous tract with many deep valleys and lofty peaks. Those who remember their first sight of a mountain landscape in their childhood, with its sunlit peaks and stretches of glittering snow; who can remember how this new mysterious world fascinated and allured them—they will understand what our feelings were this morning. We were just like children, as we sat and gazed, and followed the lines of the valleys downwards in the vain search for a glimpse of the sea. It was a fine country that lay before us, wild and grand as the western coast of Norway. Fresh snow lay sprinkled about the mountain tops, between which were deep black gorges. At the bottom of these were the fjords, which we could fancy, but could not see. A journey to Godthaab in this kind of country looked anything but a simple matter.

We enjoyed our grand breakfast at our ease and leisure this morning, made tea unlimited, and simply revelled in cheese and oatmeal biscuits. It was glorious to have a treat like this once in a

The first crossing of Greenland • Fridtjof Nansen • 87

way. The morning was well gone before we got finally on the move. In the darkness of the evening before we had sailed into some very rough fissured ice, and we now had to bear away to the south to avoid the worst crevasses and reach smoother ground. The snow throughout this day's march was partly blown into drifts, especially where there was any unevenness in COASTING DOWN THE SLOPKS..

*(By the Author, from an instantaneous photograph.)*
the ice to catch it, and partly swept away by the wind, leaving the surface slippery and bare.

Presently we reached the top of a long, steep slope which had to be descended. Sverdrup and I started down on our " ski " and had a fine run. But our sledge was difficult to steer, and we had huge crevasses on each side, so at last we were constrained to take our "ski" off for safety's sake. We then went on, standing each on a runner of the sledge, and scraping and breaking with our feet in order to keep clear of the crevasses. The Lapps during this run were especially reckless, and let their sledge rush ahead much as it pleased. A little farther down we came upon a flat piece of ice, which was so slippery that it was quite difficult to cross. It looked like the frozen surface of a fake or pool. Beyond this we found ourselves in some nasty ice again, and after I had fallen through the snow several times I thought it best to put the " ski " on again. With them one-is of course much safer, as when one slides across the narrower crevasses their great length will generally hold one up. At this time we had a nasty experience, as our sledge came lengthways upon a crevasse, the snow-cornice of which gave way under one of the runners, and we only managed to drag it on to firm ground just as the whole mass of snow was falling in beneath it. Ravna and Balto nearly got into a worse scrape once, when they tried to take a short cut instead of following our course. They slid down on to a huge wide fissure, whereupon one of the runners cut straight through the snow and all but upset the sledge, and it

was only by the skin of their teeth that they escaped. I was furiously angry with them, of course, and rated them well for not being content to let us who went in front run such risks as were necessary. Kristiansen, too, was once on the point of losing his sledge in much the same way.

In the afternoon we had a hailstorm from the south and south-east. The hail stung our faces and the wind continually blew the sledges round, so that hauling became hard and difficult work. In this respect Sverdrup and 1 were worst off, as our load was very bulky and lay high on the sledge, which therefore exposed a large surface to the wind. The steel bars or keels under the runners would here have been an advantage, but they had long ago given way on the rough ice of the east coast.

We stopped for the day on a little flat, on which there was just enough drifted snow to hold our staffs, and the pitching of the tent was thus a simple matter. We had flattered ourselves that we should come within very easy distance of land, if not reach it altogether, this evening, and we werejconsider-ably disappointed when it seemed to us at the end of the day that we were almost as far off as ever.

Next day, September 21, snow was falling, and we could see nothing either of the land or the ice Found us. We had to grope our way as best we could, and there was no possibility of choosing the most advantageous course.

Towards noon we stopped in order to get an observation, if it were possible, as the sun now and again showed through the clouds. It was most important that we should know where we were, and the day before I had been too late for the purpose, having made a mistake about the time owing to my omission to wind my watch up. Luckily this time the sun was visible for a while, and I was able to get the altitude, my reckoning putting us at about lat. 64 13' N. This position was a little more northerly than I should have liked, the reason being that I had, as I have said, steered too much to the north as we were sailing after we came within sight of land. As

it will appear, we now had to pay some days' penalty for the mistake. If we had kept our original more southerly course, we should probably have been able to sail right down on to the land itself.

We now, therefore, turned more to the south when we set off again. In the course of the afternoon Sverdrup and I had a disagreement as to our best route—a thing which rarely happened. He wanted to take us more to the right up on to a ridge, as he had through the snow seen crevasses down below in front of us. I had seen nothing of the kind, and preferred to keep away to the left; but after some discussion Sverdrup prevailed, and we climbed the ridge, but only to find ourselves in the middle of some terrible crevasses. They were worse than any we had hitherto had to deal with, and we were very glad to clear out again and bear away more to the south. Here we found a tolerably smooth stretch of ice forming the bottom of a valley between two ridges, which were both quite a network of fissures. This alley or furrow narrowed in front of us, and ended in a defile, where the two ridges almost met. Here there was an abrupt fall in the ground, and the ice was uncomfortably rough. The place looked all but impracticable, and it was clearly no use trying to push on any farther while the weather was so thick. It seemed very likely that we had come too far already.

So it was settled that Dietrichson, Ravna, and Balto should pitch the tent, while Sverdrup, Kristiansen, and I should go down and see whether this broken ice would allow of a passage. Balto in his quality of under-cook was told to set the apparatus going, and have everything ready by the time we came back— some good pea-soup and plenty of hot water in the upper vessel, so that we could have some lemon-grog after supper.

We three soon had the Alpine rope round our waists and set off downwards. The ice was unusually rough and hard to pass, a simple chaos of sharp edges with fissures in between; but it was not dangerous, as the clefts were as a rule not deep.

We had not gone far before, to my astonishment, I saw a little dark spot down below us between some ridges covered with snow. It looked amazingly like water, but it was quite possible that it was only ice, so I said nothing to the others. But when I reached it and, putting my staff in, met with no resistance, our surprise and delight were quite unbounded. We threw ourselves down, put our lips to the surface, and sucked up the water like horses. After a month of incessant thirst and limited rations, the pleasure of having abundance of drink was indescribable. How many quarts we swallowed I should not like to say, but we plainly felt ourselves swell within and without during the operation. We then went on refreshed, but before we had gone far we heard some one shouting behind, and saw little Ravna running after us as fast as his short legs would carry him. We waited, fearing that there was something wrong in the camp, and I was much relieved to hear, when he came up, that all he wanted was the wicks for the spirit-lamp, which I usually carried in my pocket to keep them dry. I was anxious to know whether he had seen the water, for Ravna was the worst of all of us to drink when he had the chance, and I was half afraid that he would go at it till he made himself ill. He had seen the water, he told us, but had not had time to attend to it as he came down, though he meant to make up for the omission on the way back.

So we sent him off again and went on with our exploration. We presently found ourselves among the roughest ice I had ever seen, and all that I knew of from Captain Jensen's descriptions was nothing compared to this. Absolutely impassable it was not, but ridge upon ridge, each sharper and more impracticable than its neighbour, lay in all directions, while between them were deep clefts, often half-full of water, which was covered with a thin skin of ice not strong enough to bear.

Darkness was already coming on when we finally turned homewards. We were wretchedly done up by having to toil over this rough ground, on which

the soft snow lay deep in places, and were much comforted when we at last caught sight of the tent in the distance. As we passed the pool again we must needs have another drink. We lay down and let the water fairly flow down our throats. Our foreheads grew numb and cold, but that did not stop us. It was a truly divine pleasure to be able once more to drink to the very end of one's thirst. A cheering smell of good pea-soup met us as we entered our little tent, where we found the others squatting round the cooking machine. Balto had everything hot and ready for us, and was very proud of having carried out his orders to the letter.

His description, too, will serve to tell us what the rest of the party did while we were away.

"The other three went off with a rope round their waists to look for a way, while we—that is, Ravna, Dietrichson, and I—stayed behind to put up the tent. I had to make some pea-soup, too, for I was cook. So I got the machine out, but then found that there were no wicks, as Nansen had them in his pocket. So I sent Ravna off to get them, and when he came back he said he had found water and drunk his stomach full. When I heard this I caught up a tin box and ran as hard as I could go till I reached the pool. Then I threw myself down and began to drink. I had to lift my head up now and then to get breath, and then I went on drinking again. It tasted just like fresh, sweet milk, for we had not had any water for a whole month. Then I filled the tin and carried it up to the tent, and when Dietrichson saw it he lay down and drank till he could not hold any more. The tin was a very big one, but there was only just enough left for the pea-soup afterwards. Ve found plenty of water every day after this."

I am sure we all remember September 21, when we first found water. I really think it was one of the best days of the whole expedition.

Balto's fragrant soup was soon served out, and we set to work upon our supper with more than usual keenness, which means considerably more than it seems to say. Even Ravna could eat that

night. He used to declare he never could make a good meal because there was not enough to drink. This used to induce him to save up his rations, and he would often annoy us, and make our mouths water fruitlessly, by bringing out four or five spare biscuits at a time to show us. The truth probably was that his little body did not need as much food as our larger ones.

After supper we had lemon-grog, which consisted of citric acid, oil of lemon, sugar and hot water, a compound which to our tastes was nothing short of nectar, and which we sipped and enjoyed to the utmost as we lay in our sleeping-bags. For my own part it was a long time since I had been so tired. The laborious wading in the deep, fresh snow had tried my legs severely, and I do not fancy that the others were much better. But an evening like this in the tent brings a feeling of comfort and gratitude upon one, and a veil of forgetfulness is gently and soothingly drawn over all the pains and tribulations of the day.

A candle-end—the last we have—has been lighted for supper. This over, and all our preparations for the morrow made, we put out our light, bury our heads well beneath the hoods of the sleeping-bags, and pass swiftly and lightly over into the region of dreams.

Chapter XVIII.

*THE CROSSING OF THE "INLAND ICE"— THE*

*DESCENT TO AMERALIKFJORD.*

Before breakfast on September 22, while Balto was making the tea, Sverdrup and I climbed the ridge of ice which lay to the south of the tent for a reconnaissance. It was seamed with broad crevasses of unfathomable depth, most of them running parallel. Once I fell through a snow-bridge, but the fissure was so narrow that I could keep my hold on both its sides, and after some amount of struggling I managed to extricate myself. From the top of the ridge we had a fine view over the surrounding ice, and could see that our best course would probably be to keep a westerly direction for the present and turn southwards again lower down. As far as we can see, in front of us the ice seems to lie in fissured ridges, which all run westwards towards Godt-haabsfjord. We had been in doubt as to what valley or fjord the depression right before us could be, but we could now see that it must be Kangersunek. Altogether we were able to make out our whereabouts very well, and it was quite plain that we had come down four or five miles farther to the north than we had meant. We found breakfast ready when we got back to the tent, and afterwards it was settled that Sverdrup and I should go out again and explore the ice to the west, keeping to the north of the part we examined the previous evening. The others meanwhile must follow us with the four sledges as far as they could in the same direction, and, if they could get so far, stop at the last ridge we could see from here. As they had a fair wind behind them, I thought they would be able to manage a sledge each without much difficulty.

So Sverdrup and I started off, and with the wind behind us ran fast down on our slippery oak " ski." The ground was fairly easy till we came far enough to see down into the fjord, which was full of floating glacier-ice. Then the crevasses began, but at first they ran parallel, and we pushed a good way farther on. But presently things became utterly hopeless, a simple network of interlacing fissures, the ice protruding in small square islands from the midst of the blue abysses. Even the fancy could form no idea of the depth of these chasms, and the sight of the riven

The "inland Ice" As It Falls Into Kangkrsunkk.

*(By t/ie Author, after a photograph.)* and chaotic mass was unearthly in the extreme. Not a step farther could we go; there was nothing for us to do but eat our dinner and go back to look for the others. We found shelter in a little crevice, where the sun did its best to comfort us and temper the keenness of the biting wind.

On the way back I had the ill-luck to fall into a crevasse. I was left hanging by my arms, and the position was neither easy nor pleasant. The fissure was narrow indeed, but it was very difficult to get a footing with my " ski" on the slippery edges.

AX AWKWARD I'RKDlrAMENT. . *idrrrt.)* I was alone, too, as Sverdrup had taken a different line, and, being a long way on in front, saw nothing of my disaster. However, after struggling for a while, I at last managed to scramble out by myself. Strangely enough, none of us ever went further into these crevasses than to the armpits.

We had not gone far before we caught sight of the tent, which lay a little way to the north of us and on the very ridge where VIKW TOWAKUS KANCKKSfNKK FJORD (SF.PTEMBKR *32). ht Author.)* the party had been ordered to halt. They had reached this point about half an hour before, and the coffee was already under way. I must explain that we were now so near the coast that the coffee prohibition was not so stringently observed. It was not quite ready, and a short rest after our.little "ski" excursion did us good. After we had finished our coffee the tent was struck, and we set off in a southerly direction in order to skirt the ice stream which flowed down to the fjord, and in the middle of which we had just been. At first the ground was easy and we made good progress, though the wind did its best to hinder us by blowing the sledges round. In the evening, when it was already growing dusk, we reached a ridge of nasty, broken ice, which we had seen in the distance that morning, and which there seemed to be no way of

' ON TI1K.MORNING OF SEPTEMBER 23: ROL'CIIISH ICE.

*(/_ E. Nielsen, from a ffwto£ra/lt.)* avoiding. It was necessary to explore the ground here before moving any farther, and so there was nothing to be done but encamp and wait for daylight. While supper was preparing two of us went out again. The ice was undeniably awkward, but with enterprise we could no doubt get through. The ridge was luckily not broad, and the best route was evidently the straightest and shortest.

Next morning, September 23, Sverdrup went out upon another prospecting expedition, and came back with comparatively reassuring intelligence. The ice was not so bad as it had seemed to be at first sight, and it would be possible, if we put three men to each sledge, to get them along without carrying them.

Then we broke up camp and set out upon the heaviest bit REST AND REFLECTION (SF.PTKMRKR 23).

*(Ry the Author, from a.photograph.* of ice-travelling which we had yet had. In many places we had to carry each sledge bodily up the steep slopes of the ridges we had to cross, while as we descended the other side the unfortunate man who went behind had to hold it back with all his might. If he slipped, down went he and the sledge on to the heels of the others in front, and the whole group slid on together. Often, however, we were lucky enough to hit upon

W

§ the course of a frozen river, which gave us an easy though somewhat winding passage among the hummocks and ridges of ice, which often formed cliffs with nearly perpendicular walls. In one case we had to pass through a narrow cleft which only just gave us room, and at the bottom held a little stream only partially frozen, the water of which stood well above our ankles. In the afternoon we at last passed out of the worst of the ON THE AFTERNOON OF SEPTEMBER 23: INTO BETTER ICE AGAIN.

*(By A. Bloch, from a photograph.').*

ice, and could again take the sledges singly. The surface was now tolerably good, and it grew still better, but the wind was awkward, as it was always blowing the sledges round. A good way further on I discovered a moraine running across the ice in an easterly direction from the land. I imagined that this moraine must mark the limit between the streams of ice, more especially because it lay in a depression, and as I could not see any good in getting into the full current of another icestream, I determined to work down towards land on the north side of the moraine. We now halted, and the tent having been pitched and Balto sent out to look for water for the coffee, Sverdrup and I set off downwards towards the land to see whether the ice were practicable here. We had not gone far before we saw that our opportunity had come. We seemed to have crossed to the south side of the stream of ice which fell into Godthaab-sfjord, for the surface seemed to fall away to the south, or more correctly towards the land which lay straight before us. We went back with the encouraging news, and the whole party drank their coffee in the highest spirits. The prospect of once more feeling dry land beneath our feet was now not far off, and this was enough to fill us with delight. As soon as we could we went on again, and with the wind behind us made good progress, the ice being relatively smooth and yet often falling rapidly. We were disappointed, however, in our hope of reaching land that evening, as, owing to the gathering darkness, we presently had to stop. But on the whole we were more than satisfied with the day's work, as we had advanced a good deal farther than we had had any reason to hope in the morning.

Next day, September 24, we turned out early and set off with the determination to reach land that day. This time, too, we were not disappointed. We pushed on fast, as the gradient was often tolerably steep and gave us much help. The wind was fair, too, the ice easy, and everything promising. Some way down a reconnaissance proved necessary, as the ice here got rather rougher. I went on in front and soon found myself upon the brow of an ice-slope which overlooked a beautiful mountain tarn, the surface of which was covered with a sheet of ice. Beyond was a gorge through which a river from the tarn ran downwards, while to the right the great glacier sloped evenly down to its end moraine, and would have formed the most magnificent coasting-hill imaginable, but for the stones that lay scattered over its surface. Here was an easy descent for us, and no obstacles to separate us from our goal. I soon had the whole party by me, and we stood enjoying the sight of the land below. After I

had taken a couple of photographs, we set off down the last ice-slope. It was steep, steeper perhaps than any we had run down before, and we had to use our brakes; but the sledges went gaily, and soon we were safe and well upon the frozen tarn below the glacier, with the " Inland ice" for ever left behind.

" UPON THE BROW OF AN ICE-SLOPE WHICH OVERLOOKED A BEAUTIFUL MOUNTAIN TARN." *(By A. Block, from a fhatografk.)*

We now pushed across the tarn towards the river on the other side. The ice was not everywhere quite safe, but by moving carefully we reached the rocks beyond without mishap, took off the " crampons " which we had been using the last few days, and, like schoolboys released, ran wildly about the shore. Words cannot describe what it was for us only to have the earth and stones again beneath our feet, or the thrill that went through us as we felt the elastic heather on which we trod, and smelt the fragrant scent of grass and moss. Behind us lay the " Inland ice," its cold, grey slope sinking slowly towards the lake; before us lay the genial land. Away down the valley we could see headland beyond headland, covering and overlapping each other .

" BEHIND US LAY THE ' INLAND ICE,' ITS COLD, GKEY SLOPK SINKING SLOWLY TOWARDS THE LAKE." *(frartt a fhotografh.)* as far as the eye could reach. Here lay our course, the way-down to the fjord.

But it was high time to think of dinner. Neither the highest spiritual enjoyment nor the overwhelming sense of an end attained is sufficient to make one oblivious of bodily wants, but on the contrary, the consciousness of difficulty overcome renders material indulgence doubly sweet. There was now a trace of gladness to be discovered even in Ravna's face. He had over and over again abandoned all hope of feeling solid earth beneath his feet again, poor fellow I and the first thing he and Balto did when they had brought their sledge safe to shore was to run straight away up the mountain side.

While dinner was preparing and the

last remnant of our much regretted jam being weighed out, Sverdrup and I went on a little way down the valley to examine the ground. We passed a couple of small lakes with a moraine between, and beyond the second we climbed up the mountain side and got a good view downwards. The valley, at least as far as we could see, seemed tolerably easy of passage. When we got back dinner was waiting for us under the shelter of some great boulders, where stretched in the heather we could enjoy its pleasures to the full.

Afterwards we went to work to prepare each his burden for the land march down to the fjord. Our object was to take as much as possible of the most necessary things, but not to overload ourselves, or we should get over the ground too slowly, seeing that we wished to despatch two men to Godthaab as soon as could be. So that we might have the necessary material for boat-building to begin upon at once, we took some bamboo poles with the idea that we could fetch some more while the work of construction was going on.

I now for the first time was able to form some idea of Ravna's real strength. During the crossing he. had had a lighter load than any of us, and nevertheless he was always complaining that it was so heavy for an old man like him, while not seldom he lagged behind and kept us waiting for him. But now there were six piles of necessary things, as large as we thought we could manage, and I was fairly astonished when I saw Ravna catch up his bag of clothes and other private property in addition to his load. I told him that it would be too much for him and that I did not mean him to carry both, but he declared that he would not part with his clothes-bag, which had his Testament in it, and that he could manage the whole very well. And though his load was thus nearly double as heavy as ours, which we found quite heavy enough, he actually managed to carry it, and went quite as well as any of us. No doubt he thought that there was no need to save up his strength now, and that he would show us for once in a way what he was good for. It was quite true what Balto was always saying in admiration, " Ah! he is a strong chap, that Ravna, and no mistake about it."

The rest of our things were packed on the sledges and well covered with tarpaulins. These preparations together with our afternoon tea being finished, we set off down the valley. The descent was steep in many places: our course lay over piles of debris and stretches of bog, and as our loads were heavy, the progress was naturally only slow. Several times on the way Ravna exclaimed enthusiastically, " It does smell good here, just like the mountains in Finmarken, where there is good reindeer pasture." And, true enough, the whole valley was redolent of mountain grasses and reindeer-moss, and we all breathed the fragrant air slowly and with infinite delight.

Late in the afternoon we reached a long, narrow lake, into which we saw, to our surprise, that a huge glacier projected from the western side of the valley. It was evidently an arm which protruded from the main body of the " Inland ice " beyond the mountain which lay to the west of us. When after descending a steep slope we came to the lake, Sverdrup and Balto hit upon the idea of putting their two loads together and dragging them across the ice on a sledge hastily made of the bamboo poles which they carried. Ravna and I, the smallest and biggest of the party, then followed their example, and put our burdens together; but it was no easy matter to construct a sledge which we could use out of nothing but a " ski "-staff and the wooden theodolite-stand. After a number of attempts, however, we succeeded fairly well, but by this time the others had pushed on a long way ahead, and we had to hurry. The ice on the lake was anything but strong, and it rocked uncomfortably under our tread in many places. When we reached the middle of the lake, and had passed a little island, we found it worse than ever. Here the ice had been much broken up, apparently by the fall of fragments from the glacier opposite, many of which lay

scattered round about us. We now proceeded with rather

"WE HKACHED A LONG AND NARROW LAKE INTO WHICH.
GLACIEK PROJECTED FROM THE WESTERN SIDK."
(f-'rvtn aphotoffrafh.) more care, and I presently discovered in the dusk a dark patch of open water lying right in front of us. The pieces of ice on which we now stood were not even frozen together, and they rocked so violently beneath us that it was quite difficult to keep one's balance. The others shouted to us from shore with all their might, but without their warning it was plain that we must beat a hurried retreat, and we were glad indeed to get on to firmer ground again without having had a ducking. We now kept closer to the others and closer in to shore, but as we went on the ice grew worse and worse, and presently we had finally to take to the land. We now found an excellent camping-place, and as it was already late in the evening, and our unaccustomed loads had made us tired, we determined to halt for the night. For the first time we had real good springy heather to lie upon, and we stretched ourselves upon the soft couch with supreme delight, while the mountain air blew over us with a peculiar resinous and narcotic fragrance which comes from a kind of heath abundant in Greenland.

While we were eating our supper inside the tent, Ravna, who sat next the door, was told to light up a fire of heather outside. The necessary material had been already collected, and we thought we should like to have the cheering blaze of a camp-fire to look at. But Ravna did not see it in this light at all, and, with the usual perversity of a nomad Lapp, had a number of objections ready at hand. He did not see any use in it, as we should want the fuel next morning to boil our water with. I considered there was plenty of stuff lying round about us, but this argument Ravna met by asserting that he had no birchbark to make a fire with. At this we all burst out laughing, and I represented to him that this obstinacy was not at all

amiable, that he would not have more birch-bark at his disposal if he waited till the next morning, and that we should be much obliged to him if he would go and light the fire at once. Thereupon he went out, and it was not long before we had a great fire crackling and blazing outside and throwing a warm and romantic glow into the dark little tent and upon the figures of its occupants, whose weather-beaten faces shone strangely and picturesquely in the fitful light. It was quite a novelty to us to be able to see what we were eating, and a very welcome change after the absolute darkness to which we had often been accustomed.

I now asked Ravna several times to come in again, as there was no need to attend to the fire any longer, which would burn quite well by itself; but now that he had once undertaken the work he was not to be prevailed upon to abandon it.

After supper the smokers had a pipe of moss or grass, and we all stretched ourselves at length round the blazing fire, comforting ourselves to the full with the feeling that we had seen the last of the " Inland ice," and had gained our long-wished-for goal. The light of our camp-fire spread out into the night, and the flames rose high against the dark starry sky, where the familiar northern lights were playing and the yet unrisen moon showed faint signs of her approach.

I lay and amused myself by watching the look of glee and something approaching to roguishness which was visible in Ravna's hitherto discontented face. He was all smiles now, and to the question what he thought of the country, he answered with enthusiasm that he would like to live here. I then asked him seriously whether he would like to bring his reindeer over. He said he would indeed, but it would cost him too much; but when I suggested that in that case the Danish or Norwegian Government might send him over free, he declared that he would not hesitate a moment. Good pasture there was, and plenty of wild reindeer, for he had seen their tracks that afternoon, and he would get rich in no time. The only difficulty would be to find anything to burn in the winter, but no doubt he could manage as some Lapps had done on an island at home in Finmarken—cut peat for winter fuel. Old Ravna finished his eulogy by saying, " I like the west coast well: it is a good place for an old Lapp to live in: there are plenty of reindeer; it is just like the mountains in Finmarken." He evidently felt almost as if he were back in his native haunts.

It was a glorious night, with the peculiar mild air of a summer evening at home. The conversation dies away of itself, thought follows thought out into space, each seeking and attaching itself to the rays of the moon which is just rising above the distant ridges, and all arc at last spun together into one tangle of ideas, till every thread is lost in the confusion, and the thinker drops into a comfortable dose. It was late at night before we recovered ourselves sufficiently to go decently to bed. Sverdrup declares that never in his life has he had so glorious an evening as when he lay by that heather fire and smoked his pipe of moss. Several of us no doubt are ready to support him here.

THE MOKNI.NG Ol bEPTEMBEK 25: PREPARING FOR THE START.

*(From a photograph.*

Next morning, September 25, after I had taken a photograph of the glacier opposite, we set off again with our loads on our backs across the ridg on which the tent had stood. On the top we found a well-trodden reindeer path which led down to an arm of the lake below. This arm was not entirely frozen, but we managed to find a passage across it. At the farther end of the lake we halted for a rest, and while there saw a hare come

Y bounding along in the distance and stop under a rock. I got a rifle out at once and stalked her to within a hundred yards or so. I could scarcely distinguish her yellowish white coat from the snow, and the distance was long. But as there seemed no hope of getting nearer, I fired, and she fell stone-dead with the ball through her neck. The others were much delighted, as they had been waiting in great excitement to see whether they were going to have fresh meat for supper or not.

Then we went on again down the narrow valley, scrambling down steep declivities and over stony moraines. Some way farther on on the west side another arm of the " Inland ice " reached into the valley. This drove a huge moraine in front of it, and formed here and there high pinnacles and ridges, which were, however, so covered with clay and stones that it was often difficult to distinguish ice from bare land.

Later in the morning we came upon the top of a precipitous slope, at the foot of which was a lake, into which the " Inland ice " descended from the east. From here we could see a long way over the great icefield, as far as Nunatarsuk, the land on the eastern side of Kangersunek. The river we had been following hitherto now joined that which flowed out of this lake not far from its point of exit The map we had been trusting to proved completely wrong; we had still some twelve-miles at least to go before we reached the fjord, and our hope of getting there to-night was vain.

At noon we reached another lake with broad, flat shores. Here we saw abundant traces of geese, which showed it to be a very favourite resort. Possibly it was a general resting-place during the autumn passage down the edge of the " Inland ice " while the lakes are still open.

Here, too, in the clay, as all along our route where such marks could be left, the tracks of reindeer were very numerous, and some of them at least were not more than two or three days old, but they all pointed downwards towards the fjord. I kept my eyes well about me, and scanned unremittingly the brown slopes that lay around us on every side, but to no purpose, as not a sign of deer was to be seen. On the south shore of the lake, which we christened " Goose Pool," we camped in the deep heather to enjoy our dinner.

It was a splendid day: the sun shone warm and bright, the sky lay clear and blue above, and round about us was as fine shooting-ground as a sportsman could wish to see. It must be a simple Eldorado earlier in the year, when the reindeer are here in their numbers, and the wild geese fly screaming along the lake, in concert, perhaps, with duck and snipe and many other of the Greenland waders.

In the evening we camped on a flat piece of ground by a little tarn amid brown slopes of heather and the best reindeer ground imaginable. We set about to cook our hare in a vessel which had originally been a spirit-can. Just as it was ready the pot upset into the fire, and we lost all our soup. The hare was rescued and divided, but her poor meagre little body gave little enough to each of six hungry men. The small portion we got, however, was enjoyed amazingly. Ve were not accustomed to fresh meat, and it was marvellously easier to bite than the hard pemmican, which is very difficult for any one with defective teeth to deal with. Sverdrup and I, who were the worst off of the party in this respect, used always to select the most mouldy parts, as they were softer and easier to masticate. The evening was clear, like yesterday; the northern lights were playing above us, the camp-fire burning brightly by our side, and our spirits were perhaps even brighter still.

On September 26 we had at last a reasonable expectation of reaching the fjord. We followed the'river downwards, passing at times over sandy hills and terraces, at times across flat, sandy stretches in which the river ran in a deep channel between steep banks. The ground was often covered with thickets of willow and alder, the bushes of a man's height or so. The alders were still green, but the willow leaves yellow and withered, the result apparently of the early frost of some few nights ago. Now, on the contrary, we had 55 Fahr. in the daytime in the shade, while the nights were mild as September nights at home. The cause of this high temperature was evidently a warm and dry easterly or south-easterly wind very like the "fohn" of the Alps. Such winds are not unusual on the west coast of Greenland.

These flat stretches of ground are often, too, cut transversely by watercourses which come from the adjacent slopes. These have ploughed deep in the soft, sandy clay, and they were sometimes unpleasant enough to cross when their steep banks were thickly overgrown with willow scrub. Geologically this valley was extremely interesting, and very instructive to the observant eye. At one spot a long way down, the sand-bank had lately fallen into the stream, and masses of old mussel shells were exposed to view. These shells tell us plainly how these great, sandy stretches have been formed. Once the fjord has filled this valley, and the clay and sand brought down by the river from the glacier moraines have settled upon the sea-floor, forming a gradually increasing deposit which has finally taken the water's place. Subsequently the land has risen, and that it has done so is clearly shown by the presence here of these shells of a salt-water mussel (*Afytilus edulis*) of a post-glacial period. Whether this rise of the land has taken place at intervals and by jerks, or gently and continuously, is as yet uncertain. The latter view is commonly adopted, and is supported by most of the phenomena. No doubt the layers of sand and clay lie in terraces, but even if the land has risen gently and continually, it is held that this might be explained by the supposition that during certain climatic periods of heavy rain-and-snow-fall, the river has brought down considerably more matter than during the intervening and less productive periods, an alternation of conditions which might well lead to this step-like formation. I cannot for several reasons subscribe to this view, but as the subject is difficult and its discussion would take too much space here, I must be content to acknowledge the question as still open.

The sea-floor thus having at one time or other risen, the river proceeded to cut its winding channel through the deposits of sand and clay which now lie high and dry. Soft stuff like this is easy to cut through and undermine, and bank after bank has therefore slipped into the river, and in the course of ages been carried along by the stream to its outflow

in the fjord, where it has gone to form new but precisely similar deposits. The mighty forces of nature which work in these regions are never at rest; some are chiselling out valleys and fjords, leaving peaks and ridges behind; others, or, more correctly, other forms of the same forces, are striving to level and fill up the excavations already made.

The glaciers are excavating and hollowing out the valleys and fjords— these characteristic narrow glacier-fjords with their smooth, precipitous sides, simple chasms gouged out of the hard gneiss rock. The same streams of ice are driving before them their huge moraines, which, as the great moving mass from time to time draws back, are left as long barriers stretching across the fjord-mouth or valley-floor. At the same time the clay and grit of which these moraines consist, as well as that of the so-called "ground-moraines" which lie beneath the ice, are carried off again by the milky glacier river and deposited in the fjord at its mouth. Here the material does its filling up and levelling work, and forms eventually the flat, sandy stretches that lie at the head of Greenland and Scandinavian fjords. These are the " orer " which appear so commonly in such Norwegian place-names as Trondhjesmoren and Laerdal-soren, and are to be seen in hundreds on the Greenland coast.

For the geologist, therefore, Greenland, which is now passing through its ice-age, is of great importance. Phenomena, which would be otherwise unintelligible to him, are here made clear throughout their history; here he can see close at hand, and in their full activity, the mighty forces which he can behold elsewhere only in the mirror of his fancy, or which he can at most study in the pigmy remnants which we still have in Europe —remnants from the time when the north of the continent and the high regions of the Alps were buried under mantles of ice like that which now forms the great " Inland ice " of Greenland.

A long way down the valley we had to wade the river, but soon afterwards discovered, to our annoyance, that the

other side was impracticable. Here the river was too deep to wade, and it was either a case of going back or of climbing the shoulder of the mountain to the west to see if we could thus obtain a passage. While we were discussing the point we thought we would stop and have our dinner, and then see what was to be done.

After we had finished, Balto disappeared, and presently I caught sight of him high up on the mountain side. He was waving his hat in high glee and looking westwards: he could evidently see the fjord. He soon joined us again, carrying a big reindeer-horn, and told us that he had seen a great sheet of blue water which must be the fjord, and that the inner end was covered with ice. We all now climbed the slope as fast as our legs would take us; we longed to get a sight of the sea; possibly the whortle-berries which Balto promised enticed us too; and, what was more, the flies down below made a longer stay there unendurable. From the ridge we had a glorious view down the valley. The river went winding along through the sandy flat, and beyond lay the fjord, a blue expanse stretching far away among the high mountains which hemmed it in. What Balto had taken to be ice we could now see to be the estuary-sands, which quite filled the head of the fjord.

We had not far to go now. Our joy was great when we found a little lower down some old footprints from a Greenlander's boots in the sand by the river-side. They were probably the tracks of some reindeer hunter, who some months ago had visited the now deserted valley, in which the well-trodden paths showed that at certain seasons it must be frequented by numbers of deer. Here we rested by the first signs of human life which we had found on the western side, if we except certain equivocal traces Balto had hit upon, and doubtfully attributed by him to either man or bear.

After we had climbed one more willow-grown ridge we had the fjord at last straight before us, and to the bare sands, through which the river still wound for a long way farther, we had only a short slope to descend. Just below us was a little flat stretch grown with heather and scrub and close by a tarn. This was the very spot for our camp, as the hill would shelter us from the east wind, which was now blowing down the valley straight from the "Inland ice." We ran down, threw our burdens into the heather and ourselves by their side, and allowed the consciousness of having reached our destination to comfort and soothe our wearied bodies. Much remained for us yet to do certainly; four were to go back and fetch the rest of the baggage, while Sverdrup and I were to go to Godthaab and take measures— of what kind we had as yet but vague ideas —for the relief of the others. One thing at least is certain, that we are once more at the sea level, if not exactly at its edge, and are in all probability at the end of our toils and sufferings. A difficulty has been overcome, a difficulty which many, perhaps most, of those qualified to judge have deemed insuperable. It is no wonder then that the mood of the party was at this moment one of pure, unalloyed satisfaction.

After a little rest and refreshment two of us went up the mountain side to the east to have a look down the fjord. On its north side the ground, as far as we could see from here, was so rough that there was very little probability of our being able to reach Godthaab that way. To get to Narsak, which lies on the south side, would no doubt be easier, but we were not certain of finding any people who understood a European language. The sea route was obviously the safest, and after determining to set to work with our boat-building at once, we went back to the tent.

We had brought down with us two bamboos and one " ski" staff, but had nothing for the ribs. For these the bent ash rods fixed at the back of the sledges would have been just the thing, but they were up by the ice, and it would have taken two or three days to get them. So it was necessary to find something else, and our thoughts went straight, of course, to the willow bushes, which lay in plenty round about us, and were sometimes as much as six or seven feet

high. Ribs made of these would not be as straight as we could wish, and would not stretch the canvas very evenly. Our boat was not likely to prove very fast in these circumstances, but the main thing was to get her to carry us. We set about detaching the tent floor at once, so as to have it ready for next morning. It was settled that Balto should stay and help us with the sewing, while the other three were to go back for the rest of our goods after breakfast.

We turned out early on the morning of September 27 and made a very meagre breakfast of bread and pemmican, to which our last ration of tea was added. Of the pemmican we had brought down a good provision, but it had disappeared amazingly fast, and of the remainder Sverdrup and I wanted as much as we could get for our voyage, seeing that it was impossible to tell how long it would last.

After breakfast Sverdrup and Balto went to work upon the boat at once, while I took some observations and the others made preparations for their return. After having received their rations for the day, they were ready to start, and I gave them their final instructions. First and foremost they were to secure the instruments and diaries, and then bring as much of the rest as they could, including of course all the provisions. Balto was to join them later.

Then they started off up the valley with our best wishes and in the most glorious weather, while we went on with our work. Originally it had been my idea to build the boat long and narrow in order that she might travel better, but Sverdrup considered that this would entail too much sewing, and that it would be better to use the tent-floor just as it was, giving it the form of a boat and patching it wherever necessary. This would not make an ornamental craft of her, but it would save an immense deal of sewing, and to Sverdrup, as a sailor, I of course at once gave way. Unluckily, as I have already said, we had left our sailmaker's palm behind in our cache on the east coast. If we had had it now we should have got through our work a good deal faster, for as it

was we had to drive the needle through the hard canvas with our bare hands. Another difficulty, and a worse one, which we had to contend against, was a plague of small black flies, which swarmed round us, settled on our faces, necks, and hands, and bit us villainously. It was impossible OUR CAMPING-PLACE NEAR AMERALIKFJORD ON THE EVENING OF SEPTEMBER 27. *From a photograph*.) to escape them, and they were almost worse than the mosquitoes on the other side of Greenland.

After I had tried my hand at the sailmaker's needle for a while, and found that it was work to which I was eminently unsuited, I left the task to the others, who at this kind of thing, as well as at much else, were simply masters, and went off with my axe to the forest, or, more correctly speaking, to the nearest thicket of willows, to look for some branches which would make ribs for the boat In many places the bushes of the thicket were so high that I quite disappeared in them, and the tops of some I could scarcely touch with the tips of my fingers. There were plenty of branches that were thick enough, and one bush had THE BOAT AND IIEK BVII.IIF.R stems as massive at the root as a grown man's thigh, but they were as a rule desperately crooked, and to find any that would serve our purpose was by no means an easy matter. At last I managed to collect as many as we wanted. They were anything but straight and even, but as we had nothing else we must needs put up with them. By the evening the boat was finished. She was no boat for a prize competition indeed; in shape she was more like a tortoise-shell than anything else, but when we tried her in a pool close by we found she carried us both well, and altogether we were hugely pleased with her. Her dimensions, I may add, were: length, 8 ft. 5 in.; breadth, 4 ft. 8 in.; depth, 2 ft.

As yet, however, we had no oars made. I had found some forked willow branches, which I intended to stretch canvas across, so that we could use them as blades, while for the shafts we had pieces of bamboo. I had not got on very far with this job, however, as on this particular day, as well as on the two or three preceding, I had a racking headache, and was not up to much work of any kind.

Next morning, September 28, Balto also left us. We watched him stride away up the valley, and the active fellow joined the others up by the edge of the ice the very same evening. By noon our two pair of sculls were made, and the boat ready to be launched. The most difficult part had been the thwarts, as we had nothing to make them of but a slender round ash theodolite-stand and two thin pieces of bamboo. They were, indeed, the scantiest seats it has ever been my ill luck to sit upon, and I devoutly hope never again to have to go through a similar penance.

After we had had our dinner—which was as meagre a meal as our breakfast had been—we packed up the sleeping-bags, our clothes, and everything that we were not going to take, in the tent, which was covered with stones, and protected as well as we could manage it against the weather. In the boat we stowed our clothes-bags with as much clothing as we thought necessary. To sleep in we had borrowed the two reindeer-skin tunics of the Lapps, and we each also had our pair of Lapp boots with the necessary grass lining. We took also the camera, a gun and cartridges, a stock of provisions packed partly in tins and partly in canvas, a supply of biscuits being stowed away in my canvas trousers, two cups which were also to do duty as balers, and lastly a cooking-pot, which was really the upper vessel of our great cooker deprived of the original felt covering.

As soon as all our preparations were made we got under way. First we took our baggage down to the sands, and then the boat itself. We had hoped to be able to row all the way down the river and straight out to sea, but here, again, we met with the most unexpected difficulties, as the water was so shallow that rowing was out of the question. When we were both in the boat it was an absolute impossibility, so I, as the heavier, got out to walk across the sands, while

Sverdrup sat in to try and punt himself along alone. But this was no great improvement, as he had soon to get out and wade in the cold water, while he towed the boat behind him, which was no agreeable work. It was seldom that he could punt, and still more rarely that he could row, and progress was therefore very slow.

Nor was it much fun for me to tramp over the sands, for the ground was soft and I often sank well up to my knees. We both had incredibly hard work in one way and another; again and again we were buried to the hips in mud and water, and half a day's toil of this kind told terribly on our legs. The sticky stuff held our feet fast at every step, and we were thoroughly tired out when we at last reached a certain point well out in the fjord, where we had hoped to be able to finally put to sea.

But here we discovered that we were by no means at the end, as the river now spread out in a delta, the branches of which were so shallow that it became impossible even to drag the boat, and it had to be carried for the rest of the way. But it was now evening, and we thought we might as well halt for the night. So we carried the boat up on to higher ground with the idea of turning it over and using it as a tent to sleep under. Then we brought up our things, and to our great comfort got some dry clothes on after our long wade in the icy water. Next we found a good place for a fire, put a hoop of copper wire on our cooking-pot, and I went off to get some water while Sverdrup made the fire up. There was no lack of fuel round about us, and by the time I got back the pile was blazing well. The pot was hung over it, and when we had put our reindeer-skin coats on and drawn up to the fire we felt thoroughly comfortable. We had enjoyed our comfort just long enough to see the water begin to boil, when the pot and all its contents fell into the fire and completely extinguished it. The ears of the vessel to which the hoop had been fastened had melted off and caused the disaster. There was nothing to be done but begin from the beginning again. We put a new hoop on the pot—

this time with more solidity—more water was fetched, the fire resuscitated, and we were soon able to enjoy the sight of boiling water again. The pea-soup was excellent, and we had another splendid evening. The last flush of day soon vanished behind the mountains in the west; the stars grew more and more distinct in the darkening sky, and presently the moon came too and shone down upon us as we sat by our sinking fire and talked of the " Inland ice " as a distant dream.

Afterwards we each chose out a willow-bush, crept under, curled ourselves up in our fur coats, and were soon asleep. To use the boat as a tent, we thought, when it came to the point, was an unnecessary waste of energy.

Chapter XIX.

*OUR VOYAGE, AND ARRIVAL AT GODTHAAB.*

Next morning, September 29, we carried the boat down to the water. It was desperate work plodding along with it through this sticky sand, in which our feet sank deep, and fixed themselves, and wheezed like the piston of an air-pump as we pulled them out again at each step. But at last we reached the water's edge, and set the boat down, to go back and get the rest of our things. There were any number of gulls down here, and we had looked forward to the prospect of a supply of fresh meat; but, unfortunately, they kept at a respectful distance, and we had no chance of a shot. When we got back to our camping-place, we came to the conclusion that we had had quite enough of the sands, and determined to carry the other things over the higher ground, rough and difficult though it was.

When we got down to the shore again, we saw that the boat was now afloat a long way out in the water, as, while we had been away, the fjord had risen to such an extent as to flood all the outer part of the sands. Luckily Sverdrup had been thoughtful enough to moor her fast by driving a stake into the ground, though we had left her so far from the edge of the water that we thought she was quite safe. He now waded out to her, and rowed her in to a point of land close by, while I moved the baggage to meet him at the same spot. Thus, at last, after a day's labour, we had overcome one more obstacle, and were ready to embark on a good sea-way.

After we had had our dinner we set out upon our first voyage, our destination being the farther side of the fjord, along which we meant to coast on our way outwards. We discovered at once that our boat travelled much better than we had expected. She did not prove to be a fast craft, certainly, but we could get along in her, and reached the other side of the fjord after what we considered to be a remarkably quick passage. Nor was water-tightness one of our boat's virtues, for we had to take to baling with one of the soup-bowls about every ten minutes.

Just here, the head of the fjord formed a little bay or inlet, which seemed to us, in our present state of mind, an unusually attractive spot. It ended in a peaceful, gentle valley—a valley of long, brown slopes and stretches of moss and stones, and skirted by low, round hills; just the ground that is most welcome to the reindeer and his pursuer. Our interests still centred in all that we could connect with food and the pursuit of game, and the more poetic reader must forgive us. To us, at this time, this was the most beautiful side of Nature; and for her true beauty—the lofty peaks, the snow-clad mountains, the precipitous cliffs, and all the glories of barrenness, glories of which Ameralikfjord has enough and to spare—we had no eyes of appreciation. Such delights are for that true lover of Nature, the tourist, as he wanders among them on his comfortable steamer, with abundance of warm clothing and good food.

Then we worked along the stupendous cliffs which form the northern shore of Ameragdla, as the inmost branch of Ameralikfjord is called, and stopped for the night at a spot where we could land our boat and find flat ground enough to sleep upon —accommodation not to be procured everywhere. We had not advanced much that day, but we were quite satisfied, and

very pleased to be on the sea once more. Our chief delight, however, was the prospect of eating our fill of good fresh meat after nearly seven weeks of the driest of food. During our row I had shot six big blue gulls. At first I missed several times, as the birds kept out of range, but at last one ventured nearer, and then I had no further trouble. Gulls, as most people know, are inquisitive birds; so when I had thrown one dead body out to float, the others must needs come to look at it, and I brought down one after the other, and stocked our larder for the time.

These gulls are big birds, and we determined to have two apiece for our evening meal. They were skinned, put two at a time into boiling water, and cooked as little as possible.

SHOOTING GULLS 1 ROM TIIK BOAT. *(By A. Bloch, after photosrnfh aiut s/iclcli* Sverdrup was afterwards asked whether he took care to clean them properly. " Oh, I don't know," he answered; " I saw Nansen pull something out of them, and I suppose it was part of the inside; and some more came out in the pot while they were cooking. All I can say is, I never tasted better birds in my life." And he was quite right: we both thought we had never had anything which could be compared with those gulls; the tenderest of chickens could not have been better. Whether the cause lay in our appetites, or the peculiar method of preparation, I will not attempt to decide. We looked for no reason at the time, but tore our birds in pieces as fast as teeth and fingers would allow. It was not long before the first two had disappeared, and then we set to work upon the second with greater deliberation and more prolonged enjoyment. We finished with the broth in which they had all been boiled. This had a very characteristic, gamey taste, which added much to its peculiarity, though we were not quite certain to what we should attribute its origin. language, in fact, has no words which can adequately describe the satisfaction of the two savages who sat that evening on the northern shore of Anieragdla, and dipped each his hands into the pot, fished out the body of a gull, and con-

veyed it, piece by piece, head, feet, and all, into the depths of his hungry stomach. The light of the fire meanwhile was almost dimmed by the brighter glory of the northern lights. The whole heaven blazed, both north and south; the lights swept onwards, and then returned again; and suddenly a whirlwind seemed to pass across the sky, driving the flames before it, and gathering them together at the zenith, where there was a sparkling and a crackling as of burning fire, which almost dazzled the eyes of the onlooker. Then the storm seemed to cease, the light died slowly away, there was nothing left but a few hazy flecks, which sailed across the starlit sky as we stood there still gazing. Such a display of northern lights I have never seen, either before or since. And there, below us, lay the fjord, cold and impassive, dark and deep, and girt round about by steep walls of rock and towering mountains, the familiar fjord landscape of the west of Norway.

Next day things did not go quite so well with us, as in the course of the morning a head-wind sprang up, which blew so z hard that, instead of making progress, we were almost driven backwards, and our little cockle-shell danced up and down upon the waves to such an extent that there seemed every chance of our capsizing. She proved a good sea-boat, however, and never shipped a drop of water, except that which ran in unceasing streams through her bottom. Against the breeze, though, she travelled very heavily, and there was nothing to be done but land, rest meanwhile, and hope that the wind would drop towards evening. This it eventually did, and we embarked again. It was not long before we reached Nua, as the point is called which lies at the mouth of Itivdlek Fjord, the northern branch of Ameralik. Here the country was less wild and broken, and, with its low ridges covered with moss and heather, promised excellent reindeer-ground.

It was a fine, still evening, and we now set about to cross the fjord. This was the longest sea-passage we had as yet attempted; but all went well, and we were soon across by the opposite shore. It was dark by this time, and we put to land to get some supper. Here, however, we found neither fuel nor water, and had to eat our food cold and without drink, a state of things to which we were, nevertheless, well used. We had thought of pushing on farther during the night, but we now saw some ominous storm-clouds coming up from the west, and gathering about the sharp, wild peaks on the north side of the.fjord. The night, too, was so dark that it would have been difficult to cross the fjord again, as we wished; and so we determined to bring the boat ashore, and get a little sleep, in the hope that the moon might come to our help later. During the operation of beaching the boat, Sverdrup was unlucky enough to fall into the water, which is not very pleasant just before bedtime, and when one has so little in the way of a change of clothes.

There was no improvement in the weather, and we slept till the morning of October i. It was a splendid sunny day, and there was a gentle wind blowing to help us.

In the course of the morning we crossed the fjord again, and went ashore to get ready a substantial dinner of two gulls apiece and a soup of unsurpassed excellence. To the broth in which the birds had been cooked we added peas and bread, and the compound was so invigorating that we literally felt the strength grow in us as we took down one basin after another.

Unluckily, at this spot where we had landed there was a great abundance of crowberries, and as a matter of course we added BY AMF.RALIKFJORD ON TIIK MOKNING OF OCTOBER I.

*(l"rim (i photograph.)*

them to our bill-of-fare. It was long since we had had access to fresh, wholesome, vegetable food, and we actually indulged ourselves beyond the bounds of reason. First we ate the berries standing; and then, when we could stand no longer, we ate them sitting; and when this posture became at last too wearisome, we lay prone at our ease, and prolonged the debauch to incredible lengths. When we landed there had been no wind, but now a stiff northerly

breeze sprang up, which blew up the fjord, and made any attempt at farther progress on our part quite out of the question. All we could do, therefore, was to lie here, and go on with our crowberries. At last we grew so torpid that we had not the energy to pick the berries any longer with our hands, and so we turned on our faces, and went on gathering them with our lips till we fell asleep. We slept till evening, and when we woke, there hung the great black, luscious berries still before our very lips, and on we went eating them till we dozed off again. If what people say is true, that gluttony is one of the deadly sins, then may Heaven's mercy save us from the dire punishment that must await us for what we did that day in Ameralikfjord. It has always been a cause for wonder to me that we did not pay the penalty then and there; but, as a matter of fact, we suffered no ill-effects from our excesses.

At midnight the wind dropped, and I turned the crew out. In spite of the crowberries, Sverdrup had had sufficient energy in the course of the evening to collect some wood and fetch water in the event of our needing a meal in the night. Ve now, therefore, fortified ourselves for work, and by one o'clock we were afloat, ready to push on with renewed energy. We made our way quickly along the shore in intense darkness. The phosphorescence of the water was almost as brilliant as anything that tropical seas can show. The blades of our oars gleamed like molten silver, and as they stirred the surface the effect was seen in the glittering radiance that stretched far below. The whole scene was very grand as we passed along under the beetling cliffs, where we could see scarcely anything but the flashes of phosphorescence which flitted upon the water round about us, and danced and played far away in the eddies of our wake.

We seemed to have luck with us just now—a state of things to which we were not much accustomed. The weather was fine, and there was no wind; so, to make the best use of our opportunities, and keep the steam up, we had

recourse to frequent stimulants, in the way of meat-chocolate. Rations were served out often and liberally, and with apparent effect, for we made rapid progress.

At dawn, while we were resting at a certain spot, we heard numbers of ptarmigan calling in the scrub close by us. It would have been easy to bag some, and I was tempted to try; but we thought we had no time to waste on land for such a purpose, so we showed an heroic determination by rowing away from the enticing spot.

We rowed on all the morning without stopping, except for chocolate. Along the whole stretch of shore the rocks fell SO FULL SHEKI) AHLiAU FOR GODTHAAB. *(By Tk. Holmboe, after a. f holograph.)* abruptly into the water that there were but two or three places where a landing was possible. About noon, to our great astonishment, we found ourselves approaching the mouth of the fjord. Here we came upon a point with a nice flat stretch of beach, and pulled in to land. The spot seemed a favourite camping-place, for there were several rings of stones marking the sites of Eskimo tents, and masses of seals' bones and similar refuse strewn about the place.

The consciousness of having got so far made us unusually reckless. We felt that we should soon be in Godthaab now, and in honour of the occasion we contrived a dinner which, in magnificence, suqiassed even that of the day before. We had now no need for parsimony or self-restraint, and no meal throughout the course of the expedition came up to this in extravagance. We began with sea-urchins, or sea-eggs, which I collected in numbers on the beach close by. The ovaries of these are especially good, and little inferior to oysters, and of this delicacy we consumed huge quantities. We then went on to gulls and guillemots, which were followed by the usual excellent soup. Biscuit and butter we had in abundance, and there were plenty of crowberries for him that had recovered from the surfeit of the preceding day. It was, indeed, a dinner worthy of the name, as Sverdrup said. It was no easy matter for us to convey ourselves into the boat again, and bend over the oars to do our proper work. If at any time afterwards I wished to bring Sverdrup into a thoroughly good humour, I had only to call to mind our notable dinner at the great camping-place in Ameralikfjord.

Fortune was strangely kind to us that day: we now had a fair wind behind us, and, in spite of our torpor and laziness, we made rapid progress during the afternoon. Everything was rosy to us now, and we pulled away in sheer fulness of heart. There was one thorn in the side of our happiness, nevertheless. This came from the absurdly thin little rails on which which we had to sit instead of thwarts. I suffered so much that I felt I could well do without a certain part of the body altogether. We shifted, and shifted again, but with little relief to our soreness and discomfort. The happiness of this world is, indeed, seldom pure and unalloyed.

Thus we passed out of the fjord, and saw the sea, islands, and scattered rocks spread out before us, and lighted by the most glorious of sunsets. The whole expanse seemed to be suspended in an atmosphere of gently-glowing light. The vision stopped us, barbarians as we were, and deprived us of speech and power of action. A feeling of home and familiar scenes came over us; for just so lie the weather-beaten islands of the Norwegian coast, caressed by flying spray and summer haze, the outskirts of the fjords and valleys that lie behind. It is not to be wondered at that our forefathers were drawn to this land of Greenland.

We had set ourselves the task of passing the mouth of Kobbefjord, an inlet which lies just to the south of Godthaab, that evening, so that, in the event of bad weather next day, we could, nevertheless, easily reach our destination overland. We now came to a little fjord which is not marked sufficiently clearly on the map we had, and which we therefore wrongly assumed to be Kobbefjord, though I thought at the time that it lay suspiciously near to the mouth of Ameralik.

Consequently, we thought we might as well land there and then, as we sat simply in torture, and our legs were stiff with the pain and discomfort of the position. But then it struck us that we had better keep on till we could see the lights of Godthaab, for, in our innocence, we supposed them to be visible from the south. We saw, however, nothing at all, and, as the current now ran hard against us, we were at last obliged to desist and go ashore. This was at a point which lies at the foot of a high mountain, which we afterwards found to be Hjortetakken. It was now about nine o'clock, and, with the exception of short intervals for breakfast and dinner, we had been fixed to those seats of affliction for a good twenty hours. It was indeed a welcome change to have a broad surface to stretch ourselves upon.

Phenomenal as our dinner had been, the supper which now followed was not much less so. For the first time since we left the *Jason* we could go to work upon bread, butter, and liver "pate'" without restraint and stingy weighing out of rations. We drank lemonade to our heart's desire, and did our very best to prevent any of that provender which we had been economising so long from remaining over, to be carried to people among whom it would have no value. This thought it was that harassed us, and urged us to further effort; but in the end we were obliged to desist, with our task as yet undone.

This was the last of these wonderful nights which we had a chance of enjoying before our re-entrance into civilisation. We felt that it was our farewell to Nature and to the life which had now grown so familiar and so dear to us. The southern sky was as usual radiant with the northern lights, streamer after streamer shooting up to the zenith, each more brilliant than the last; while the stars glittered in their usual impassive way, their brightness more or less eclipsed as the rival lights waxed or waned in intensity.

We were both of us in a strange mood: our wanderings were all but ended; we had met with many mishaps and many unforeseen obstacles, but we had succeeded in spite of all. We had passed

through the drifting ice, and pushed our way up along the coast; we had crossed over the snow-fields of the continent, and made our way out of the fjord in our miserable little boat, in defiance of adverse winds; we had worked hard, and undeniably gone through a deal of tribulation to reach the goal which now lay so near to us. And what were our feelings now? Were they feelings of triumph or exultation? For my own part, I must confess that mine were not of this lofty order; to no other feeling could I attain than a sense of gross repletion. It was a feeling grateful enough to me; but as for our goal, we had been kept waiting too long—there was too little surprise about its eventual attainment for us to give much thought to it.

We curled ourselves up in our fur pelisses, chose each a stretch of heather among the rocks, and slept our last night under the open sky as well as we had seldom slept before.

It was late before we woke next morning, October 3, and when we at last shook off our sleep, the wind had long been blowing freshly up the channel leading to Godthaab, and calling us to work. But we felt that for once we need not hurry—we could sleep to the end, and yet reach our destination in good time.

We began breakfast again with the worthiest intentions of consuming to the last morsel the provisions which remained; but though we attacked them manfully, we had to put to sea once more with this end still unattained. With the wind behind us we made rapid progress northwards, and when we passed the spit of land on which we had camped for the night, we found that we had been all the time on the south side of Kobbefjord. This fjord now lay before us set in a circle of wild, lofty mountains, among which Hjortetakken was most conspicuous, with its sides sprinkled with fresh snow, and its peak from time to time wrapped in light, drifting mist.

We now set about to cross the fjord to the south side of the promontory on which Godthaab itself lies. As we reached the middle we heard, for the first time for many weeks, the sound of unfamiliar voices They were evidently Eskimo women and children from whom the sounds came. They were screaming and shouting; but, though we listened, we could make out nothing, and though we looked, there was no one to be seen. Some time afterwards we learned that these voices must have come from a party of folk who had gone over to "Store Malene," a mountain lying to the east of Godthaab, to gather berries. They had caught sight of us, and were shouting to one another that they could see two men in half a boat, and were much exercised to know what new sorcery this could be. Such a vessel they had never seen before, and they did not at all like the look of it.

This Eskimo description of our little craft as half a boat was really very happy, as it did much resemble the forepart of an ordinary boat. Some way farther on we saw in the distance the figure of a man sitting, as it were, in the water. This was the first "kayaker" we came across on the west coast. Presently we caught sight of two more; they were out after seal, and took no notice of us. This was either because they preferred their own business, or because they thought there was something wrong about u.s. There is no doubt that they saw us long before we saw them, for the Eskimo has the keenest of eyes, and never fails to use them.

As we rounded the next point, Sverdrup, who was rowing bow, caught sight of some houses which he thought must be Godthaab. I turned my head in astonishment, and saw some Eskimo huts, but could not think them to be Godthaab, as, according to the map, the settlement did not lie just there. Sverdrup then said: " But those big houses can't belong to these wretched Eskimo. " I then turned quite round, and could now see the slated roof of a long building, surmounted by a little tower, and was quite ready to agree that this could not be an Eskimo abode, though it struck me that it might very well be a warehouse. But as we passed another point, we found we had before us no warehouse, but a church and a number

of Eskimo huts lying by a little bay. We did not think it was any use landing here, and were for keeping straight on; but suddenly a fresh bree/e sprang up, and made it very heavy work to row, and we concluded that it would be better to go ashore at once, and proceed to Godthaab overland.

So we turned our little tub shorewards, and found that a number of Eskimo, chiefly old women, were already swarming out of the houses, and coming down to the beach to receive us. Here they gathered, chattering, and bustling to and fro, and gesticulating in the same strange way as we had seen their fellows of the east coast often do. Ve could see little or no difference between the two branches of this people we had met; here there was just the same outward aspect—the same ugliness, and the same beaming friendliness and good humour.

When we landed they thronged round us, and helped us disembark our goods, and bring the boat ashore, all the while jabbering unceasingly, and laughing, in wonder and amusement, at us two poor strangers. While we were standing there, mounting guard over our gun and the more valuable of our possessions, and ignoring the crowd of people round us, whom, of course, we could not understand one whit, Sverdrup said: " Here comes a European!" I looked up, and saw a young man advancing towards us. He was clad in an attempt at a Greenlander's dress, but had a Tam-o'-Shanter cap upon his head, and a fair, good-looking face, which was as little like an Eskimo's as could well be. There could be no mistake about him; he and his whole demeanour were, so to say, a direct importation from "the King's Copenhagen," as it is called here. He came up to us, we exchanged salutations; then he asked, " Do you speak English? " The accent was distinctly Danish, and the question somewhat discomfited me, as I thought it a little absurd for us to set to work at English instead of our own mother-tongue. But before I could answer, he luckily inquired: " Are you Englishmen? "

To this I could safely answer, in good Norse: " No; we are Norwegians." "

May I ask your name?" " My name is Nansen, and we have just come from the interior." " Oh, allow me to congratulate you on taking your Doctor's degree." This came like a thunderbolt from a blue sky, and it was all I could do to keep myself from laughing outright. To put it very mildly, it struck me as comical that I should cross Greenland to receive congratulations upon my Doctor's degree, which I happened to have taken just before I left home. Nothing, of course, could have been more remote from my thoughts at the moment.

The stranger's name was Baumann. He was a good-natured, sociable native of Copenhagen, who was now in the Greenland Service, and acting as assistant, or, as they call it, " Volontor," to the Superintendent of the colony of Godthaab. We subsequently had a good deal of his society. The Superintendent, he told us, was just now away from home, and in the name of his superior he offered us a hearty welcome to the colony. Godthaab itself was close by, and it was quite by chance that he had just walked out to Ny Herrnhut, the spot where we landed, to see the missionary. This is one of the few stations established by the German Moravian Mission in Greenland.

The first question I asked, as soon as I could get an opportunity, was about communication with Denmark, and whether the last ship had sailed. From Godthaab I learned that the last ship had gone two months or more ago, and there was none now that we could catch. The only possible chance was the *Fox,* at Ivigtut, but she was to leave in the middle of October, and the place was 300 miles away.

These tidings were anything but welcome. It had been the thought of catching a ship to Europe which had spurred us on during our crossing of the ice; the vision of a ship had haunted us unceasingly, and never allowed us the enjoyment of rest or ease. We had consoled ourselves with the thought that we could make up for lost time on board, during our voyage home; and now, when the time came, we found that our ship had sailed before ever we started upon our journey across the continent. It was a magnificent structure of hopes and longings that now sank into the sea before our eyes. As far as I was concerned personally, this was not of much account, for, on the contrary, I was quite ready to spend a winter in Greenland; but for the other poor fellows it was another matter. They had friends and relatives—one of them wife and children—away at home, whom they longed to see, and they had often talked of the joys of their return. And now they would have to wait through the long winter here, while their people at home would think them long since dead. This must never be; a message must be sent off at once to the *Fox,* our last hope of relief. While we were talking the matter over, we were joined by another European—the Moravian missionary, Herr Voged. He greeted us very kindly, gave us a heart)' welcome, and would not hear of our going by his door unentertained.

He lived in the building with the tower which had first caught our attention, and which served both as church and as a residence for him. We were received here by the missionary and his wife with unaffected heartiness, and it was with a strange mixture of feelings that we set foot once more in a civilised dwelling, after four months of wild life on shipboard, in our tent, and in the open air. The room we were taken into will always remain vividly impressed upon my memory. Its dimensions were not grand, and its features were uniformity and simplicity; but for us, who were used to a cramped tent, and the still greater simplicity of the open air, the appointments of this house were nothing less than luxury itself. The mere sitting upon a chair was a thing to he remembered, and the cigars to which we were treated were a source of unconcealed satisfaction. Then the cup of welcome was handed round, while coffee and food were being prepared for us. It was a queer change to be sitting at a table again and before a white cloth, and to be using knife and fork upon earthenware plates. I will not say, unreservedly, that the change was altogether for the

better, for we had been thoroughly comfortable when sitting by the camp-fire, and tearing our gulls to pieces with our teeth and fingers, without forks, plates, and formalities.

While the meal was in progress, the pastor of Godthaab, Herr Balle, arrived; soon after him came the doctor of the place, whose name was Bin/er. The news of our coming had already reached the colony, and they had hurried out at once to bid us welcome. We were now beset with questions as to our journey: as to why we had changed our route, how we had got out of the fjord, where we had left the others, and so on; all our accounts being followed with the most lively interest. Then the party broke up, and we took our leave of our kind host and hostess.

When we got out of doors, we found, to our surprise, that it was raining. Our luck was true to us this time, and we had reached the habitations of men none too soon, for the rain would have been very unpleasant to us in our little boat.

We were assured that our boat and things should be taken care of and sent on, and then we started off to walk in the rain over the hills to Godthaab.

After a time our way brought us out upon a projecting point of rock, and we saw the colony lying below us. There were not a great number of buildings—four or five European houses, a church perched upon an eminence, and a good many Eskimo huts. The whole group lay in a small hollow between two hills, and by a pleasant little bay. The Danish flag was flying on its high mast, which stood on a mound down by the water. Crowds of people were swarming about. They had all come out to see the mysterious strangers from the interior who had arrived in half a boat.

Then we made our way down; but we had hardly reached the houses before a gunshot rang out over the water, and was followed by one after another, in all a complete salute. We had parted from civilisation amid the thunder of cannon, and with this same thunder we were received into the civilised world again, for to such the west coast of Greenland must certainly be reckoned. It might

have been supposed that we were individuals of the most warlike tendencies. How many shots they fired in our honour I cannot say, but the salute was well sustained. The little natives had all their work to do round the guns under the flagstaff, as we were passing among the houses and between long rows of Greenlanders of both sexes, who crowded round and lined the way. They—and especially the women—were a striking sight in their picturesque attire. Smiles, good nature, and here and there, perhaps, a little unaffected wonder, beamed from all the faces about us, and added a new sunshine to the surroundings.

Then our eyes fell upon a more familiar sight—the figures of the four Danish ladies of the colony, who were coming to meet us, and to whom we were duly presented. At the same time, it struck us somewhat curiously to see European petticoats again among all the skin jackets and trousers of the fair Eskimo.

As we reached the Superintendent's house, the salute was brought to an end, and the native gunners, under the lead of one Frederiksen, gave us a ringing cheer. The Superintendent's wife now welcomed us, on her own part and that of her husband. Here, again, we were temporarily entertained, and also invited to dine with the doctor at four o'clock.

We had still a long time to get through before then, however, though we had plenty to do in the way of washing and decorating ourselves. We were shown up into our new friend Baumann's room, the aspect of which, again, was sufficiently unfamiliar to us to make a very vivid impression upon our minds. Here a musical-box played to us "The last Rose of Summer," an air which will hereafter never fade from my memory; and here we were, for the first time, horrified by the sight in a glass of our sunburnt and weather-beaten faces. After our long neglect in the way of washing and dressing, we seemed to ourselves little fit for presentation in society, and, both in our faces and clothes, a considerable number of the hues of the rainbow were intrusively conspicuous.

It was an indescribable delight to plunge the head into a basin of water once more, and to go through the ceremony of an honest Saturday night's wash. Cleanness was not, however, to be obtained at the first attempt. Then we attired ourselves in the clean linen, so to say, which we had brought all the way across Greenland for the purpose; and, thus reconstituted, we felt ourselves quite ready for the good things of the doctor's well-provided dinner-table.

By all the Danish inhabitants of Godthaab we were entertained with unprecedented hospitality, and the luxury displayed on all sides was quite astonishing. We had expected to find that the Europeans exiled to this corner of the world would be so influenced by the nature of their surroundings, and the primitive section of humanity amid which they dwelt, that they would have inevitably forgotten a certain amount of their native etiquette. And therefore our surprise was great when we saw the ladies appear at social gatherings in the longest of trains and gloves, and the men in black coats and shirt-fronts of irreproachable stiffness, and even on occasions going to the extremity of the conventional swallow-tail. Surrounded, as we were, by the natives in their natural and picturesque attire, and thoroughly unaccustomed as we had grown to all these things, to us the absurdity of European taste in such matters seemed altogether incongruous.

We two were now safe in port, and the next thing to be done was to send relief to our comrades in Ameralikfjord with the least possible delay. They had no means of knowing whether we had reached our destination, or had gone to the bottom of the fjord, and left them to starve to death out there. And after this was done, we must despatch a message to the *fox*.

In the course of the afternoon we tried, therefore, to arrange matters, but without success. No sooner had we arrived than a storm from the south had sprung up, and the weather was so bad that the Eskimo, who are bad sailors in anything but their " kayaks," would not venture upon the voyage into Amera-

lik-fjord. The letter to the *Fox* was to be sent by one or two " kayakers," but we could find no one in the colony who would undertake to start in this weather, and we were therefore obliged to wait till next day.

When night came, and lodging had to be found for us, Sver-drup was quartered upon the before-mentioned Frederiksen, the carpenter and boat-builder of the place, while Herr Baumann's room was put at my disposal. It was strange, too, to find myself in a real bed again after six months' absence. There can be few who have enjoyed a bed as completely as I did this one. Every limb thrilled with delight as I stretched myself on the soft mattress. The sleep which followed was not so sound as I could have expected. I had grown so used to the bag of skin, with the ice or rock beneath it, that I felt my present couch too soft, and I am not sure that, after a while, I did not feel a faint longing for the old order of things.

On the morning of October 4 I was roused from my unquiet dreams by the gaze of the Eskimo maid-servant who had come with the morning supply of tea and sandwiches. After this early meal I got up, and went out to look round the place.

Down by the beach there was just now a deal of life and movement, for a boat's load of seals, which had been caught not far off, had just come in, and the so-called " flensing," or process of cutting the blubber out, was now in progress. I went down with Baumann to study this new phase of life. The Eskimo women, with their sleeves rolled up, knelt in numbers round the gashed and mangled seal. From some the blood was taken, and collected in pails, to be afterwards used in the manufacture of black puddings, or analogous delicacies; from others the intestines were being drawn, or the blubber or flesh being cut. All parts were carefully set aside for future use.

After having seen enough of the sanguinary spectacle, and duly admired the dexterity and grace displayed by the Eskimo women, as well as the good looks of some among them, we went

across to see Sverdrup and, if he were up, to ask him to come and have breakfast at the Superintendent's house.

When we entered, however, we found him already at table with his host, Herr Frederiksen, and engaged upon a breakfast of roast ptarmigan and other delicacies. I expressed my regret that this was the case, as I had hoped that we should breakfast together. But Sverdrup could see no reason why we should not do so still. He was now occupied with his first breakfast, certainly, but so good a thing would easily bear repetition, and he expressed himself ready at once to begin again. So he actually did; and, as a matter of fact, he made at this time a regular practice of eating his meals twice over. For three days he stood the strain; but after this he succumbed, and had to keep his bed for some hours in consequence. It was a long time, indeed, before any of us returned to decent ways again, and were content to take our food like civilised beings.

In the course of the morning a man was found who was considered equal to the task of carrying our despatches southwards, and was at the same time willing to undertake the journey. The man's name was David, and he was a resident of Ny Herrnhut. He was to go to Fiskernass, a small settlement some ninety miles to the south, and there to send the letters on by other "kayakers." An errand of this kind is usually undertaken by two men in company, as risks of a fatality-are thus much lessened. But as the same David was not afraid of the undertaking, and had expressed his readiness to start the same afternoon, I, of course, had no objection to make. I promised him, as well as the others to whom he was to hand the despatches on, extra pay in case they caught the *Fox*.

I then wrote a hurried letter to Herr Smith, the manager of the Cryolite quarry at Ivigtut. The *Fox* being the property of the company who own this quarry, it lay really with the local manager to decide what course the vessel should take; but I also wrote to the captain of the ship. In both these letters I asked that the vessel should be allowed to come up to Godthaab to fetch us, if possible. I did not propose that she should wait at Ivigtut till we could join her there, because, in the present uncertain state of the weather, it was quite impossible to calculate how long it would take us to get the rest of the party from Ameralikfjord, and cover the necessary 300 miles in open boats. As far as we could judge, we could not reckon upon reaching Ivigtut by the middle of the month—the date at which the ship was expected to sail—and we could not ask her to wait an indefinite time for us down there. On the other hand, it seemed to me that, if she thought of doing anything on our behalf, it would be to come and fetch us. By these means she could save time, and it would be possible to reckon, with a fair amount of accuracy, how many days the voyage to Godthaab and back would take her.

Furthermore, in case my messengers should catch the *fox,* but she could not see her way to fetching us, I hastily wrote a few lines to Herr Gamel, of Copenhagen.

This letter, and one from Sverdrup to his father, brought to Europe the first news of our having reached the west coast of Greenland, and contained all that was known of our journey for six months. In one respect they hold, perhaps, a somewhat unusual position, for their postage came to no less than 17.

Our messenger promised me that he would start that very afternoon. He did make the attempt, but, as far as I could learn, was driven back by stress of weather.

As things were just as bad in this respect when evening came, and it was the general opinion that no boat would be able to make the voyage into Ameralikfjord next day either, the Pastor proposed that a couple of men should be despatched in " kayaks " to take to our companions the news of our safe arrival, together with a temporary supply of provisions, with which they could console themselves until the boats could be sent to fetch them away. This proposal I accepted, of course, most gratefully; and while the Pastor went to secure his " kayakers," two plucky brothers, named

Terkel and Hoseas, who belonged to Sardlok, but happened at this moment to be at Godthaab, the ladies of the colony set busily to work to collect a supply of the most unheard-of delicacies. These were stowed away in the two canoes, while I supplemented them with some simpler articles of food, such as butter, bacon, and bread, and last, but not least, some pipes and tobacco. Among the latter was a big Danish porcelain pipe with a long stem, and a pound of tobacco, for Balto's private delectation—a present which I had promised him up on the " Inland ice " on some occasion when he had surpassed himself in handiness. As soon as the " kayaks " were ready packed, I gave Terkel, the elder of the two brothers, through the medium of the Pastor, an exact description of the spot where the others were to be found, and pointed it out to him on the map, which he understood well.

Next morning, therefore, October 5, three Eskimo left Godthaab—two bound for Ameralikfjord, and the third for Fiskernass. The first two, who were excellent hands at their work, made good use of their time, and found our companions on the morning of the following day. But the latter, who was an inferior " kayaker," had to turn back, and was a long time-before he finally got off. As far as I could make out, he was seen hanging about Ny Herrnhut, which was his home, some days later.

This same morning, too, a boat for Ameralikfjord made an attempt to start, but only to come back a couple of hours afterwards. As I have already said, these Greenlanders are no great performers with the oar. In the afternoon they had another try, and this time, strange to say, we saw no more of them; but, as we subsequently learned, they got no farther than to an island a little way to the south, where they disembarked, and passed the next few days in a tent instead of returning, though they were no more than an hour's row distant all the while. There was a very good reason for this odd conduct, as it appeared, for had they come back they would have lost all the pay which they now managed to put to their credit; and, besides, they would

have had nothing like so good a time at home as in their tent on the island, and therefore they felt no call to move till they had consumed their whole supply of provisions.

Next day the Superintendent of the colony, Herr Bistrup, returned, together with Herr Heincke, the German missionary from Uinanak, a Moravian station up the fjord, some forty miles from Godthaab. The Superintendent had been in Umanak, when a "kayaker," who had been sent off from the colony, brought him the news of our arrival. He and the missionary had thereupon at once despatched a couple of men in canoes into Ameralikfjord. They also carried a supply of provisions sent by the missionary and his wife, and were told to remain with our party, and help them in every possible way.

On October 7, Terkel and Hoseas came back from Ameralikfjord with a letter from Dietrichson, telling us that they now felt quite comfortable in there, as they had an abundance of provisions, and now knew of our safe arrival at Godthaab.

Two days later, or on October 9, the weather was sufficiently favourable to allow of my sending off an ordinary Eskimo boat, which I had borrowed of Herr Voged, the German missionary whom we had first met. The crew consisted as usual chiefly of women. The same day, too, the first boat, commonly known as " the whaler," finally left the island on which its crew had hitherto been picnicking.

Several days now passed, and as we had heard nothing of our companions, we began to expect their arrival every moment. The Greenlanders in particular were extremely anxious to see them.

Like all Eskimo, they have the liveliest imaginations, of the fruits of which we had some noteworthy examples. The very day after our arrival the strangest rumours were flying about among the natives of the colony as to our experiences upon the " Inland ice." We were said to have taken our meals in the company of the strange inhabitants of the interior, who are double the size of ordinary men. We had also come across the tiny race of dwarfs who inhabit the rocks in the recesses of the fjords. Of the feet of these little people we had seen numerous traces in the sand, and we even had two specimens of the race in our company.

On the other hand, it was reported that two of the members of the expedition had died on the way; but of this sad occurrence we, as was quite natural, had no desire to speak.

At first, indeed, we were regarded as possessing certain almost supernatural attributes, and it was feared that we had achieved the heroic feat of crossing the dreaded " Inland ice" by the aid of means not strictly orthodox. And, therefore, as soon as Sverdrup or I showed ourselves in public, the natives assembled in their numbers to gaze at us. I, especially, on account of my size, was a favourite object of their regard. We received appropriate names at once: Sverdrup was called " Akortok "—that is to say, " he who steers a ship "; while I was honoured with two appellations— " Angisorsuak," or " the very big one," and " Umitormiut nalagak," which means " the leader of the men with the great beards,' under which description the Norwegians are generally known.

It had also come to the knowledge of these good people that we had two Lapps in our company—members of a race which they had never seen. The two " kayakers " who had come back from Ameralikfjord had minutely described their meeting with the strangers. "There were two men," they said, "of the people who commonly wear great beards, and two who were like us, but were clad in a wonderful dress." They were thus quite acute enough to see that the Lapps, in spite of all distinctions, belonged to a race somewhat on a level with themselves, and were widely different from all Danes and Norwegians.

At last, early on the morning of October 12, the two Eskimo who had been sent into the fjord from Umanak arrived with a note from Dietrichson, saying that the whole party were now on the way.

The entire colony, Europeans as well as natives, now turned out, and awaited

their arrival in great excitement. At last we could see, by a movement among the " kayaks," which lay below us, that the boats must be in sight. Presently, too, "the whaler" appeared from behind a projecting point. The "kayaks" simply swarmed round her, and we soon caught sight of our four companions, seated in the stern, in front of the steersman, and already waving their caps in the air by way of salutation. It was a little strange to me to see them sitting there as passengers, instead of working at the oars.

The boat came slowly on, with a long string of " kayaks"' tailing out behind, and soon put in to shore under the flagstaff mound, where the four strange beings from the interior landed, and were heartily welcomed by the Europeans of the colony, as well as by crowds of Eskimo, to whom, of course, they were a source of renewed wonder and admiration. The Lapps came in for marked attention. The Greenlanders set them down as women, because they wore long tunics something like the cloaks of European ladies, as well as trousers of reindeer skin, which particular garments are only used by the women of the Eskimo. Balto seemed to take the attention which fell to his share with the greatest complacency and nonchalance. He talked away, related his experiences, and was soon on an intimate footing with all the inhabitants of the place. Ravna, as usual, went his own silent way; he came up to me, ducked his head, gave me his hand, and, though he said very little, I could see his small eyes twinkle with joy and self-satisfaction.

They were all glad enough to have reached their destination, and the announcement that there was a very doubtful prospect of their getting home this year did not seem to have much effect upon their good spirits.

Of course, there now followed an interminable series of questions and answers. I will leave chiefly to Dietrichson the task of chronicling the events which occurred after Sverdrup'and I parted from the others in Ameralikfjord.

Chapter XX.

*WAITING IN AMERALIKFJORD.*

This short account of the movements of the rest of the party after Sverdrup and I set out upon our voyage to Godthaab is the work of Lieutenant Dietrichson, who was left in charge of the detachment; but I have also thought it as well to insert an extract or two from Balto's narrative:—

" The task which had been entrusted to us, the remainder of the party, was to fetch the baggage, which we had been obliged to leave meanwhile up by the ice, down to Ameralikfjord, and on September 27 Kristiansen, Ravna, and I set off on our errand, leaving the other three busy at their boat. We had about eighteen miles to go, but hoped to reach our destination before dusk, as we expected to be able to shorten the distance to a certain extent by crossing some of the lakes on the ice. The upper lakes indeed were just frozen, but the ice was altogether too thin to bear us, so we had to make our way as best we could along the steep valley-side and over the rough surface of the moraines, while the swollen streams also contributed not a little to delay our progress. It was therefore not till half-past seven or so, or long after the sun had gone down, that we eventually came to the end of our day's march. After a somewhat primitive and miscellaneous supper of fragments we crept into our sleeping-bag and spent the night in the open air.

" The morning of the next day was devoted to arranging and packing our goods, so that they could be carried on the back with tolerable comfort, and we were not ready to make a start till noon. We considered it best to move the things in sections and by short stages, and began by conveying our first lot down to a certain lake, to which we had given the name of ' Langvand.' When we got back to the starting-place we found Balto already there. He told us that after a day's work the boat had progressed so far that his aid was thought no longer necessary, and so he had been despatched to help us. He had taken about the same route as that we had followed on the way down, except that he had had to go round nearly all the lakes. Langvand, however, for the sake of the short cut, he had tried to cross. At first the ice was tolerably firm, but in the middle of the lake it was so weak that he had had to go on all fours, and even then only just managed to get across without going through.

" Next morning, September 29, we carried our last load down to Langvand. Balto again tried the ice and crossed a little arm of the lake, going on his ' ski' and dragging a sledge behind him. I was busy making a map of the valley, and as I had fallen a good deal behind, I thought I would make up for lost time by following Balto's example. So I set off like him on my 'ski 'and pulling a sledge behind me. When I was half-way across I felt that the ice was on the point of giving way under me, but as I saw there was a second layer below, I went confidently on. The upper layer, however, now grew weaker and weaker, the lower came to an end, and the only course left me was to scramble to shore by the shortest way. But the ice now re-fused to bear me altogether, and I sank slowly down into the water, 'ski' and all. The ' ski,' however, were luckily not bound fast to my feet, so I slipped them off at once and swam to land."

Balto, who had gone on before and only crossed the same ice with great dif-ficulty, thus describes the situation:—" As I was afraid that Dietrichson would try and cross this bad ice, I pulled out my whistle "—he means by this one of the small horns that we carried for sig-nalling purposes—"and ran up on to some high ground and blew away. Di-etrichson answered at once, and I then ran in his direction to see what was go-ing to happen. Just as I got down to the lake, he was well out in the middle, and I could see that the ice was very weak. So I called to him to come straight to shore, but after a few steps he went in through the ice. Then I told him to leave the sledge and 'ski' and swim to land, which he did, and when he got out we pulled the instruments out of his pockets to prevent them getting wetter than was good for them. Ve were now at our wits' end to know how we should get the sledge and ' ski,' and Dietrichson want-ed to swim out again and fetch them.

But I said, ' Don't do that, man, you'll freeze to death!' and I shouted to Kris-tiansen to bring one of the long bamboo poles and a rope. But Dietrichson would not wait, and went on to the ice again. He got on to a loose piece at once, which tipped up, and he went head first into the water once more. Then he swam back to shore again. I now ran up on to a hillock and blew with all my might. Kristiansen then shouted, 'What's the matter?' I shouted back, ' Bring a bamboo and a rope! Dietrichson has fallen into the lake, and the sledge is left out on the ice.' Kristiansen was much frightened at this; he thought Di-etrichson was drowned, and that only the sledge was left on the ice. He came running as hard as he could go with the pole and rope, and we drew the sledge and gun to shore. We then went on to the place where the others had a fire and were making coffee, and where we stopped for the night, for Dietrichson of course was quite wet through."

" After getting the things ashore," re-sumes Dietrichson, " we went on to the others, who were getting a meal ready. A cup of coffee and a partial change, for I had not enough for a complete one, soon made me warm and comfortable again.

"We now had all our goods collected at this spot, but we could see that we should not be able to carry the large loads we had brought so far all the way. On the other hand, if we took them in three portages, instead of two, we should lose so much time, and should not reach the fjord as soon as we wished. So I determined to abandon one sledge and one pair of ' ski,' and then to make sure that every man had a fair share of the weight, I made a pair of scales out of' ski,' bamboos, and rope, and while the others were busy distrib-uting the things equally, I went on down the valley surveying for my map in or-der to avoid being delayed by these op-erations next day.

" Next morning we started at six o'clock, and after a hard day's work got all our things down to another lake, which we had called 'Gaasedammen," or 'Goose Pool,' where we spent the

night.

"Next day, October i, after two hours' march, we came to a long and steep, but fairly smooth and grassy slope, down which our loaded sledges ran capitally. But when we came to the river below we met with an unexpected obstacle. The volume of water was quite four times as large as it had been five days before. Cross it we must, however, as farther down, and on the same side on which we stood, it ran close under a steep wall of rock quite impassable to us, and furthermore the tent and our oth-er things lay on the opposite side. At the best wading-place we could find the river was some seventy yards wide, and this breadth of water we had to pass three times before we conveyed all our loads over. The two Ipps kept all their clothes on to protect themselves better against the cold water, but Kristiansen and I preferred to divest ourselves of trousers and stockings. The stream ran very fast, and we had to use our bamboo poles diligently and carefully, for had we lost our footing the loads on our backs would have made it very difficult to recover ourselves. It was a chilly business, indeed, wading this seventy yards three times over, and with the wa-ter nearly up to our waists. Kristiansen's and my legs were simply blue with cold when it was all over, but a good rub and our dry clothes soon brought back the warmth again, and then we were in bet-ter case than the Lapps, who had noth-ing dry to change into. A couple of days later we should have found it quite im-possible to get our things across the riv-er, had it gone on increasing in the same way.

"Though it was not yet noon, we de-termined, as there was plenty of fuel hereabouts, to light a fire and have our dinner. We all felt that some hot soup would be very grateful and comforting after our cold bath.

"At two o'clock in the afternoon of October 2 we reached the fjord with our first loads. The rest of the things we left where they were for the present, and spent the remainder of the day getting the tent in order. The original tent-poles had been used for the boat, and we now had to supply their place with others.

" During the six days which had passed since we were here last we had been unusually lucky in the weather. The days had been bright, but not too hot, and the nights clear, but mild enough to make it a simple pleasure to spend them in the open air with no other protection than our sleeping-bag.

" Early next morning, October 3, we were on the move, and, after breakfast, we started up the valley to fetch the rest of our things. By noon, we had them all down by the fjord, and as there was now a prospect of our having to spend some days here inactive, we unpacked a number of our goods and made the tent and camp generally as comfortable as we could. We took stock of our provisions also, and found that, besides a good supply of pemmican, we had biscuit for six days and pea-soup for five. In the way of fat we had nothing left, and our stock of salt had also come to an end.

" Every day now we might expect to hear from Godthaab; we had even had faint hopes of finding a boat already arrived to fetch us when we got down to the fjord with our baggage. As yet we had no reason to feel anxious about our two comrades, but if another week were to go by without our receiving news of them, we should have to try and reach the colony by land, for in that case we should be justified in supposing that they had come to grief. By that time, too, we should have come to the end of all our provisions, except the pemmican, which would just suffice for the proposed land journey.

" Outside the tent we made a campfire, and lying round it enjoyed to the full a hardly-earned rest. The whole afternoon we thus spent stretched on the elastic heather, and gloating over the thought that our worst labours and trials were over, and that we had now a few days of ease and leisure before us.

"We turned in early, and it was not till late next morning that we left the tent again. I spent the first part of the day finishing my surveying, and Kristiansen went out with the gun, but came back an hour or two afterwards empty-handed. This day and the next as well we practically devoted to rest.

" On the morning of October 6 I started off along the stretch of higher ground which ran out into the fjord to the end of the river sands, partly to look for a landing-place for the boat we expected, and partly to see if there was anything to shoot. When I was about half-way to the point I heard a shot. I hurried up to the top of the ridge to see who it could be, and soon caught sight of two Greenlanders coming up from the water and carrying packs on their backs, attached by the peculiar broad forehead-strap which the Eskimo use for this purpose. I shouted and they stopped, and then came to meet me. As I had, of course, guessed, they proved to be two men sent off in 'kayaks' by Nansen. A letter they brought told me that he and Sverdrup had arrived safely at Godthaab, that he had sent off a temporary supply of provisions herewith, that a boat with more things of the kind would be soon despatched, but that owing to stormy weather no one had yet been found willing to undertake the voyage.

" We three now started for the camp, our way lying over a high headland of rock which jutted out towards the river. When we reached the top of this I shouted to the others in the tent, who all came rushing out and, at once apprehending the situation, set up shrieks and cheers of joy. I had gone out to look for game, but though I had found nothing I have never in my life come back from shooting with a better bag than these two Eskimo.

" The whole party now gathered round the welcome supplies. First I read the letter, which contained nothing but pleasant news except the announcement that there was little hope of our reaching home this year. But in the first rush of joy we had not much room for this disappointment. Then we began to unpack, with all the curiosity of children round the Christmas tree. We feasted our eyes on the sight of all these good things —bread, meat, coffee, tobacco, and all the rest, and above all upon the butter and bacon, for which we simply craved.

Cakes even and sweetmeats were not wanting, for the Danish ladies of the colony had collected for us all manner of delicacies. We set to work upon them at once and with unprecedented fury."

Balto's account of this incident may be added. He writes:—

" While Dietrichson was out I climbed up on to a crag which was 300 feet high. When I reached the top I saw three men coming towards me. One of them I knew, for it was Dietrich-son, and he had met the two men who had been sent from Godthaab to bring us victuals. I ran straight down to the tent and told the others that I could see some men coming. They would not believe it, but I began to collect dry wood and made a fire, fetched some water, filled the coffee-pot, and put it on, as I knew these people must have some coffee with them. As soon as they all reached the tent Dietrichson began to look at what had been sent us. I saw Nansen had sent me a pipe and some tobacco, which I caught hold of at once and began to smoke, while the others set about eating. We cut slices of bread an inch thick, spread half an inch of butter on them, put bacon on the top of that, and then we had coffee afterwards."

"While we were still engaged upon our meal," Dietrichson continues, "we heard two or three more shots in the direction of the point, and presently two men appeared on the high ground above. When they came down they handed us some letters, one from Herr Bistrup, the Superintendent of Godthaab; another from Herr Moller, a Greenlander of the same place; and a third from Herr Heincke, the German missionary at Umanak, at which settlement the two former were on a visit. Besides these letters they also brought a supply of provisions from the Superintendent and the missionary.

"We asked our new visitors to come into the tent and inspect our arrangements. When they saw the sleeping-bags they pointed first to themselves, then to the bags, laid their hands on their cheeks, and shut their eyes. Then they pointed to the tent and all it contained, pretended to lie down on their backs, and finally nodded in the direction of the fjord. From all this pantomime we understood that they meant to spend the night with us, and that they would conduct us to the colony. The provisions they had brought were down by the fjord with their canoes, and so Kristiansen and Balto prepared to go and help to bring them up. The two Eskimo from Godthaab also made signs of moving, and as I managed to get out of them that they meant to go back at once, I wrote a few lines to Nansen thanking him for the supply of provisions and telling him how we were getting on.

" When the new consignment of good things arrived another solemn unpacking began. The names of the different things were shouted as they were turned out, and as soon as some one named spirits, another sugar, and a third candles, we determined to make the evening memorable by drinking a bowl of punch in the tent. It was already late, and we set to work at once. The water was boiled and sugar and spirits added, the latter being a luxury which we had not tasted since we left the *Jason.* Our grog did not promise to be of much strength, however, for Balto had boiled an absurd amount of water. But this was perhaps as well, as the spirits proved to be the ordinary Scandinavian 'akvavit,' which is really impossible in combination with water, and a stronger mixture would therefore have been most undrinkable. As it was we thought it excellent."

Balto, however, a connoisseur in these matters, reproachfully observes in his narrative that " one cannot expect grog to be anything but weak when one has to add five bottles of water to one of spirits," and that " this did not taste of anything at all."

"Cigars too had been sent us, and we were soon working away at them with a will to make up for lost time. Nansen's letter said that he and Sverdrup were living like princes at Godthaab, but we were just as well pleased with our fate and ourselves in the little tent, and we all agreed that this was undoubtedly the pleasantest evening we had spent together. There were six of us again in our little dwelling, and as we grew lively a bewildering confusion of tongues prevailed. With the Greenlanders we managed to carry on a fairly satisfactory conversation by means of gestures and the aid of our Eskimo dictionary and conversation-book. Our two guests, Peter, a seal-catcher from Godthaab, and Silas, a mighty hunter of Umanak, were both intelligent and well-informed men, who could not only read and write but even draw. Their sketches of some of the buildings of Godthaab and Umanak were so true that we afterwards recognised the originals at first sight.

" We enjoyed ourselves so thoroughly that evening that we were all loth to go to bed. Eventually Kristiansen, Balto, and I packed ourselves into one bag, while Ravna and the two Greenlanders occupied the other. Sleep did not come at once, however, as our two guests presently set to work to sing hymns. They went through three in all, then finished with a prayer. This little service was probably due to the fact that the day was Sunday, though it may have been called forth by their apprehension at the prospect of a night in the midst of strangers.

"Next morning Silas went out to look for reindeer. He told us that in August last he had some sport among these very mountains, but I must confess that I had not much faith in his luck when he started off this morning with his rusty old muzzle-loader over his shoulder, though at the same time I felt a strong temptation to go with him. However, I had settled that we would to-day begin to move our things down to the extreme end of the point, where was the only available landing-place. I did not like to shirk this work, and besides my help was necessary because Ravna was now of scarcely any use, as during the latter part of the crossing he had rubbed one of his feet so badly that he was now almost completely lame. So Silas went off alone, and the rest of us began to move the sledges and other things that we had no further need of down towards a new camping-place at the end of the point.

"At one of our scanty meals upon the ice we had discussed what particular preparation of food would have been most welcome to us at the moment. Most of us had given our votes for a good bowl of porridge with plenty of butter, and this delicacy Nansen had promised to treat us to as soon as we reached Godthaab). But among the good things now sent us was some meal, so we thought we would set about making the long-looked-for porridge for this day's dinner.

"This was in fact our first hot meal since the provisions arrived, and after it was over we were lying stretched on the grass smoking our after-dinner pipes, when we caught sight of Silas at some distance up the mountain-side. He was coming down towards the tent and had something large and heavy on his back. Ve scarcely dared think it was a reindeer, but presently we saw the horns sticking up above his head, and there was no longer room for doubt. We all rejoiced; the I.apps were simply wild with delight at the prospect of again enjoying some of their national food, which they had had to do without so long. Balto ran to meet the hunter, skipped and danced about him, clapped him on the back, and knew not how best to express his overflowing joy.

" Silas soon reached us, and laid down his burden before us. It was the hide, head, suet, marrow-bones, and one haunch that he brought, the rest having been left behind to be fetched next day. He distributed the marrow-bones and suet among us, and gave us to understand that we must put the pot on at once and cook the whole supply. The Greenlanders eat their meat quite as willingly raw as cooked, and our two friends had already begun their meal. For our parts it was little more than an hour since we had eaten our fill of porridge, but nevertheless we put the pot on at once, and, grouping ourselves round it in Lapp fashion, took bit after bit out with our fingers, so that by the time the larger pieces were properly done most of us were already satisfied. In the evening, however, we set to work again and finished our first supply of good fresh meat.''

Balto's recollection of the reindeer

moves him to say that " from this time things grew brighter, we began to forget the hardships we had gone through—the hunger, the thirst, the cold, and the desolation of the ice."

" Next day the two Greenlanders went off to fetch the rest of the reindeer, while we moved the tent and our other things down to the point in expectation of the boats. Ravna's foot was still so bad that he could scarcely manage to climb over the high bluff which barred our way.

"On their return the Greenlanders took the reindeer meat down to the spot where their ' kayaks' lay, and presently made their appearance at our new camping-place with a great piece, which was put on to boil at once. Peter also presented us with a ptarmigan which he had shot. First, however, he took the entrails out and devoured them forthwith, to our great consternation, but his own undisguised delight.

"Our constant watch for the boats met with nothing but disappointment. Hitherto, as I have said, we had had splendid weather, but now it began to rain, and at times so hard that we were constrained to keep within the tent, I only showing myself outside when meteorological observations had to be taken. This confinement grew at last very wearisome, and we began to await impatiently the hour of relief. On October 9 there was a fairly strong wind blowing from the east, which would delay the boats considerably, and if it went on increasing in force, there was a chance of our remaining fixed here for some time yet. So in order to provide against a possible dearth of provisions, we had to take to limited rations again, though there could be no real famine in prospect as long as we had the reindeer to rely upon.

" No pleasanter diversion than a stalk during this period of waiting could have been wished for, but all my attempts to induce Silas to go with me were in vain. He only shook his head and declared the wind to be in the wrong quarter.

"The last few evenings our twoGreenlander guests had, in spite of the incessant rain, left us and spent the night down by their canoes. I supposed that this was in order to keep watch in case the boats should arrive in the middle of the night, but possibly the motive was sheer modesty and consideration for us, from the idea that they were a burden to us, seeing that the boats were so long in coming. Even before this they had disappeared from the tent once or twice just before a meal was going to begin.

"At last, at seven o'clock on the morning of October n, we were awoke by the sound of several shots. We guessed at once what they meant, and jumped from our bags and fired in answer out of the tent-door. Very soon afterwards we were dressed and outside on the look-out for the new arrivals. Presently, above a little rise in the ground, we saw one Eskimo head after the other appear. We began to count, but their number actually baffled us, as they seemed to swarm. Fourteen there were in all, men and women, chattering eagerly together as they neared the tent. When they reached us one of the party advanced, and, in a mixture of Danish and Eskimo, announced that they had come with two boats to carry us away. It was one Terkel, a smith in the Danish service, who thus acted as interpreter. The result of the performance was that we understood a little of what he said, and he practically nothing of all the questions we put to him. We extracted from him, however, that they had arrived at the point the night before, after having spent five days on the voyage. It was less than sixty miles from Godthaab, but there had been a storm on the coast outside which had forced them to put in and wait when they were only four or five miles from the colony.

" Often as we had struck our tent and broke up camp, we had never performed these operations so speedily as to-day. The things were packed, each of the new-comers took his burden, and the whole caravan moved off towards the boats, which lay a short half-mile from the encampment. Down at the point stood the Greenlanders' tent in which they had spent the night. Terkel now informed me that they had run out of provisions, owing to the length of their voyage, and asked if we would give them something, so that they could make a meal before we started, as they had now eaten nothing for a long while. They had brought us another good supply, so we now had plenty for everybody, and I promised that they should have what they wanted, but not till we reached the other side of the fjord. It was just now high water, and I feared that if we delayed we might not be able to get the boats off.

"The relief party had come in one wooden boat, belonging to the Danish Greenland Service, and one ordinary Eskimo skin-boat, the property of the German Mission. We embarked in the former and stowed our baggage on board the latter. The packing seemed likely to take some time, so leaving Balto to see that nothing was left behind, the rest of us started and rowed across the fjord to look for a convenient landing-place and make ready for the distribution of food to the Greenlanders.

"As soon as the other boat arrived supplies were served out, and the natives were presently hard at work upon the long-expected food. I have already mentioned that we had seen to our astonishment Peter devour the entrails of a ptarmigan. We were now introduced to another Greenland delicacy. Silas produced the stomach of the reindeer he had shot, and the very sight of it made the mouths of his fellow-countrymen water. It was then cautiously opened and the contents distributed among the party, all of whom, after eating their share with evident satisfaction, carefully licked their fingers lest they should lose even a stray fragment of the highly pri/ed delicacy.

" At last we were ready to start in earnest and got under way, Peter escorting us and Silas the other boat in their quality of 'kayakers.' It was not long, however, before our companions had to put in to land again. Their boat had now been so many days in the water that the skin was soaked to such a degree that it was quite necessary to take it ashore and dry it. We therefore gave the crew a quantity of provisions and went on our way alone.

" The weather had grown finer and finer as the day wore on, and at noon the sun was shining brilliantly. We lay at our ease in the stern of the little white boat, leisurely contemplating the grandeur of the landscape round us. Towards evening, as the sun sank lower and the mountains thrust their long shadows far over the surface of the fjord, the solemnity of the scene seemed to inspire even the Eskimo, who had hitherto been so gay and lively. The cheerful conversation and merry laughter by degrees died away and gave place to absolute silence. Thus we rowed on for a long while, with not a sound but the monotonous splash of the oars, and not a sign of life to be seen. At last the intensity of the silence became too much for the Greenlanders, and with an earnestness which seemed the outcome of the surrounding nature they broke out into a hymn. This was followed by another, and to the accompaniment of their chants we now rowed on through the gathering darkness.

" Except for a break of half-an-hour our crew had been at their oars since nine o'clock in the morning. So at eleven we put in to land, to give them a well-earned rest, and pitched our tents for the night.

"Though we were up at five next morning, we found that the other crew whom we had left behind the day before had been astir still earlier. Their boat was already in sight, but only Silas, their 'kayaker,' caught us up before we started, and henceforward he kept us company as well as our own attendant Peter.

"We calculated that we should reach the colony somewhere about noon today. We got under way at six o'clock, and, as a nice breeze was blowing from the east, we hoisted sail and our boat shot quickly by one little spit of land after the other. The wind soon dropped, however, and the crew had to take to their oars again. We now left Ameralikfjord and turned northwards among all the islands which lie between it and Godthaab. When we came within two or three miles of the colony our two '

kayakers' went on in front to announce our approach.

" As we turned the point of one little promontory we came within sight of a long, low, red house with a little tower and surrounded by Eskimo stone-huts. This we supposed to be Godthaab, but the boats passed on, and we were told it was the German missionary station, Ny Herrnhut. Another promontory was passed, and we saw the settlement itself lying before us. There were already a number of people down by the beach, and the Danish flag was hoisted as we came into view. We landed and were received in the heartiest way by the Superintendent. Herr Bistrup, and his wife, to whom we were afterwards indebted for so much kindness and hospitality, and by the other Danish families, all of whom had come down to offer us a welcome."

Chapter XXI.

*WINTER QUARTERS AT GODTHAAB.*

The first thing to be done, now that we were all together again, was to find lodgings for the whole party. It was not yet quite certain that we should spend the winter here, but at all events we needed shelter for a time. Dietrichson, Sverdrup, and I were hospitably received by the Superintendent, while the other three were assigned a room in the building known as the "Old Doctor's House." Here they cooked for themselves, and did their own housekeeping generally.

The new-comers were, of course, for a long time a source of great interest to the Greenlanders. Of their arrival Balto writes:—

" The first evening, all the time we had a light in the room —there were no blinds or curtains before the windows—as soon as we had a light, there came a crowd of Eskimo girls outside the window, and peeped in at us as long as we were up. They came every single evening all the time we had no blind to the window."

It was not long before we were all on good terms with the natives, and made many friends among them. The three in the " Doctor's House " had an unbroken stream of visitors, and card-playing,

fiddling, and talking went on from early morning till late at night. Here Balto, of course, was supreme. He took upon himself the duties of host, as he would say, " quite and altogether alone." He held forth to the devoutly listening Greenlanders, partly in his broken Norwegian, to which a flavour of Danish was soon added, and partly in excruciating Eskimo. He had quickly picked up a number of words of this ANK AND LAKS HE1LMAX. A GOOD SEAL-CATCHER AND HIS WIFE FROM GODTHAAB (OK HYBRID RACE).

*(/'/am a photograph by C, Ryberg.)* formidable language, and these he twisted and turned to his purposes with the greatest confidence and self-satisfaction. The subject of his discourse, which was always attended by an abundance of illustrative gestures, was at one time our journey across " Sermersuak," or " the great Inland ice "—when he would describe how we Norwegians, who were evidently, in his estimation, the finest of fine fellows, had managed to find our way across this terrible desert of snow, where there was no coffee to be had and only a pipe of tobacco every Sunday; and at another time the frightful perils of the ice-floes, where " these Norwegians ate raw flesh, and we Lapps were almost *(i.e.,* very much) afraid."

All this, of course, was highly interesting to the Greenlanders, but I think Balto impressed his hearers most when he discoursed to them of his own native country, and told and showed them " how we Lapps drive reindeer," and how " clothes and boots are made in the land of the Lapps." Here he was in touch with the Greenlanders' own manner of life, and had their full sympathy and interest. There are few of them, indeed, who understand any Danish or Norwegian, but pantomime is a " Volapük " which is intelligible all the world over.

Kristiansen, on the other hand, who rarely let his tongue get the better of him, assumed a humbler position, and gladly left the leading part to Balto. If there was card-playing, however, Kristiansen would readily join in, while old

Ravna wandered silently about, mutely protesting against the whole proceedings. Often he would plaintively say to me, " I am an old Lapp, and I don't like all these people about." When the room was crammed full with smoking, card-playing, chattering Green-landers, Ravna would either be sitting up on a bed in a corner, looking indescribably miserable, or else he would steal out, and go and pay a visit to one of the Eskimo houses, where he was always welcome, and where he would take his place upon a bench. Here he would sit for hours, gazing at the ground in front of him, and saying never a word, and then would go out again. Why these visits of his were so highly appreciated, and why he went through the performance day after day, is still a mystery to me.

This want of sympathy between Ravna and his younger companions is easily to be explained if it be remembered that he was an elderly and sedate father of a family, while the other two were young and lusty. Not that, as far as I could )! HYHK1U K.U.I: 1-KOM bl'KKKK-TOI'I'KX.

*(Frcm a fknlcfrafli.')*

learn, anything that could shock him was ever done in the room. The visitors were of one sex only, for, to avoid possible complications, it had been decided that the feminine part of the population should not be allowed admittance.

This rigorous prohibition was not, however, sufficient to prevent Balto being deeply enamoured of a young Eskimo, who was rather attractive than really pretty. Unfortunately, she was already betrothed to an Eskimo Catechist, who was now stationed at a colony further to the north, and to whom she was to be married the following year. This state of things was, however, no obstacle to the growth of a pretty platonic attachment between Balto and his beloved Sophie. It was a romantic story altogether, and Balto was in course of time moved to write Sophie a long letter, which a Greenlander helped him to turn into Eskimo. In this he told her of his affection, explaining that he loved her, but that she must not misunderstand his love. He had no intention of mar-

rying her, not only because she was already bound to another—this engagement, I think I may say with confidence, would as a matter of fact have gone little way to deter either of them— but because, if he took her with him to the land of the Lapps, she would not be comfortable, as she would never accustom herself to the ways of this strange people; while, on the other hand, if he were to settle here in Greenland, he would always be pining for his relatives and friends at Karasjok. For this reason he would now say good-bye to her, and tell her that he was very fond of her, but did not wish to marry her.

This letter was a great source of joy to Sophie, as well as to her mother, who was very proud of the direction which Balto's affection had taken. She, indeed, used to say quite openly that she would much rather have Balto for a son-in-law than the unfortunate Catechist.

In spite of the letter the two lovers saw just as much of one another as before, and when Balto began to talk about Sophie his eloquence would rise to its highest pitch. She was not like the others, he declared; she was so modest, so retiring: she never ran up and down the road after the men-folk, as the other girls did. When he went away in the spring, I am sure he left some portion of his heart behind him. The parting was a hard one. On the voyage he spoke of Sophie several times, and it was only the fair ones of Copenhagen that completely effaced her memory from his mind.

The first Sunday evening after our installment at Godthaab there was dancing in the assembly-rooms of the colony—that is to say, in the cooper's workshop. I hope it is unnecessary to say that all the members of our party, except Ravna, were present on the occasion, and whenever there was a dance, which was not seldom.

"krktora," A Native Girl Of Gouthaab.

*(Ry A. BU'ck.frwt n pkotogr.tph ty Carl lyberg, Itispfftor South Greenland.)*

I fear I can scarcely describe how I was impressed the first time I saw these Greenlanders dance. The picturesque coloured dresses in closely-packed, swaying groups, the graceful forms in

rapid movement, the beaming faces every muscle of which was full of life, the boisterous voices, the infectious laughter, the nimble little legs and feet clad in boots of white, red, or blue, the perfect time which they all kept in their reels and other numerous dances—the whole was a scene of teeming life and unrestrained enjoyment.

It was all so new at that time to us wanderers from the deserts, so strange and attractive, that we were carried away in spite of ourselves. It was as if we had suddenly discovered what a spring of pleasure and delight life really contains. Among these folk at least joy is not yet a forgotten thing.

It really does one good to see the way in which they dance in Greenland. Here they do it to move their limbs and refresh their minds. Here there are no bitter-sweet visages of uncompromising propriety, no misshapen forms or extravagant dresses, no bored wearers of black coats, white shirts, and gloves; none, in fact, of all that futility that stalks about a European ballroom and takes the place of the Graces and other good spirits that should be found there. How these Greenlanders would laugh were they to see the funereal performance which we entitle a fashionable ball!

I need hardly say that we did not remain spectators for long. Our absolute ignorance of the dances was no bar, we were unceremoniously seized and set in motion by the little Eskimo. Here there was no modest waiting for engagements; all our partners were obviously proud when they c6uld get possession of one of us, which was, as a rule, no difficult matter. But at the same time they laughed at us most unmercifully when we danced wrong or awkwardly, as we all did of course at the beginning. For a long time afterwards, indeed, we used to seethe more mischievous among the girls dancing for the benefit of their friends in the road before the houses, and mimicking our ways and movements so accurately that we could well recognise ourselves as we passed by. These Greenlanders have a wonderfully keen eye for the comic side of things.

We were industrious pupils, however, and after a time one or two of us learnt to dance well enough to inspire respect. The Lapps, however, were quite hopeless. As a people they have no dances, and Ravna was not even to be induced to go and look on. Balto both looked on and joined in, but he remained to the very end a simple caricature, whether it was a BOl-KITl., LSK-IMO 01-HYBRID KACK, I ROM COD T11AAB.

*(f-'rani a jihviosrafk by C. Ryi'frg.)*
reel or round dance in which he performed. He sprawled and jumped about like a man of wood, while the Green-landers laughed at him till they nearly died. This ridicule did not deter him in the smallest degree, however. He was only too glad to manage the whole concern, to officiate as master of the ceremonies, to lead off or arrange a dance, and tell every one what he had to do. In the qualities of enterprise and self-confidence he was rarely wanting.

The Eskimo dances are not national. They are for the most part reels imported by English and American whalers, but adopted with such appreciation by the natives that they have become general along the whole west coast, and have in time assumed a certain national character. A few round dances, such as the waltz and the polka, are also in favour, but they are not held so high in estimation as the reels.

The only Greenlanders who do not dance, or, more strictly speaking, are not allowed to dance, are the so-called " German Greenlanders," who are members of the Moravian congregations. According to the teaching of the Moravian missionaries it is a great sin to dance or look at others dancing, and they have therefore been narrow-minded enough to forbid these poor people to practise one of their few amusements. The idea may hav'e been to protect the morality of their charges, but as far as I could learn, this does not stand higher among the German congregations than elsewhere in Greenland. The answer to this might be, however, that the charges dance in spite of the prohibition.

However this be, I feel sure that every one who has witnessed and taken part in a Greenland dance must see at once what a healthy and glorious recreation it is, as well as a most attractive sight. Many an evening, too, did we commit the sin of taking our enjoyment with these childlike folk, while the floor rocked under the rhythmic tread, and the fiddler sat on the carpenter's bench, and worked till his strings gave way.

The first period of our stay at Godthaab was strangely delightful after our march across the snow. Danes and Green-landers alike did all they could to make things pleasant for us, and I think we could all say with Balto that we very soon forgot " our hard life and all the desolation of the ice." At the same time we all grew in bulk to such an astonishing extent that it was reported that the difference could be seen from day _to day.

In spite of all this, however, there was one thing which prevented our being thoroughly comfortable—the uncertainty whether we should be here for the winter or not. None of us had much hope that our messenger had caught the *fox,* but all the same we felt as if we were expecting every day to see a ship come under steam and sail inwards from the horizon. The presentiment that something might happen was for a long time in our minds.

But the ship did not come, and I had long ago persuaded myself that the *Fox* had never had my message. Sverdrup and I, however, had for a time been thinking over another idea. There was an old sloop at the colony, belonging to the Greenland Trade Service, which was used to take goods to the neighbouring settlements. Now we thought that, if we could get this sloop, it would be an easy matter to put across to America and get home that way. This project came to nothing, however, because the Superintendent conceived that he had not the right to lend this vessel, which, as is set forth in his instructions, must not leave the colony except for official purposes, and a voyage to America could scarcely be brought under that head. So we must needs be content to stay where we were.

Then one day, while we were sitting at dinner, word was brought that there were " kayaks " coming up from the south, and soon afterwards a packet of letters was given me. They were opened in silent expectation, no one understanding what they could be, and our suqmse was great when they proved to be from Herr Smith, the manager of the cryolite mine at Ivigtut, and several of the Superintendents farther south. The first letter told me that my messenger had caught the *Fox* at the last moment. The ship had started the day before, but had been obliged by stress of weather to seek shelter close by. The following day she was just about to weigh anchor, when two " kayakers " were seen in the distance paddling at full speed and signalling to her to wait. Thus the captain got my letter, and was induced to go in to consult with the manager as to what was to be done, though in his opinion there could be no question of the *Fox* going up to Godthaab. The two agreed that this was impossible, as the captain did not know the water and was afraid of the dark nights, while the deciding argument was that he had forty passengers on board, men from the mine who were on their way home. They dared not run the risk of the ship being wrecked up north, and of these men having to winter somewhere, as, for instance, at Godthaab. An increase of this magnitude to the number of consumers might possibly have led to serious consequences in the way of famine.

The result was that the *Fox* went off without us, but taking my letter to Herr Game'l and Sverdrup's to his father. Thus it came about that the old *Fox,* the same vessel that had carried McClintock on his celebrated search for Franklin, brought to Europe the first news of our having successfully crossed Greenland.

Had these two Eskimo paddled very little less vigorously, no intelligence would have come. But in that case what heroes we should have been, and what a welcome back to life we should have received, if in the spring we had suddenly risen from our laurel-crowned graves in the ice! It was an unlucky thing indeed for ourselves as well as the newspapers.

With the voyage of the *Fox* on her way home we need not concern ourselves, though I may mention as worthy of note that she was obliged by want of coals to put in at Skudesnaes, and it was therefore my own country after all that received our first greeting. As to the arrival of the news in Europe on November 9, 1888, I need say nothing, but leave it to the reader to supply a description which I do not feel myself qualified to give, for this reason among others, that I was over in Greenland at the time, and little suspected what giants we suddenly became in the eyes of the world that day.

As we now knew that we had no chance of getting home this year, we became resigned to our fate, and reconciled to the idea of spending the winter where we were.

As time went on our intercourse with the natives grew closer, and the interest we took in them of course increased. It was not only the Eskimo of Godthaab and Ny Herrnhut whose acquaintance we made, but we also paid visits to other settlements in the neighbourhood. Thus in the middle of October some of us made an excursion in the company of the Superintendent to Kangek, some ten miles from Godthaab, and another in November to Narsak, which lies beyond the mouth of Ameralikfjord. I myself spent most of the winter in studying the peculiarities THE INTERIOR OK AN ESKIMO HUT.

*(Fn-ni a photograph taken fry tlte A uthor tit Sukkertppf'cn )*
of native life. I lived with the Eskimo in their huts, studied their methods of hunting and seal-catching, their customs and manner of life generally, and learnt, as far as I could in the short time at my disposal, their difficult language, in which latter task I received at the outset valuable assistance from the doctor of the place.

Upon the occasion of our arrival a poem was composed by a Greenlander of the name of Christian Rosing, and published in the same " Atuagagdliutit." As it will give the reader some idea of modern Eskimo poetry, I insert it here with a translation.

Angutit arfinigdit Norgemit autdlarput, Sisamat Norskiussut mardluk Lappiussut Norskinut ilauvdlutik tunumut niiiput, sakutitik tamaisa nagsataralugit.

Sermikut ingerdlaput nagdliokakttik, takuakarpiarnatik ardluatakaralik; kavfinik nungOtsiput tuparugtarputdlo, taimaiidlutingme klsa ituikasakaut.

Mardluk Nungmut tikipiit Ameralikortut,
umiatsiakarput tupingnangartumik,
ilatik sisamaussut kimagsimavdlugit,
Lappinik tusarpiigiit erininakautdle.

Klsame likilcrput
Lappit ilaiigdlo,
fcitdlime uvagut aterfiorpavut;
aipangussakulua tusiavigdlune,
mikissunguvdlunilo kumukuj6kartok.
Aiparssuakulua sisamavililik,
m'sunik kardiekartok anorarssualik,
inugsiarn i n garpok okalugkajokaok,
taimaingmat kalalfirkat nuanarivigpat.

Chr. Rosing.

Six men
Journeyed from Norway;
Four were Norwegians,
Two were Lapps;
They sailed upon a Norwegian ship,
Landed on the eastern coast,
And carried all their implements
With them.
They journeyed across the "Inland ice"
And suffered much by the way;
They had no great store of food
And only one suit of clothes;
Their coffee came to an early end
And likewise their tobacco.
And yet they crossed the " Inland ice "
And reached the western coast.
Two of them came to Godthaab
Out of Ameralikfjord;
They had a boat,
Which was exceeding strange.
Four of them
Had been left behind; them;
We heard that there were Lapps among
We longed much to see them.
At last they came,
The Lapps and ihe other two;
We went as usual down
To the sea-shore to receive them.

One of the Lapps
Was somewhat lame;
He was very small
And had a tall, pointed cap.
The other big one ol the Lapps
Had a four-cornered cap;
He had trousers upon his legs
And a great pelisse.
He was very kind
And very talkative;
For this reason the little Greenlanders
Grew very fond of him.

AN ESKIMO IN HIS "KAYAK." *(By A. Block, from photographs.)*

Chapter XXII.

*FIRST LESSONS IN THE "KAYAK."*

The Eskimo " kayaks " were, of course, a great attraction to us strangers, and as soon as possible I possessed myself of one. The necessary balance in this narrow, crank little vessel is very difficult for a beginner to acquire. One feels as if he were swinging on a knife-edge, and it is very necessary, so to speak, to keep your hair parted well in the middle. Yet when one sees the Eskimo dancing like sea-birds on the crests of the waves the whole performance ·seems simply child's play.

As soon as my "kayak" was ready I took it down to the shore. I found it no easy matter to force my legs and as much else of me as was necessary through the narrow opening into the place where I was to sit. This done, I was carefully pushed out into the water, but the feeling that seized me just as I left dry land was one of unspeakable insecurity. The little craft rocked first to one side and then to the other, and 403 every moment promised an immediate capsize. It seemed to me a simple impossibility that I should ever learn to sit it, and I looked with despairing envy and desire at the Eskimo, who were of course out to enjoy the sight of Nalagak in a " kayak," and were darting hither and thither over the water, and throwing their little spears about with as much ease and indifference as if they were sitting safe on the floor at home.

—— i. HOMKN KNGAGED IN COVERING A "KAYAK.' *(Payment for this-work is ahitiys made in coffic.) (/!' E. Nielsen, from a photograph.)*

But practice has a wonderful effect, and after one or two outings I began to feel tolerably comfortable. I got on better still when I had a pair of outriggers or supports made to help me. These are miniature " kayaks," about two feet long, and are fastened one on each side of the canoe, just behind the seat. They make things considerably easier for the uninitiated of course, but the Eskimo themselves rarely use them, and I myself abandoned them after a while.

One day, when I was out shooting, I found myself in the middle of a shoal of white whales, which I followed up. They took me well out to sea, and in my excitement I did not notice that the day was closing in. When at last I turned homewards it was already beginning to get dark. Unfortunately, too, before I had gone far a strongish breeze from the south got up, and as it caught me sideways it made paddling hard work, and I did not reach Godthaab till well into the evening. The folk there had meanwhile been getting very anxious on my account, for all the native " kayakers " had come in a long time ago, and the whole settlement was on the move.

As I passed the last point and entered the bay I thought I saw some dark objects against the snow, and heard at the same time the sound of childlike voices. I answered with a vigorous shout, which at once seemed to turn the whole place into one prolonged shriek. Then as I rode on the top of a wave in to the landing-place, there came a general rush of black forms down the white hillside to meet me. The snow swarmed with figures large and small, which pressed round partly to help scrape the ice from the canoe, and partly to look upon one who had risen, as it were, from the dead.

This little event Balto describes as follows:—

"When it began to grow dark, we fell to wondering that Nansen had not yet come. We waited for him a good while, but he did not appear, and then we all began to be very sorrowful. We had heard that he had not gone to Ny Herrn-hut, where there was a birthday-party at the missionary's. Ve sent a message, however, to ask, but he was not there,

and then I stretched myself upon my bed and the tears began to flow. Bistrup called all the people of the colony together and told them to get ready to go out and look for Nansen. They were soon ready, and Dietrichson took a gun, a lantern, and a horn to make him hear. Just as they were putting off in the boat Nansen came in to shore safe and well. The Greenlanders set up a frightful yell, and shouted ' Kujunak, Kujunak, Nansen tigipok, ajungilak,' which means 'Thank God, Nansen has come home!' or, ' Let us give thanks, Nansen has come; all is well.' Then my heart returned to its own place, and we were as happy as before."

After I had been some time practising, and the others saw that I got on tolerably well, some of them felt inclined to try too. Sverdrup.was the first to get himself a "kayak," and he soon became very proficient. Balto had begun to express his eagerness to try as soon as he arrived at Godthaab, and had

A " KAYAKKR" THROWING HIS HAR-POON AT A SEAL.

*(By A. Black.)*

asked me whether I thought it was difficult. The Danes ot the place meanwhile, none of whom understood the art, represented to him the danger of it, and told him how many lost their lives over it.

Balto, at no time distinguished for his courage, had given up the idea, and quietly looked on while I was out on the water. But now that Sverdrup had begun too, the temptation became too strong.

Both Sverdrup and I told him that it was not the easiest thing in the world to sit a " kayak," and that he would have to mind what he was about. But Balto was just now in a great state of elation, and said he was sure he could manage it, as he was used to driving a Lapp reindeer-sledge. Sverdrup pointed out to him that the two processes were not exactly identical, but Balto stood his ground and determined to make the experiment. Sverdrup's canoe was carried down; there were a number of spectators gathered round to watch, and I paddled about a little way from shore ready to fish him out.

Balto placed himself in the " kayak,"

made himself comfortable, and tucked his great pelisse round him. He made all his preparations with the most confident air, and evidently intended to show us what a Lapp really could do when he tried. When he was ready he eagerly seized the paddle in both hands, and boldly gave orders to push off.

But no sooner did the canoe touch the water than its steadiness began very perceptibly to diminish, and Balto's expression grew less confident. Yet he was determined to carry it off well, and even helped to push the canoe along. At last it was so far out that only the point was left resting upon the shore. Balto's valour now gave place to the most absolute terror, while at the same time the " kayak " slid out into the water and began to rock uncomfortably. Then came some desperate flourishes with the paddle in the air, which were apparently preparatory to strokes in the water; his face was one picture of horror and despair; he made frantic efforts at some unholy ejaculation, but no further than the first letter, "D D D," could he get. His mouth and the whole concern went under together, and his emotion vanished in a simple gurgle. All we could see was the bottom of the canoe and his great square cap floating on the surface of the water.

I paddled up, but luckily the water was so shallow that Balto could touch the bottom with his hands, and the " kayak " was so near the shore that the spectators could pull it and its occupant out. Balto was greeted with a pitiless shout of laughter from the bystanders, especially the girls. Then he got out of the canoe, and as he stood there on the rocks, throwing his arms and legs about, while the water poured out of his voluminous garments, which now hung close and lank about his body, he looked for all the world like an ordinary scarecrow.

The first thing he said was, " Well, I am almost wet." Then he reflected a moment, and added with all the fervour of con-

Tin: MEMBERS OF THE EXPEDITION IN THEIR "KAYAKS IN GODTHAAB HAR-BOUR.

*(From a pki'tograph* V *C. Ryl'frg.)* vic-
tion, "And I will say that that 'kayak' is
a very devil of a boat."

It was some time before Balto tried the
"kayak" again. Soon after this Dietrichson had one made, and was not long in
learning the use of it. His success induced Kristiansen to try his luck, and
even brought Balto to the point once
more.

Both of them set to work to build
their own vessels. The Greenlanders
helped them with the frames, and they
were then covered with skin, as usual
by the Eskimo women. As soon as they
were ready both the beginners set about
practising vigorously. Balto's experience had, however, made him cautious,
and he had the outriggers put on at once.
Kris-tiansen was more reckless, and
frightened us all by starting without
these supports and going right out to
sea. But, for the first time, he got on surprisingly well.

Towards the end of the winter all the
members of our party, except old Ravna, were often to be seen out in their
"kayaks " after sea-birds.

There are not many seal about in the
winter, so it does not pay to go after
them for mere amusement. We found the
birds better worth our attention, and the
flight-shooting of the eider-duck was
especially attractive. In the earlier part
of the winter this generally goes on in
the evenings, when the duck come flying in large or small flocks along the
shore on their way into the fjords. The
"kayaks" are drawn up in line, especially just off the promontories. It was quite
exciting work to lie there in wait for the
duck, and reminded me of the flight-
shooting at home when the woodcock
come back in the spring. One's eyes are
turned southwards, whence the duck
should come. Suddenly you see the man
in the furthest canoe stoop forward and
paddle away as hard as he can go, while
the rest of the line meanwhile dress up
to him. Then he stops, there is a moment's waiting, and then come a flash
and a report, which are taken up by the
next, and so follow down the line. You
see a dark mass to the south of you
silently skimming the water. You bring

your canoe up a bit to get better into
range; you put your paddle in under its
strap and get your gun ready. By this
time you can distinguish every bird. Just
as they sweep by you, you let fly into
the thickest part of the flock, and if you
are lucky you get a couple or more to
your shot. Then you load again, gather
up your birds, and wait for the next
flight. So you go on till it is dark, the
line of "kayaks" shifting backwards and
forwards just as the duck happen to fly
close to or further from the shore.

This shooting needs a considerable
amount of skill, for the duck fly strongly, and a good command of your canoe
is necessary if you are to keep within
range and shoot tolerably straight.
Many of the natives are amazingly good
hands at it. The quickness with which
they bring the canoe up to the point,
secure the paddle, and get the gun to
the shoulder, as well as the accuracy of
their aim, even if they have only one
bird to cover, is enough to secure the admiration of the best of shots, especially
as the little boats in which they sit are
the whole time bobbing up and down
upon the waves.

KSK1MO BOY PROM GODTHAAH. *(/"rvr-
rt a photograph by C.*

Chapter XXIII.

*CHRISTMAS AT GODTHAAB.*

In due time Christmas came, in the
keeping of which the Greenlanders cannot be said to be far behind the rest
of the world. The preparations begin
months before; the women have their
hands full with the making of any
amount of fine new clothes, tunics,
breeches, and boots, all with the most
garish decorations. The whole family,
from the youngest children to the aged
grandparents, must appear as smart as
possible, and in new things from top to
toe.

The young unmarried women, of
course, are the most extravagant. If they
belong to the more well-to-do families,
who are employed by the " Service,"
the parents will generally have ordered
something from Copenhagen for the occasion; something really good, better
than anything the colonial store supplies, of silk may he, though it is even

said that some have had velvet imported
for them. In this new finery, which is
generally made up in secret, these girls
suddenly appear on the festal day, each
one more irresistible than he,r neighbour.

If women are in the habit of talking
about dress and decorations elsewhere
in the world, the Christian Greenlander
is by IN WINTER GAKB.

*(From a fliofcgrafh by C. Kyl'crg.)*

no means behind her sisters. But I cannot deny that she really does look be-
witchingly attractive at Christmas-time
in her picturesque Eskimo costume. I
fear a competition would not always
prove the superiority of her rivals across
the sea, in spite of all their European advantages.

But it is not only dress that engages
the attention on the approach of Christmas. With the idea of simply revelling
in creature-comforts, the Eskimo saves
up his money, so far indeed as he can
contrive to do so, for a long while before. If he has no money when the season comes, why, he simply raises it by
selling one of his chief necessaries. It
has been no uncommon practice to take
the down out of the coverlets and sell it
to the Trade for the purpose of buying
some luxury or other. The thriftless one
must then, of course, lie and shiver un-
der.nothing but cotton for the rest of the
winter. The first thing of all that there
must be an abundance of is coffee.

So it will be seen that our great festival has not been improved in character
by its transplantation to Greenland soil.
It is, in fact, here as elsewhere, the despair of the father and the ruin of the
stomach. It brings a transitory joy perhaps, but one that is followed by a more
permanent privation. It is needless to
say that an institution of this nature is
thoroughly appreciated by the Eskimo,
who has made the Christian precept, "
Take no thought for the morrow," pre-
eminently his own.

In our host's house the usual preparations were also in full swing. Our hostess, Sverdrup, and Dietrichson had long
been busy making bags, baskets, and
other receptacles of coloured paper,
while the Superintendent himself was

at work upon a Christmas-tree, which he constructed by fastening branches of Greenland juniper into a piece of wood which did duty for a stem.

On the morning of Christmas Eve this tree was dressed. At two o'clock there was a grand ceremony in the church. The children were to be catechised, and no Eskimo could fail to be present at so amusing a function. As soon as this was over the children, in accordance with old custom, rushed one and all across to the Superintendent's to receive each his bag of figs. These they carried home, and then they presented themselves at our rooms to receive another supply. There was a regular stampede of all these little skin-clad creatures. All who could walk came by themselves; those who were too young were carried by their mothers, while the smallest of all appeared by proxy.

At five o'clock there was choral service in church. Hymns, written in or translated into Eskimo by the "catechists," were sung by a large choir of natives, who had surreptitiously been practising a long while before. The performance impressed one by its charm of simplicity, and the melodies were fresh and cheerful. An elderly half-civilised Greenlander, who never hid his light under a bushel if he could help it, declared that the singing was not so good as when he had a hand in it, but it was *very* pretty" all the same. It reminded one so much, he said, of a gull-rock, where the birds are always flying up and down and screaming.

After supper at the Superintendent's, to which all our party were invited, the tree was lighted and general excitement prevailed.

Just as the merriment was at its highest the door opened and a great round head with a huge shock of hair appeared. This was part of our friend Joel, who had come to inquire about a bottle of beer he had received from the Lapps in exchange for some eider-ducks, but which he had left behind with something else when he went to pay a visit to the doctor on the chance of getting a dram or two in honour of the occasion. As far as this errand went he seemed

to have been eminently successful. He set us all laughing at the lively-gestures by which he described that everything had disappeared, and that he had found " Bovase nami, mitit nami, elisa nami, damase nami;" that is to say, " No bottle, no duck, no fishing-line, no anything." He was, however, soon consoled with another bottle of beer. His astonishment, and the glitter of his dark eyes, which turned to two bright round beads, when he saw the Christmas-tree and all the lights and decorations, were most amusing to see; but the wildness of his delight was still greater when he was given some bags of sugar-plums. As rich as Croesus and far happier, he reeled off across the rocks to join his charming consort at Ny Herrnhut.

On Christmas morning, about six or seven o'clock, just as I was sleeping my sweetest and fancying myself back at home, the songs of children were suddenly wafted through the air and took their place in my wandering dreams. The sound grew louder, and I woke to hear the carolling of a large choir in the passage outside our door. They had been singing at the Eskimo houses all night long, and had now come, faithful to tradition, to wake the Europeans of the place. I allow that the custom is charming, and that I had never been woke in so pleasant a

A ME.M. IN AN KSK1.MO HUT. (/fy *E. Nielsen, from a photograph.*) way before; but I must add that when the strains had ceased, and the choir departed to sing at other doors, I gently dozed off again to pick up the lost thread of my interrupted dream.

When I went into the kitchen that morning I found Balto there haranguing the girls. He was holding forth at length on the virtues of the Eskimo Christmas, which he had found " very jolly." He was fluent as usual. He had been wandering from house to house the whole night; and what a place it was for coffee! It was not yet ten o'clock, and he had had twenty-four big cups already " that morning." As his eyes and speech showed, something stronger than coffee had also been exhibited, but this was not mentioned. He had never had such a

Christmas before; it all really was "very jolly."

Soon after noon the adult Eskimo of the place, men and women alike, came round as usual to all the Europeans, to shake hands with them and wish them a merry Christmas. To this greeting it is only necessary to answer " Itlidlo," or " The same to you," but even this gets somewhat monotonous when it has to be repeated to fifty people or more.

At three o'clock the leading natives—that is to say, the "catechists," the printer, the men employed by the "Service," and the seal-catchers—were invited, together with their wives, to an entertainment of chocolate, coffee, and cakes at the Superintendent's. They came in their best Christmas array, paid their respects to the host and hostess, and ranged themselves in silence along the walls. It was a very solemn performance, but that is not to be wondered at, since these poor folk were now in the state apartment of "the Merchant," one of the highest in the land. Presently, however, the refreshments had their usual effect, and the gathering assumed a more genial tone. One of the men, who had been in Copenhagen and wished to show his fellow-countrymen how things were done in the great world, went up to one of the more prominent of the native ladies and offered her his arm with an awkward bow. She, of course, did not understand the manoeuvre, and he was obliged to drag her away by force in order to conduct her, as he said, to a worthier place further up the room. When he had accomplished this he turned to me to explain how stupid his compatriots were, and how often they had to be instructed how they should behave in polite society. " Now," he went on, " suppose you take my wife and lead her up to a more honourable place." I thanked him for the great compliment he was paying me, and deplored that I did not feel myself at all worthy of the distinction. The man had evidently had a little more than was good for him. He was one of the few Greenlanders who are so far trusted that they have spirits given into their keeping on such occasions. He was celebrating the festival by indulging himself as long as his supply lasted. Every night he was quite unmanageable, and his nice little wife had to leave the house or sleep in the garret, though she had taken all possible precautions beforehand, by making signs and binding amulets under the seats of the chairs, with a view to charming her husband into a gentle drunkenness, as Eskimo superstition ordains.

At last the guests took their leave, and went off on their Christmas pilgrimage to another house, there to begin the festivities again.

Two days later the Superintendent gave another entertainment to the employé's in the " Service " and the leading seal-catchers. On this occasion rooms were borrowed in the hospital, and there was a great supply of peasoup, bacon, salt reindeer, and stewed apples; spirits were not wanting, and afterwards came punch, coffee, and cigars. On such field-days the combatants come armed with plate, cup or bowl, spoon, and some vessel for the punch. All that a man does not eat of his ration he carries home to his wife and children, who, indeed, often put in an appearance at the meal itself to make their share secure.

This entertainment came to an end in the course of the evening, and the company then adjourned to the coopers workshop for further jollification.

AN ESKIMO HOUSE IN THE WINTER. *(Ky the Autlwr.)*

Chapter XXIV.

*SARDLOK AND KANGEK—NOTES FROM MY DIARY. February 6.*—I am now living half underground in an earth-hut, which is so low inside that I can scarcely stand upright. As in all Eskimo houses, the entrance is a long passage, which is so small that one is almost obliged to go through it on all-fours. Outside the snow is deep enough to bury the hut. All that is to be seen is part of the window, which is kept as clear as possible, and the hole which serves as entrance to the above passage.

I had long had it in my mind to pay a visit to Sardlok, and as the doctor, one day in January, was coming out here to

see a sick man, I started off at the same time in the company of Joel.
4'7 2 D

The distance is thirteen or. fourteen miles: my arms were not quite used to the exercise, and the cramped position which the "kayak" entails upon one tired me considerably before I reached my journey's end, and as the afternoon went on I began to long for Sardlok. In Joel, however, as the reader will surmise, I had a cheery companion. At one time he sang songs, "Den evig glade kobbersmed" among them of course; at another he gave me any amount of unintelligible information about the places we passed; then whenever he saw a flock of eider-duck come flying by he made desperate attempts to get his gun out, which he only did once in time, and then he shot wide. Then, again, he would grunt out that he must go ashore to empty his canoe, and would paddle off as if his life depended on it. The little vessel was half full of water indeed, as, like the rest of him, it was in very bad repair and leaked unmercifully.

It was a dark evening: the " Saddle " and other peaks rose menacingly above us and shut in the east side of the fjord: over our heads the net of stars shone brilliantly, and while we worked along silently side by side there was no sound to be heard save the splash of the paddles and the rippling of the water against the sides of the canoes.

At last we rounded a point, saw a friendly light shining to greet us, and found ourselves at our destination. The doctor had arrived a little while before. The passage of the narrow little tunnel, the entry into a small but cosy room like this, and the welcome of Eskimo hospitality, all have attractions of their own.

I am staying in the house of Johan Ludvig, an old "cate-chist." Its other occupants are his wife, one daughter, and two sons. Johan Ludvig told me with obvious pride that his grandfather was a Norwegian, and had been renowned for his gigantic strength. He has himself been a clever seal-catcher in his day, but he goes out no longer, as he is more than seventy years old. He has had several sons, who have done him credit, though

two of them were lost in their "kayaks. ' The youngest, who is now at home, a boy of eighteen, is no seal-catcher. His parents are afraid to let him go out.

It is no active life I am leading here; in fact, I am fast turning Eskimo. I live as the natives do, eat their food, and am learning to appreciate such dainties as raw blubber, raw halibut-skin, frozen crowberries mixed with rancid blubber, and so on. I talk to the people as well as I can, go out in my "kayak" with them, fish, and shoot on land and water. In fact I begin to see that there really is nothing to prevent a European turning Eskimo if he only have his time before him.

"SADI.EN " OR "THE SADDLE," A MOUNTAIN TO THE NORTH OF GODTHAAB. *(From a flwtfra/h l-y C. Ryfarg.)*

One cannot help being comfortable in these people's society. Their innocent, careless ways, their humble contentment with life as it is, and their kindness are very catching, and must clear one's mind of all dissatisfaction and restlessness.

My original idea had been to do some reindeer-stalking, and I went out one day on " ski,'' but as there was not even a track to be seen I have done nothing more in that way. My chief amusement is to go halibut-fishing. Pulling up these huge, strong fish, which are big enough to upset a boat, from a little canoe is the best sport in the way of sea-fishing that I have yet come across.

To begin with, one may wait half or even the whole day and not get a bite. This is no pleasant work in thirty or forty degrees of frost, with a bitter north wind blowing, and perhaps in driving snow. Care has to be taken or some part or other of the face will be caught by the frost.

But if the bite does come at last, all hardships are forgotten. At first, as a rule, there is no violent tug, but the line is drawn down by a slow and irresistible force; then come some distinct jerks; the paddle is slipped under its strap, you take the line in both hands and pull as hard and violently as you can; then you feel if the fish is still on, and if he is you go at it again. You tug and tug and tug again, time after time, for it is necessary to get him well hooked. You look like a lunatic all the while this is going on, but if one has to transmit the jerks the whole length of a hundred fathom line it is indispensable to put one's back into the work.

At last you have him fast and you begin to haul in. It is a slow business, as the fish resists and the line is long, and the strain tells on the arms. The line is coiled up on the " kayak " meanwhile, and drenched with water from time to time to prevent its freezing into a mass. In case the fish should make for the bottom again and take all the line out, you throw the bladder which is fastened to the end out to the side; if he does do this you simply follow the bladder, which remains on the surface, and take the line up again when he is more exhausted.

The length of one of these lines is extraordinary. At last the end comes; you can see the cord twisting with the fish's movements. The resistance increases, and it is all you can do to pull; hand over hand, however, the line comes in; the sinking-stone appears, and then a huge head rises above the water with a mouth and eyes that are enough to make your blood run cold. You seize the club which lies behind you and give him a couple of prodigious whacks in the region of his brain, but with a desperate effort he drags his head under water and with the speed of lightning darts off to the bottom again. 'oe betide you now if you It is passed through certain straps which are fixed to the " kayak ' just in front of the occupant, and then projects from the vessel laterally. The blade thus lying on the water of course very much increases the steadiness of the canoe.

HALIBUT-FISHING KKUM THE "KAYAK."
*(Hy A. Black, after a iviigli sketch hy the Author.)*

have not your line clear and it hitches anywhere; you are upside down before you know where you are. As the fish reaches the bottom the pace slackens, and you can begin to haul in again. A second time you get him up, and perhaps a second time he returns to the depths. To pull a big halibut up three or possibly four times from a hundred fath-

oms of water is fairly exhausting work. When you really have him in hand at last you give him a few well-directed blows, which make him somewhat quieter; then you let fly at him as hard and fast as you can manage; perhaps he makes one or two more despairing attempts to break away, but as the blows shower down upon him he gradually grows stupid and inactive. Then you drive your knife into his brain and spine till he is as dead as you can manage to make him for the time being. You now attach the bladder to his mouth to make him float, and tow him ashore in order to fasten him properly to the canoe. While I was at this work one day I found I had got both cheeks, as well as my nose and chin, well fro/en. However, by rubbing them with salt water and ice, of which there was plenty on the "kayak," I succeeded in reviving them and preventing further consequences.

To get your fish to land you take the line between your teeth and then paddle away. I must confess that I found this towing the least agreeable part of the whole business. Every time the canoe is carried on the top of a wave you are suddenly pulled up by the line with a jerk almost hard enough to wrench your teeth out. This is a difficulty, perhaps, which does not present itself to the Eskimo, whom nature has provided with teeth so strong that he can easily pull nails out with them.

When you have brought your fish ashore you tie him fast to the side of the canoe, with his head foremost, so that he is as little drag upon you as possible. To arrive at Sardlok with one of these huge fish in tow, and to be received on the beach with the same beaming welcome that awaits every one who brings in a catch, was an experience which recalled the triumphant return home with one's first game in the days of childhood.

This fishing is a sport well worthy of the name. The fish weigh from two to four hundred pounds, and they make good food at a time when there is little else to be had. On two which I caught we lived, five of us, for nearly three weeks, and ate scarcely anything else

the whole time.

One day as we were out fishing in still, calm weather, the sky suddenly darkened to the south. We knew the wind was coming, and gathered up our lines with all haste. But before ve were ready the storm was upon us, first with a few preparatory gusts, and then in all its wild fury. The sea flew black and white before it, the calm surface was soon one sheet of foam. The current and the wind met here; the green waves broke in crests of white spray, and the canoes were lost to each other in the hollows. We had to make for shore to save our fish and ourselves, and we paddled away as fast as we could go with the sea on our beam.

An occasion like this, which was, of course, a regular experience of the Greenlanders, had all the charm of novelty to me, and my mastery of the "kayak" was put to a hard test. You have to keep a sharp eye on these big breaking seas, for if one of them catches the canoe before the paddle is well out on the lee-side there is every chance of its occupant going to the bottom for ever and a day.

When we reached the shore we kept along it under shelter. Then we ran northwards fast before the wind, and now the " kayak " was even harder to manage than before. The big seas came rolling up from behind, and it was no easy matter to keep an even keel. As the wave comes you give a couple of powerful strokes and let the paddle float out to the side. Then the stern is lifted high in the air and you lean hard back. As the wave breaks you feel a heavy blow on the back, while the spray showers round you, and you seem to fly through space on the foaming crest. Then it rolls by you, you sink into the hollow, and with a few more vigorous strokes you ride again on to the back of the next wave.

I had a good companion and instructor in Eliase, who kept the whole time as close to my side as the sea would let him. Now he would shoot past me on the top of one wave, and then I would ride by him on the next. It was a dance with the waves and a game with danger.

Presently the shore turned westwards

and again offered us shelter. But first there was a belt of ice to pass, and it was necessary to bring the canoes through without getting them crushed between the moving floes. We found an opening and seized the opportunity, and with a few quick strokes sailed through on the top of a sea.

Terkel, the leading seal-catcher of Sardlok, and his brother

' j TKKKKL, THK LEADING SEAL-CATCHtK OK SARDI.OK.

*(By A. Bloch, from a photograph by C. Kyterg.)*

Hoseas, were of our party. They each had a halibut in tow, and came into shelter a little while after us. We hoped that while the fish were being lashed fast and other preparations were being made the wind would drop. But it was equally strong when we started again for Sardlok. We had it all behind us, however, made a good passage, and were soon safe at home.

I am often asked out to eat halibut in the other houses, generally just after I have had my fill of it here at home. But I have to go from one to the other and continue eating as long as my system will consent to be imposed upon. I go most to Terkel's, which is the biggest house in the place. The other evening as I sat there I witnessed a very comical performance. Hoseas' son, a little boy rather more than twelve months old, was dancing the " mardluk," a kind of reel, with Terkel's daughter, a child of three. The boy had nothing but his shirt on, which reached about half-way down his stomach; his arms were held out stiff like pump-handles; with an air as grave as any professor's he went through his steps. First he hopped on one leg and then on the other, then he twirled round, and all was executed in perfect time with the singing of the air, and with the same grave contemplation of his partner. She was a pretty little girl, was dressed just like a woman, and had her hair tied on the top of her head in the orthodox way, and an arch, coquettish look on her face which suggested that this was not the first time she had been in masculine company. The whole sight was enough to make a hermit laugh.

The Eskimo children are precocious indeed.

On February 14 I went back to Godthaab, having already-been at Sardlok nearly a month. We were a party of three, Hoseas joining Joel and me. All our " kayaks " were well laden with halibut, birds, and such things, and very inopportunely a strongish west wind sprang up on the way. As long as we kept close under the western shore we did well enough, but when we were about to cross over to Godthaab things grew worse. The further we got out the bigger the waves became, and we quite disappeared between them. As it came on to snow, too, and we could see nothing, the Eskimo began to hesitate, and called to me to turn back and shelter under the land again. I thought we could find our way across well enough in spite of the snow, and wanted to push on. So we went on for a while, with the waves rolling in on our quarter; but things grew worse and worse, my companions would listen no longer, and turned towards shore without waiting for my consent. So we worked back against the wind, and lay in shelter to see if the weather meant to improve. Meanwhile we landed a good deal of our cargo, and packed it away under stones and snow, so that we could fetch it next day if the weather were better. It is bad, of

"KAVAKKKS IN TIIK OPKN SKA.

*(/ty Th. lltituilif,/row a. rough sketch ty the Author.)*

course, to have too much on the canoes in a sea, as they capsize so much the more easily. A little later, as the snow cleared off and the wind dropped a little, we went on our way again, and got safely across to Godthaab.

I came out to Kangek on February 17. It is a good place for practice in the " kayak.' The current is exceptionally fast, and off the headlands and between the islands it runs like a river. Where it meets the great waves coming from the open sea they rise and break like the surf over a sunken rock. So it is no wonder that the natives of Kangek are the cleverest " kayakers " hereabouts, and I doubt whether there are better in all Greenland. They get their living in the

open sea at the risk of their lives, and though many are lost they go out calmly to their daily task. It is a pleasure to see them on the great sea-waves, riding them like horses, while the foam floats round them like a long white mane. There is scarcely a sea they can-

" AND AS THK WAVE HKKAKS THKOW TIIEMSKl.VES INTO ITS VKRY JAWS." *(By A. Bloc/i, after a rough sketch ty the Author.)* not ride; if a wave presses them too hard, they fasten the paddle under the strap on the weather side, stoop down, and let it roll over them. Or they lay the paddle out flat, and as the wave breaks throw themselves into its very jaws, and so lessen the shock, rising again on the paddle when all is over. I have even been told that really masterly " kayakers " have a prettier manoeuvre still. When a sea is so heavy that they think they cannot manage it in any other way, they capsize at the moment the wave breaks, and let the bottom of the canoe receive the shock.

The blow such a wave can give must be very severe. I have heard of a man who was struck by the full force of a sea, which bent him down in the canoe and wrenched his back so badly

Simon, "catkchist" And Skai.-catchkr Of Kangek.

*(From a fkolafrafli ty C. Ryterg.)*

that he became a cripple for life; and yet he was not upset. The presence of mind and command of their little craft that these men can show is simply marvellous.

A skilful seal-catcher from Karusuk, Anton by name, came out to Kangek one day in his canoe. There was a high sea running, and as he did not know the water he was carried by a big wave over a sunken rock and there left high and dry. Here another sea rolled in upon him; he thought all was over, but bent forward and held his paddle fast, while the wave floated him clear and left him riding as gaily as before.

The sport I cultivate most here is eider-duck shooting. One of the best places is a small group of islands known as Imerigsok. Far out on the sea side of these the birds are especially abundant, but here there is always a swell and the current runs fast, so that for a new hand the shooting is difficult. But on the whole it is the best form of sport that I have yet had in the " kayak."

Here the method is different from that practised at Godthaab, as we paddle about to find our duck. When you catch sight of them you work well off to windward before you bear down on them. As a rule you cannot get very close in, but as they must rise against the wind they are generally forced to fly by you within range. But the thing is to get your canoe into the right position to give you a shot. As the " kayak " does not give one much turning room, a man who does not shoot from his left shoulder cannot cover his right side, but must be content with straight ahead or left side shots. So, as the duck rise, and you see which direction they are going to take, you swing the canoe round if necessary, fix the paddle, slip your right mitten off, fetch out the gun and bring it to your shoulder; but if you are to have any chance of dropping your bird this must all be done in an instant. And if there is any sea running you must be so thoroughly at home in the canoe that you can handle your gun with as much certainty as if you were ashore, to say nothing of keeping your balance at the moment of firing.

Many of the Kangek men are masters at all this, and I have seen them, in a heavy sea, bring their half-score birds down without a miss. Now and then I have met out at sea a man of the name of Pedersuak—that is to say, " the great Peter "— and we have generally gone on in company. Sometimes we have tried our skill together, but as he is an excellent shot at these birds I have come off second best, much to his amusement and satisfaction.

One day when we were together two duck came sweeping by us down the wind. They were out of range for me, but were making for Pedersuak. I shouted to him and he saw them, but quietly let them pass him. I could not understand what he meant, but presently he raised his gun and brought them both down. He explained to me afterwards that he had only waited to get them in

line before he fired. I thought it was simply a fluke, but we had not paddled far before two more duck came by, and still better within my companion's reach. He fixed his paddle and held his gun ready, but did not fire. Then, when they were a long way past, the report came and both birds fell. I have often witnessed this performance, and have even seen three birds brought down at one shot in the same way. These folk have only muzzle-loaders, but they use heavy charges, and shoot at what we should call absurdly long distances. I have often been out with them and have let birds pass me as being out of range, while an Eskimo by my side has not hesitated to fire, and has, moreover, brought off his shot. The loading of these guns when the sea is breaking over the " kayak " is not easy. The natives put the butt of the gun forward on the canoe, and hold the muzzle against the face, or rest it on the shoulder, while they take out powder, cap, and wadding, which they always carry in their caps to keep them dry. In this way they manage to load in almost any sea without getting water down the barrel. There is a special bag to contain the gun on the canoe in front, so that it is always ready to hand.

Another way of getting these birds, which is really better sport still, is spearing them with the dart; but it is exceedingly difficult, and needs a great deal of practice. Here, again, the Kangek people are supreme. It is truly delightful to see the darts fly from the throwing-stick as if they were shot from a bow, and birds hit from the same distance at which one would fire with a gun if they were lying on the water. I understand that birds are even killed flying in this way. It is the auk especially that they use their darts upon, and in November and December, when these birds are most plentiful, though they have no more than one or two of these little weapons lying before them on the "kayak," they come home often with a bag of sixty or seventy. This is more than one can get with a gun, which

TOBIAS, ONK OK THK LEADING SEAL-CATCHKKS OF KANGKK.
*(From a. photograph by C. Ryberg.)*

frightens the birds a long way round, while by the dart only the very nearest are disturbed.

While I have been here this sport has not been very good, as the birds are said to be shyer now the sun has got so high. Yet the men will bring home twenty, which have been killed in the course of the morning, all by the strength of the arm and an instrument made of wood and bone. Where, then, are the great advantages which our firearms were to bring these people? The advances of civilisation are not always so huge as we are often ready to imagine them.

After spending three weeks at Kangek I returned, and on the home journey fell in with a good instance of Greenland superstition. When I reached Godthaab I was received as usual on the beach by a number of fair Eskimo. I must have been more surly and taciturn than usual, possibly because I was tired from having paddled about among the islands after BOAS. ONE OF THE LEADING SKAI.-CATCHERS OF KANGEK.
*(FrvtH a photograph by C, Rybcrg.*
birds the whole day. But the Greenlanders at once came to the conclusion that I had come across a horrid big ogre or supernatural being named "Tupilik," because of his tent-like shape, who haunts some of the islands, and has the uncomfortable habit of displaying himself to solitary "kayakers" who trespass upon his domain, and frightening them out of their wits. When the men come back after seeing this apparition they are always silent and moody for a season. The belief in this is absolute, and the men therefore dare not go out to these islands by themselves. It was considered, too, that I ought not to be allowed to paddle about alone so much, but now my friends hoped that I had had my experience and paid for it.

Chapter XXV.

*FURTHER ATTEMPTS ON THE "INLAND ICE"—THE SHIP! THE SHIP.'—THE VOYAGE HOME.*

We had long had it on our minds to make a little expedition to the "Inland ice" as soon as spring came, to see whether that season were not likely to be the best for exploration of the outer margin. We thought, from what we had observed in September, that all the fissures and irregularities would be filled up and smoothed down by the heavy snowfalls and continual wind of the winter.

It was my idea, therefore, that future " ski" expeditions which are intended to investigate the outskirts of the icefield ought to utilise the months of April and May, and perhaps a part of June, and that then they would be able to pass over with comparative ease ground on which they would be otherwise much hampered by the obstacles which are exposed by the subsequent melting of the snow. Again, if such an expedition contemplated using a special vessel built for sailing on the snow, which 1 am persuaded would be a great help, the spring and early summer would be best for this purpose, since not only would the snow be in good condition, but there would be more wind. It is quite possible that with such a vessel one could easily sail along the edge of the ice-field from the southern part of the country a very long way north, if not to its extreme end.

There was much, therefore, to urge me to visit the " Inland ice" again, and I thought it would be most interesting to explore first that part where we came down, in order to see what changes there had been since we were there in the autumn.

434

But it was thought possible at the colony that the ship from Europe which was to take us home might arrive as early as April i, and after that time, of course, we should not be able to leave the place for long. So some of us determined to make an attempt in March, though this was too early to produce any great result. Our equipment this time was in several respects very poor. The only provisions we could scrape together were dried capelan fish, ship's biscuit, and butter. Of spirit for melting snow we had a very small supply. With what we could get, however, three of us, Sverdrup, Kristiansen, and I, started for Ameralikfjord on March 21, I in my "kayak," and the other two in a boat.

We reached Kasigianguit, where we hoped to get a few reindeer to stock our larder with, but here we were kept by snowstorms and mild weather for five days. Most of the time we spent in the tent, and lived on our fish, biscuits, and butter, while the wet snow accumulated on the top of us, and that on which we lay melted away underneath. The last day or two, in fact, we lived in a simple pool, and once, as we thought the sleeping-bag was rather damp, we examined it, and found so much water inside that we could bale it out with our hands. This was of little use, however, as it found its way in again just as fast. Sverdrup opined that our life in the tent up on the " Inland ice " had been pure enjoyment compared with this.

As the end of the month was now near and the ship might soon be expected to arrive, we did not see the use of going on any further, so on March 28 we returned to Godthaab.

At the same time as we left for this excursion, Dietrichson and Balto had started on a " kayak " tour into Godthaabsfjord to visit the settlements of Sardlok, Kornok, Umanak, and Karusuk. They came back some days after us. The last day of their tour, as they were on the way home, and were just off the mountain known as " Sadlen," Balto called out to Dietrichson that he must go ashore, as his canoe was leaking fast and would soon be half full. Dietrichson answered that he did not see what good that would be, for the shore was so steep that there was nothing to land on; they had better paddle on a bit and try to find a better place. In the most heartrending tone Balto replied, "Then I suppose I shall have to sink. " However, they paddled for dear lite, and presently found a rock or two, on to which Balto could just crawl out, so that they could empty the canoe. They found a hole in the bottom, but all they had to plug it up with was a mitten and some butter, which they made to serve the purpose, and so went on.

Soon afterwards they were suddenly caught in a storm, but luckily just by a spot where they could land, for if this had happened a little earlier or a little later there is no saying how-things would have gone. There was no other possible place to go ashore, and the storm was so violent that they could scarcely have weathered it on the water. On this very occasion a native was lost off Umanak. Seven hours they had to spend on the little shelf of rock on which they had landed. Then the weather improved somewhat, and in the evening they arrived safely at Godthaab, where they were joyfully welcomed by the Eskimo, who thought they had done well to travel on such a day when they themselves had not ventured to go out.

After I had waited nearly a week at Godthaab and there was no sign of the much expected ship, I determined to make one more attempt on the " Inland ice.' So on April 4 I set off in my " kayak " with Aperavigssuak—that is to say, " the great Abraham"—a well-known old "kayaker" of Kangek, into Godthaabsfjord. The same day we reached Kornok, which is about 36 miles from Godthaab, and next morning I went on with two men named Karl and Larserak further up the fjord towards Ujaragsuit, where I meant to make my ascent. As the head of the fjord was frozen we went into an inlet by Kangiusak, beached the canoes and took to our " ski." Then we crossed the end of the inlet, which was also frozen, and went on over a promontory till we joined the fjord again. Here we pitched the tent, which we had carried across along with some provisions. Our supply of the latter was by no means sufficient, and it was necessary to shoot some ptarmigan. These were devoured raw in the usual Eskimo way, and treated in this very simple manner they are certainly excellent. They must be allowed to get cool, however; one day, when I was very hungry, I set to work upon one directly after I had shot it. I did not get far, and never repeated the experiment; it had a most peculiar taste, and the flesh still quivered between my teeth.

MY FRIEND APKRAViGSSUAK. *(rvttt it fil-wfografk by C, Rylerg.*

Next day, April 6, we crossed over the ice on our " ski" and went up Ujaragsuitfjord. Half-way up I went on shore after ptarmigan, and from a height I had climbed I could see that the head of the fjord was entirely open, owing to the amount of water brought down by the glacier-river that runs into it, so that it would be impossible for us to land there. To reach the " Inland ice " it would have been necessary to land at Ivisartok on the eastern shore, but we should have taken at least two days to get there by this route, and as I could not give so much time to it there was nothing to be done but turn back.

This time, however, the result of the journey was not so meagre as last time. I had not reached the edge of the ice where I wished, but I had at least seen the glacier which comes down between Ivisartok and Nunatarsuak. This proved, however, not to have so much snow on it as I had expected, and the ice was nearly as blue and fissured as ever. There was also astonishingly little snow on the ground hereabouts. The bare land showed through in long stretches, and the difference between this place and Godthaab was very striking. Evidently the high mountains to the west and south had attracted most of the moisture.

The change that takes place in the surface of the ice during the winter is possibly not so great as I had expected where there is a broad strip of land separating it from the sea, as there is just at this part of the coast. The land in this case attracts to itself a large portion of the snow. Another result of this little excursion was the observation of the great quantity of water which this glacial river had brought down into the fjord even in the winter-time. It had not yet been warm enough for any real melting of the snow along the coast even at Godthaab. Now it is well known that it is always considerably colder in here by the edge of the ice than outside, and the difference that there is between the temperature on the surface of the icefield and on the land which skirts it we had had an opportunity of seeing on our journey. But in spite of all this the river was now running, as it were, in flood, and, according to the Eskimo, it was in the

habit of so running the whole winter through. The consequence is, in the lower layers of the great ice-sheet melting must go on independently of the temperature of the surface.

In the evening we camped on a point at the mouth of Ujaragsuitfjord. As we were in no real hurry we arranged things as comfortably as possible. Of grass we could collect any amount on the bare spots, and with this we covered the floor of the tent and made ourselves a good dry couch. *We* then made some coffee, and the Eskimo produced one of their dainties, the red fish "bergylt," which was eaten frozen and raw; besides this we had our ptarmigan, and altogether enjoyed ourselves immensely. Then we slept just as we were, as we had brought no bag this time, because I thought it would be too heavy to carry.

Next morning we crossed the fjord again. I was very much inclined to stay a little longer in this hunter's paradise, for Ivisartok and Nunatarsuak are well known as excellent reindeer-ground. Besides, there were a number of seal on the ice, and they afford most exciting sport. The old Norsemen knew what they were about when they settled in here. This and Ameralikfjord were probably the richest part of the old "Western Settlement," and there are many traces of their occupation still left, Ujaragsuit in particular being celebrated for its extensive ruins.

When we crossed the ridge which we had passed over on our way up, we had rather a steep descent to Kangiusak, where we had left our "kayaks." I now found to my cost how bad these Greenlanders are on their "ski." They had already been lagging behind the whole way, and I had had to relieve one of them of nearly all he was carrying to enable him to keep up at all. When they came to this descent they did not hesitate to take their " ski" off and carry them. I rushed down, and then had the pleasure of waiting nearly an hour at the bottom while they plunged along through the deep snow down the cliffs. Nor was it till they reached the ice on the fjord that they ventured to put their "ski" on again. One of them certainly

did try once on a little slope, but he began by falling and made no further attempt.

On the ice, too, Karl shot a ringed seal, which also had to be dragged along to the " kayaks." We reached them in the course of the afternoon, but did not know how late it was, as the sky was clouded and none of us had a watch. I wanted to reach Kornok that day, as there might possibly be news of the shij). So, though Larserak especially was very little inclined for it, we got into the "kayaks'" and set off. But we had not gone far before we saw that it was much later than we thought, for it was already quite dark; and as we were met in the fjord by a stiffish westerly breeze things became anything but pleasant.

A NIGHT PADDLE TO KORNOK.

*(/ T. Halmtat,fivm a skclck fy He Author. )*

As long as we could hug the shore we got on tolerably well, but when we reached the headland of Kangersuak it was a case of crossing the fjord to get to Kornok. This was worst of all, as off the point we met the full force of tht sea, and in the dark it was not easy to keep one's eye on the big waves. So we stopped and considered matters; the two Greenlanders asked me if I thought I could manage it, but I did not like to show the white feather, and inquired in return whether they thought they could. Finally they started, but we soon found that it was not altogether a joke. Karl was worst off, as he had the seal lying on the "kayak" behind him. He shouted out that he must go ashore to take it off, but there was no place to land along these precipitous cliffs. So we pulled his seal off for him, and he towed it for a while. This, however, kept him back, so we had to help him put it on to the " kayak " again. At first the night had been completely dark, but now the clouds lifted a little, and occasionally the wind parted them enough for the moon to shine through and help us to see the waves and find our way. It was hard work to paddle against the wind, but at last we reached the opposite shore. Here, too, we met with a new difficulty in the shape of masses of drift-ice, which for a time quite shut us in.

It was not till one o'clock that we reached Kornok, much to the consternation of the inhabitants, as the natives rarely travel at this time of night.

There was no news of the ship yet, so next day I went in to Umanak to see the place, which is one of the Moravian stations, and to visit the missionary, Herr Heincke, with whom I spent four pleasant days.

On April 12 I was in Kornok again. The next day it rained, and my companion on the way out, Aperavigssuak, did not care for the journey. He had spent the whole time while I was in the fjord in going the round of all the houses at Kornok and Umanak. So instead of going back I gave a great ball to all the inhabitants of Kornok. Dancing began at four in the afternoon, and the entertainment consisted of coffee and ship's biscuits. We amused ourselves thoroughly till late in the evening, when I grew so sleepy that I had to ask my guests to go.

The following day, April 14, we paddled back to Godthaab in tolerably fine weather. As an instance of the rate one can travel in the "kayak," I may say that, though for the first three hours we had the current against us, and for the last hour a stiff breeze, we covered the thirty-six miles in eight hours. This is little compared with what a really good " kayaker " can do. Herr Heincke told me that when his wife had been taken very ill a couple of years before, in December, a seal-catcher named Luclvig, belonging to Urnanak, had gone off before dawn to Godthaab to consult the doctor. In spite of the shortness of the day he was back before evening, the whole distance that he had travelled being over eighty miles.

On April 15 we had thick weather and snow, and we all VIKW TO THK SOUTH FROM KORNOK.

*(From a photograph,*

agreed that the ship would not come that day. But after dinner, as we were sitting over our coffee at the Superintendent's, and having a chat with the doctor, suddenly the whole settlement rang with a single shriek, " Umiarsuit! Umiarsuit! " (" The ship! The ship! ") We rushed out

and gazed seawards, but could see nothing but the flying snow. All at once we caught sight of some dark object looming high up in the air. It was the *Hvidbjornetfs* rigging, and the vessel was already nearly in the bay. We jumped into boats and " kayaks," and as we boarded the ship the Norwegian flag was hoisted and a thundering salute fired in our honour. We were welcomed and congratulated by the captain, Lieutenant Garde, whom I have already mentioned more than once in connection with the Danish east coast expedition, and by some of the Greenland officials who had spent the winter in Europe.

1IARBOI R OF Sl'KKKRTOPPFX.

*(ffatti a photograph.)*

Greetings were given us from home, and there was a general questioning and exchange of news. An entertainment was at once prepared on board, and it was late in the evening before we escaped from the festive scene and got back to Godthaab.

Then came the hour of departure. I had long shrunk from the thought of leaving, but now there was no way of avoiding it. It was not without sorrow that most of us left this place and these people, among whom we had enjoyed ourselves so well.

The day before we started one of my best friends among the Eskimo, in whose house I had often been, said to me: "Now you are going back into the great world from which you came to us; you will find much that is new there, and perhaps you will soon forget us. But we shall never forget you."

Next day we started, and (iodthaab, still in its winter garb, smiled a melancholy farewell in the beams of the spring sun. We stood looking at it for long, and the many happy hours we had spent there with Greenlanders and Europeans alike came ' back into our minds. Just as we were leaving the fjord we passed three "kayaks," in which were Lars, Michael, and Jonathan, the three best seal-catchers in Godthaab. They had paddled out *(Pram a sketch ky tht Autlior.')* VCQ to give US a last touching farewell, by a salute from their three guns. We were steaming fast out to sea,

and for a time saw them bobbing up and down upon the waves, till at last they disappeared.

Our ship had to go northwards to Sukkertoppen and Hol-stensborg before she set her course for home. We reached the first place on April 26. Here we found a good instance of the postal facilities in Greenland, for no one knew that we had been spending the winter at Godthaab, which is only ninety miles to the south. On May 3, after six days at Sukkertoppen, and a deal of merrymaking, we left again for Holstensborg. On the way we fell in with the *Nordlystt,* a bark belonging to the " Trade Service." She was fast in the ice, so we went to her help, and towed her in to Sukkertoppen. In the evening we left again to go northwards, but we found the whole sea full of ice ten inches thick, through which it was impossible to push.

KSKIMO POVERTY—A GIRL FROM SUKKKKTOITEN. UUK 1..!)T 1AKKVF.I.I. TO GBKKNLAND.

*(Frottl an instantaneous photograph.)*

There was, therefore, nothing to be done but give up Holstensborg and turn back. On the morning of May 4 we anchored at Sukkertoppen for the third time, and the same day said our last farewell to Greenland.

That evening, when we were well out in Davis Strait, Balto was standing at the taffrail in deep thought, and gazing towards land, though it had long since disappeared from view. Dietrich-son asked him why he was so melancholy. " Have you forgotten Sofia? " he answered.

We were now seventeen days on board the *Hvidbjornen.* In the captain we had excellent company, for-few could have taken more interest in our expedition than he. Thanks to hospitality the time went pleasantly, and in spite of wind and sea we drew slowly nearer home. Many of us will remember the morning revels, at which we drank the champagne and ate the good things sent out from Europe for us—very different entertainment from that of the " Inland ice."

On May 21 we were in Copenhagen.

To describe the welcome and hospitality accorded us here, as well as in Norway afterwards, my pen would be far too feeble, and I will forbear to make the attempt. Nor will I try to account to the reader for all the speeches that had to be heard, and all those that had to be made in return; nor for all that had to be eaten or drunk on such occasions; nor to give him an idea of the incredible sufferings that those tormentors of the human race, those ghouls of modern life, by courtesy called interviewers, are allowed to inflict on people as innocent as ourselves. It was no pleasant or easy thing to cross Greenland, but I must say, in full earnest, that the toils and hardships of our return were even worse to bear.

In glorious weather, on May 30, we entered Christiania Fjord, and were received by hundreds of sailing-boats and a whole fleet of steamers. It was a day that I do not think any of us will forget.

Even Ravna, I am sure, was impressed in his own way. When we got near to the harbour, and saw the ramparts of the old fortress and the quays on all sides black with people, Dietrichson said to Ravna: " Are not all these people a fine sight, Ravna?" "Yes, it is fine, very fine;—but if they had only been reindeer!" was Ravna's answer.

PLAUDITli!

CPSIA information can be obtained
at www.ICGtesting.com
Printed in the USA
BVHW060143290619
552236BV00004B/205/P